Reimagining the Library of the Future

Public Buildings and Civic Space for Tomorrow's Knowledge Society

T0344533

Reimagining the Library of the Future

Public Buildings and Civic Space for Tomorrow's Knowledge Society

Steffen Lehmann

With a Foreword by Kelvin Watson, a Prologue by Michelle Jeffrey Delk, an Epilogue by Keith Webster, and a Photo Series by Cida de Aragon

ORO Editions
Publishers of Architecture, Art, and Design
Gordon Goff: Publisher

www.oroeditions.com
info@oroeditions.com

Published by ORO Editions.
Copyright © 2022 Steffen Lehmann. All rights reserved.

All rights reserved. No part of this book may be reproduced, stored in a retrieval system, or transmitted in any form or by any means, including electronic, mechanical, photocopying or microfilming, recording, or otherwise (except that copying permitted by Sections 107 and 108 of the US Copyright Law and except by reviewers for the public press) without written permission from the publisher.

You must not circulate this book in any other binding or cover and you must impose this same condition on any acquirer.

Author of this book: Steffen Lehmann, Las Vegas and London
Preface text: Michelle Jeffrey Delk, Snøhetta, New York and Oslo
Foreword text: Kelvin Watson, Las Vegas-Clark County Library District, Nevada
Epilogue: Keith Webster, Carnegie Mellon University Libraries, Pennsylvania
Book Cover Design: Fortino Acosta and Steffen Lehmann, Las Vegas
Drawing used for book cover: Section courtesy of Steven Holl Architects, New York
Book Graphic Design and Layout: Fortino Acosta, Las Vegas
Managing Editor: Jake Anderson, Los Angeles

10 9 8 7 6 5 4 3 2 1 First Edition

ISBN: 978-1-951541-98-9

Color Separations and Printing: ORO Group Ltd.
Printed in China
Trim size dimensions format 7" x 9" (portrait), softbound

ORO Editions makes a continuous effort to minimize the overall carbon footprint of its publications. As part of this goal, ORO Editions, in association with Global ReLeaf, arranges to plant trees to replace those used in the manufacturing of the paper produced for its books. Global ReLeaf is an international campaign run by American Forests, one of the world's oldest nonprofit conservation organizations. Global ReLeaf is American Forests' education and action program that helps individuals, organizations, agencies, and corporations improve the local and global environment by planting and caring for trees.

The author is grateful for the support provided by the International Federation of Library Associations and Institutions (IFLA) in The Hague, the American Library Association (ALA) in Chicago, the American Institute of Architects (AIA) in Washington, D.C., and the Las Vegas-Clark County Library District, Nevada. Thank you!

In a good bookroom you feel in some mysterious way that you are absorbing the wisdom contained in all the books through your skin, without even opening them.

— Mark Twain, 1885

The golden age of public libraries dawns again. An abundance of new and newly renovated libraries have recently opened their doors. In addition to being breathtakingly beautiful, many are exemplars of what great community spaces can and should be. Indoors, they are filled with natural light. Books once packed together in dark corners are now on display on bright, welcoming shelves that could rival those in an Apple store. Some libraries have added outdoor patios and roof decks. Though printed volumes remain their focal point, the best new libraries offer much more: computer labs, conference rooms of different sizes, studios for recording podcasts and editing videos; event spaces, hands-on experiences for kids, a cafe, and kitchens where people can learn to cook foods from different cultures. Call it a new golden era for public libraries worldwide.

— Washington Post, Editorial, 2022

Endorsements

Besides the pivotal question on reimagining the library of the future, the author discusses the critical topic related to public space in contemporary cities. The consolidated trend to privatize significant parts of the public space has restricted interaction, free use and expression. The libraries thus possess the opportunity to become the catalyst of several new public activities due to their renewed spatial programme, their crucial urban role and changing societal expectations. Therefore, through the lens of the library, a new idea of public space emerges, and this is where the book makes fascinating discoveries and contributes to the debate.
 — **Dario Pedrabissi, Architect and Senior Lecturer, University of Portsmouth, United Kingdom, and Milan, Italy**

As someone on the forefront of contemporary urban societal and spatial transformations, Steffen Lehmann does it again: his newest study brings a brilliant discourse on the libraries of the future, reimagined places creating a lasting civic value and destination in the new digital society framework. These open-society, genderless and inclusive agora spaces are beautiful works of architecture that resonate with people looking for a new grounding for culture, publicness and social capital. This book is a must for all urbanists and architects as libraries are maybe our last outposts of the enduring repository of history, culture, and meaning. The next generation of libraries in the network society will and are creating a renewed mission well beyond the storage of knowledge. Read it!
 — **Professor Tigran Haas, Ph.D., Associate Professor and Director of the Center for the Future of Places, KTH Royal Institute of Technology, Stockholm, Sweden**

I applaud this book's deep dive analysis into the library of the future and, frankly, the timing of this highly relevant book publication could not be better. The 2020 Census projects a demographic sea of change in the US, so as our democracy becomes more diverse, our buildings are ideally poised to become community service delivery centers. And once again, we will be called upon to reinvent our role as the great equalisers of society.
 — **Kelvin Watson, Executive Director, Las Vegas-Clark County Library District, Nevada, US**

Beyond a reservoir of information in the age of disinformation, Steffen Lehmann's timely book considers the library as a civic space for the production and dissemination of public knowledge. The prescient study of this classical building type that has been missing has finally been written! Reimagining the Library of the Future *presents numerus examples of different approaches to the design of libraries as public space. It reminds us why, despite the gradual transformation of inscriptions from ink on paper to bits per pixel, the library, with its extended media infrastructure, still occupies a visible and necessary space within our cities and societies.*
 — **Professor Iman Ansari, Ph.D., Assistant Professor, Knowlton School of Architecture, Ohio State University, Columbus, US**

Now that digital technologies have changed the way books can be stored and accessed, it is important to remember that the media also triggers our desire. They tell us not only where to buy, but also where to meet and where to kiss. They can shape communities. Therefore, this book is an important and timely reminder that libraries are also important as public places to meet and share the pleasure of reading and knowledge.
　— Professor Bart Lootsma, Ph.D., Professor for Architectural Theory, University of Innsbruck, Austria

It is always a very particular pleasure and challenge for any architect to design a library. Similar to the museum, art gallery or concert hall, libraries express more than other typologies their public character. Steffen Lehmann's new book makes a significant contribution to a better understanding of this important building type and to the architectural discourse at large, by presenting and contributing a relevant selection of projects in plans and sections. I share the opinion that architectural quality is still decided by the plan and section of a building.
　— Professor Igor Peraza, Ph.D., Founding Partner, si_architecture + urban design, Dubai, UAE, and Barcelona, Spain; Professor of Practice, American University of Sharjah, UAE

The library, as a public building and a civic space, deserves to be in a state of constant experimentation and evolution as our circumstances and needs change. Filled with a wide range of excellent case studies, this eloquent book not only showcases libraries of the past and present but also addresses the critical question, "What can a library be?" We need public libraries more than ever as places for gathering and exchanging the knowledge that is the bedrock of our society as well as places for social interaction for communities and the empowering exchange of ideas. This magisterial book brings much-needed attention back to the critical, civic and communal role of libraries in our cities and societies.
　— Professor Aseem Inam, Ph.D., Chair in Urban Design and Founding Director, TRULAB: Laboratory for Designing Urban Transformation, Cardiff University, United Kingdom

Strong in analysis and critical exploration, Steffen Lehmann's book Reimagining the Library of the Future is a well-overdue contribution to understanding the transforming typology of the library. The notion of the library is viewed not just as a conduit for knowledge sharing and creation, but as a medium for coalescing public interest and understanding the evolution and role of civic spaces. In the twenty-first century, the concept and form of the library as a significant public space is undergoing greater transformation and reshaping than ever. In this context, the author explores in depth major social questions on the role and utility of the library of the future including issues of inclusiveness, equity and multi-functionality as attached to changing notions of public, private and commercialisation. This timely interdisciplinary book by an acclaimed academic is essential reading for scholars and students keen to deepen their understanding of the history and theory of architecture, design and planning of the city through the changing lens of the typology of the library.
　— Professor Paul Jones, Ph.D., former Programme Director MURP, the University of Sydney, Australia; Global Studio Leader on Cities of the Global South, Institute of Technology Bandung, Indonesia

Other Books by Steffen Lehmann

Contents

Book Synopsis

The library is currently in the middle of a transformation, adapting to an unprecedented set of modern challenges, including digitisation, sustainability, equity and changes in research methods. To find out more, the author took a close look at recent libraries to learn what the future might hold, and spoke to those who are involved in shaping it.

The book *Reimagining the Library of the Future* investigates the various models of public buildings and civic space through the lens of the library. It takes a critical look at the history, present transformation and future prospects of this significant building typology that has recently emerged as a redefined community place, social condenser and urban incubator for knowledge generation, storage and sharing. In particular, the library has evolved as a vibrant and vital member of community development and as a basis for outreach efforts aimed at underserved and diverse populations.

This is an interdisciplinary study that challenges the conventional, traditional idea of the library as "a building to store books", and aims to make a meaningful contribution to the discourse of this particular building type by speculating on the next-generation library. It uses a critical comparative case study approach to identify and discuss alternative and hybrid models of two types: the public and the academic library. The discussion touches on the future of civic space and public buildings in general, as well as how communal places are likely to continue to evolve and change.

The book presents an exemplary collection of historically significant libraries and over 40 recent public and academic libraries from around the world, with over 250 images, rich in architectural delights. As the survey of precedents shows, the historical cases have informed the design of the recent libraries and the continuous development of the building typology over time. Well-designed libraries are now in abundance, and the wider view of this study includes mediatheques and learning centers. The selection of contemporary projects from the last 20 years focuses on libraries in Europe (in Germany, France, Italy, Austria, Netherlands, UK), the US, Canada, Mexico, Australia, Japan and China—countries where the design of libraries has been most comprehensively developed.

Libraries belong to society. The library is a unique typology undergoing great transformation, and this well-overdue analysis examines how the typology has always been a testing ground of public interest and shared civic space—again evolving in very interesting directions today. Over the next decade, the library is likely to continue to further expand its role as a free educational resource for lifelong learning of all residents, with initiatives also targeting non-traditional library users.

Libraries are dynamic and continually changing. Advocating the dissemination of knowledge while empowering the public, libraries celebrate ideas, curiosity and empathy. The historical function of libraries as storehouses, limited to collecting and storing manuscripts and books, has expanded: the library of the future is a significant public space — a place for community building, meetings and frequently a catalyst for urban revitalisation; the next-generation library is likly to be a forum – a moderated place of knowledge and debate. This supports the urban ambition for the library to become a new civic centre and genre-bending hub for social development and community support.

Will the future library resemble a densely vegetated garden? Libraries always exist in multidimesional relationships within their larger urban, cultural and societal context and the wider knowledge system they create. Libraries are more than engines of research and places for public engagement. *Reimagining the Library of the Future* explores the transformation of this established typology from the traditional format to a communal incubator of ideas and a place for new knowledge generation, exchange and sharing.

New libraries are now re-emerging everywhere, and the book-based library is making a comeback. Its spaces often exude tranquillity. But the library of the future is a phenomenon that has yet to be defined in terms of its atmosphere, performance, role and architectural appearance. Therefore, the book explores the opportunities and challenges for new hybrid types of urban libraries and the transformation of civic urban space previously known as *public*.

One of the key take-away messages of the study is that society will still need libraries in the future. Libraries are not dying, they are evolving, and they are important cornerstones of a healthy community: they give people the opportunity to find jobs, explore scientific research, experience new ideas and get lost in wonderful stories – while at the same time providing a sense of place for gathering. The author predicts that the library's important role as a symbol of shared cultural and community values will remain. The subject of the future of libraries is of great relevance to many people. For example, there are more than 117,000 libraries throughout the US alone, employing over 160,000 librarians, but in many countries user numbers have been declining over the last 10 years.

Written by an architecture professor with extensive research and professional background, and richly illustrated with relevant examples, this reference book will be useful for practitioners, students, bibliophiles, librarians and everybody who has an interest in the future of libraries.

Book Highlights
• The book presents a selection of historically significant as well as contemporary public and academic libraries, and identifies emerging trends relevant to the design of libraries.
• Among the highlights of the book are the twelve statements by leading architects and library designers specifically written for this publication.
• In general, there is currently a lack of systematic understanding of how public buildings and the collective civic spaces weave cities together through their interconnected spatial networks; thus, more research is necessary to better understand the civic character of the library of the future.
• The popularity of the library will continue (despite the digitisation of books and manuscripts), and the role of the urban library of thetwenty-first century is more relevant than ever before: it has evolved as a vibrant and vital place of community development and outreach efforts aimed at underserved and diverse populations. It offers lifelong learning, training on career advancement and social services support, addressing the growing digital divide in our society.
• Over recent years, new library spaces have become arenas for innovative concepts and utopian views of social place-making in the urban landscape.
• Experts speculate that, by 2050, sharing knowledge might be the last remaining form of public activity.
• The spotlight is now on the renewal of the urban fabric and its public space network, accommo-dating libraries in super-green adaptive-reuse projects, hence the question: what exactly will be the role of the library as a new type of public space and community building institution?

Acknowledgments

This book is presented as the open-ended research and outcome of two years of work and commitment of numerous people. I would like to express my thank you for the generosity of everyone involved, especially all the library experts, archtects and designers who made this comprehensive study possible.

Firstly, my gratitude goes to the International Federation of Library Associations and Institutions (IFLA) and to the American Library Association (ALA) for their support. In our increasingly digital world, I would like to thank my fearless publisher and his team at ORO Editions: Gordon Goff and Jake Anderson. Your trust and experience in managing the production of this publication was crucial. You all believed in the project from start to finish, and it has been a pleasure to work with you.

I owe a tremendous debt to the immensely talented architects, library innovators, colleagues and designers who made their work and ideas available. I am grateful for their participation and contribution of statements (that make up such an important part of the study) and insight presented in this book. Getting this publication done would have been impossible without the collaboration of the designers; especially a big "thank you" to the incredible firms profiled in the Part 2 section; twelve statements on the library of the future were specifically written for this book by eminent world-renown architects: Steven Holl, Antoine Predock, Craig Dykers and Michelle Delk, Charles Renfro, Francine Houben, Max Dudler, Eun Young Yi, Richard Francis-Jones, Ludovico Lombardi, Will Bruder, Winy Maas, and Gerard Evenden of Foster + Partners. — I thank you all for your time amidst of your busy schedules!

My warmest thanks go to two valuable contributors of ideas: to Michelle Jeffrey Delk, partner and discipline leader at Snøhetta in New York for the poetic "Prologue"; and Kelvin Watson, executive director of the Las Vegas-Clark County Library District in Nevada for providing an interesting "Foreword" to this book. Keith Webster provided the "Epilogue" and critical feedback. I am grateful, you all made this a better book!

We worked on this book during the 2020/2021 pandemic, which helped to make the quarantine time fly. It would not have been possible without the generosity of the University of Nevada, Las Vegas. Some colleagues have been supportive and I am grateful for their wise comments; and the conversations we had, which were relevant for the direction of this publication. My committed Ph.D. student Fortino Acosta was instrumental in the design of the book. Many thanks go to Cida de Aragon for her photo series of library spaces (presented on pages 22–29); and for constant encouragement and understanding over the years. You all made this a better book!

Furthermore, my thank you goes to the student group in my studio working on the library of the future; and the AIA Las Vegas and AIA Nevada Chapters. Without their strong support, this study would not have been possible. My friendship with many colleagues and scholars provided me thoughtful guidance and this is a daily inspiration. I thank you all for your encouragement and relentless curiosity during the preparation of this book (in alphabetical order):

Fortino Acosta, Heiko Achilles, Pal Ahluwalia, Inaki Alday, Hiba Alobaydi, Eva Alvarez, Martin Andrews, Iman Ansari, Erieta Attali, Thomas Auer, Eric Baldwin, Martin Bechthold, Vladimir Belogolovsky, Kai-Uwe Bergmann, Paola Boarin, Giovanna Borasi, Peter Bosselmann, Peter Brandon, Keith Brewis, Andrea Brizzi, Will Bruder, Andreas Bruemmel, Charlotte Skene Catling, Niccolo Casas, Javier Castanon, Cesar Ceballos, Edwin Chan, Akhtar Chauhan, Marcus Civin,

Rafaella Colombo, Annette Condello, Peter Cook, Edoardo Croci, Mario Cucinella, Luca D'Acci, Cida de Aragon, Cees de Bont, Michelle Delk, Neil Denari, Antonino Di Raimo, Paolo Di Nardo, Ralph Dlugosz, Khoa Do, Markus Dochantschi, Craig Dykers, Harry Edelman, Hisham Elkadi, Sura El-Maiyah, Beate Engelhorn, Dwayne Eshenbaugh, Eric Farr, Maggie Farrell, Elizabeth Farrelly, Billie Faircloth, George Ferguson, Richard Francis-Jones, Ruben Garcia, Georg Gewers, Edward Glaeser, Tigran Haas, Daniel Hammerman, Catherine Harper, John Hartley, Peter Head, Ulrike Heine, Tom Heneghan, Peter Herrle, Rainer Hirth, Simi Hoque, Francine Houben, Donald Houston, Alvin Huang, Kurt Hunker, Claus-Peter Hutter, Yasuhiro Imai, Arata Isozaki, Aseem Inam, Dieter Janssen, Mike Jenks, Mitchell Joachim, Charles O. Job, Paul Jones, Ahmed Z. Kahn, K.K. Philip Kang, Irma Karjalainen, Greg Keefe, Karima Kourtit, Kisa Kawakami, Lance Kirk, Thomas Kiwitt, Samia Kirchner, Barbara Klinkhammer, Joerg Knieling, Michelle Kolbe, Branko Kolarevic, Gabor Kovacs, Bodo Kraeter, Franz Krenn, Ralph Krohmer, Esa Laaksonen, Luciano Landaeta, Norbert Lechner, Margit and Werner Lehmann, Andres Lepik, Pekka Leviakangas, Nina and Daniel Libeskind, Bob and Vicki Liljestrand, Bart Lootsma, Piotr Lorens, Phil Lewis, Sergio Lopez-Pineiro, Ferdinand Ludwig, Winy Maas, Richard Marshall, Adrian McGregor, Peter Murray, Antonello Marotta, Alessandro Melis, Walter Menteth, Michael J. Monti, Mark Mueckenheim, Mark Mulligan, Gjoko Muratovski, Ethan Nelson, Boonlay Ong, Dominic Papa, Mita Patel, Emily Penn, Dario Pedrabissi, Igor Peraza, Maria Perbellini, Rodrigo Perez d'Arce, Chona E. Ponce, Alberto Pottenghi, Antoine Predock, Karim Rashid, Carlo Ratti, Victor A. Regnier, Charles Renfro, Roger Riewe, Saffa Riffat, Kristien Ring, Tom Rivard, Noel Robinson, Paco Francisco J. Rodriguez-Suarez, Stefan Rossner, Paola Ruotolo, David J. Sailor, Norma Saldivar, Dean Sakamoto, Richard Saladino, Matheos Santamouris, Saskia Sassen, Azadeh Sawyer, Ute Sievers-Gnasso, Tom and Susan Schoeman, Oliver Schuette, Ehsan Sharifi, Brigitte Shim and Howard Sutcliffe, Brian and Kay Suters, Peter Cachola Schmal, Bleyer Schneider, Mark Shapiro, Malcolm Smith, Werner Sobek, Thomas Spiegelhalter, Antje Steinmuller, Monika Szopinska-Mularz, David Turnbull, Ed Vance, Thomas Vonier, Keith Webster, Gerold Wech, Liss C. Werner, Frank Werner, Ken Worpole, Jenny Wu and Atiq U. Zaman.
You are all incredibly supportive and I feel fortunate to have been able to share my journey.

I would also like to thank all photographers, architects and archives for making images and information available. Every effort has been made to trace and identify all the copyright holders correctly, and we apologise in advance for any unintentional omission.

Lastly, as a full professor and chair of architecture for the last two decades, I am fortunate to be working on three continents, including previously as head of school and executive director of three schools of architecture in the US and in Australia. These particular leadership positions provided me with additional insight, and I am grateful to have been able to work with over a thousand inspirational, talented and hard-working students of architecture and design at various schools in the US, UK, Australia, Germany, Austria, Mexico, Singapore, China and India over the last three decades.

The popularity of the library continues (despite the digitisation of books and manuscripts) and the library in the twenty-first century is now much more than ever before: it has evolved as a vibrant and vital member of community development and outreach efforts to underserved and diverse populations. It offers lifelong learning, training on career advancement and social services support, addressing the digital divide in our society. It has also transformed into a sustainable building that is frequently generating its own energy. I am convinced that, over the next decade, the library will continue to further expand its role as a place of learning and sharing of knowledge; as a free educational resource for all residents, with initiatives targeting non-traditional library users. However, in this context, it still remains to be seen how exactly the typology of the library will continue to evolve in the coming decades.

— Steffen Lehmann, January 2022

List of Image Credits

We thank all photographers, architects and archives for making images and information available.Numerous images were available in the public domain, and made available courtesy of Wikimedia Commons, Creative Commons CC-BY-2.0. Every effort has been made to trace and identify all the copyright holders correctly, and we apologise in advance for any unintentional omission. In case we forgot someone to mention, the publisher would be pleased to insert the appropriate acknowledgment in any subsequent edition. We are particularly grateful for the images and statements provided:

Cida de Aragon: Photo series of 14 selected images on library spaces and throughout the book. Photos (2021) courtesy of Cida de Aragon, Las Vegas: 22–29; and 238 (photo author biography).

Image of the painting *St. Jerome in his Study* courtesy of The National Gallery, London: 37.

Photo Celsus,37: courtesy of Wikimedia Commons, Creative Commons CC-BY-2.0 - public domain.

Bodleian Libraries, Press and Media: Natalie Awdry, Oxford University: 41.

Maria Laach, Andrenach; Bibliothek Goerlitz, 42: courtesy of Wikimedia Commons, Creative Commons CC-BY-2.0.

British Museum, 44–45: courtesy of British Museum, London.

Trinity Library, 46: courtesy of Trinity College, Dublin, Ireland.

Boston Public Library, New York City Public Library, and Peabody Library, 48–49: courtesy of Wikimedia Commons, Creative Commons CC-BY-2.0. Berkeley Bancroft Library, 49: courtesy by Steffen Lehmann, Berlin.

Alexander von Humboldt, 69: courtesy of Deusches Historisches Museum, Berlin, Germany.

Stockholm Public Library (Asplund), 70–71: courtesy of Steffen Lehmann, Berlin.

Central City Library, Vyborg, 72–73: courtesy of Alvar Aalto Foundation, Helsinki; the Finnish Committee for the Restauration of Viipuri Library; and photo by Petri Neuvonen, Helsinki.

Phillips Exeter Academy Library (Kahn), 74–75: courtesy of Steffen Lehmann, Berlin.

History Faculty Library, Cambridge, 76–77: courtesy of Stirling Wilford & Associates, London.

Doninque Perrault Architecture: Drawings, text, and photos courtesy of Dominique Perrault Architecture, Paris: 79.

Berlin State Library, 80–81: courtesy of Steffen Lehmann, Berlin.

Beinecke Library, SOM: drawings and photos courtesy of SOM, Chicago: 82–83. SOM photo 81: courtesy of Henry Trotter, public domain.

Geisel Library, US San Diego, 84–85: courtesy of Cida de Aragon and Steffen Lehmann, Las Vegas.

David Chipperfield Architects: drawing and photo, 86: courtesy of David Chipperfield Architects, Berlin and London; and photo by Christian Richters.

Ortner & Ortner Baukunst: drawing and photo, 87: courtesy of Ortner & Ortner Baukunst, Vienna/Berlin; and photo by Stefan Mueller.

Foster + Partners, 88–89: Gerard Evenden, Nigel Young, Hiba Alobaydi and Tom Wright. Drawings and photos courtesy of Foster + Partners, London and Reinhard Gorner.

Bolles-Wilson + Partners, Peter Wilson and Julia Bolles, 90–91: drawings and photos courtesy of Bolles-Wilson + Partners, Muenster.

Herzog & de Meuron: Jacques Herzog, Pierre de Meuron; Holly Baker, 92–93: drawings and photos courtesy of Herzog & de Meuron, Basel; and photo by Stefan Mueller.

Las Vegas Central Library, 94: courtesy of Cida de Aragon and Steffen Lehmann, Las Vegas.

Lied Library UNLV, 95: courtesy of Cida de Aragon and Steffen Lehmann, Las Vegas.

Alvaro Siza Architects, 96: drawing and photo courtesy of Alvaro Siza Vieira, Porto, Portugal.

Central Library Depok, Indonesia (DCM), 97: plan by DCM; photos courtesy by Steffen Lehmann, Berlin.

OMA: Rem Koolhaas, Reinier de Graaf; Marina Maestre: 98–104: drawings, text, and photos courtesy of Office for Metropolitan Architecture, Rotterdam. Joshua Ramus, 101: text courtesy of J. Ramus, New York; photos Seattle: courtesy by Steffen Lehmann, Berlin.

SANAA: Kazuyo Sejima and Ryue Nishizawa, 105: drawing, text and photo courtesy of SANAA, Tokyo.

Arata Isozaki & Associates: Arata Isozaki, Misa Shin; Naoko Hatta and Rie Someya:106–12: drawings, text, and photos courtesy of Arata Isozaki & Associates, Tokyo; and photos by Yukio Futagawa; Yasuhiro Ishimoto.

Toyo Ito & Associates: Toyo Ito, 113–17: drawings, text and photos courtesy of Toyo Ito & Associates, Tokyo.

Snøhetta: Craig Dykers, Kjetil Trædal Thorsen, Michelle Jeffrey Delk; Eric Baldwin and Danielle DeVito, 118–29: drawings, text, and photos courtesy of Snøhetta, New York/Oslo.

Mecanoo: Francine Houben, Dick van Gameren; Eliano Felicio, 130–41: drawings, text, and photos courtesy of Mecanoo, Delft; Ossip Architectuurfotografie, 133 and 136; Christian Richters, 135; Ethan Lee, 137; and John Bartelstone, 139.

FJMT Studio: Richard Francis-Jones, Jeff Morehen, Annie Hensley; Myrrhine Fabricius, 142–54: drawings, texts, photos courtesy of FJMT Studio, Sydney; Trevor Mein and Glenn Hunter, 147 and 153; John Gollings, 154.

Will Bruder Architects: Will Bruder and Alice Sandstrom, 155–60: drawings, text, and photos courtesy of Will Bruder + Partners, Portland/Phoenix; photos by Bill Timmerman.

Yi Architects, 161–67: photos, text, and drawings courtesy of Eun Young Yi, Yi Architects, Cologne and Seoul; photos by Yi Architects, Stefan Mueller, 162–63; and Cida de Aragon, 164–67.

Kerry Hill Architects, Patrick Kosky, and Sean McGivern, 168–69: drawings and photos courtesy of Kerry Hill Architects, Singapore/Perth.

Max Dudler Architekten, 170–171: drawings and, photos courtesy of Max Dudller Architekten, Berlin; Monika Krauss, Annette Kern, Svea Weiss; and photos by Stefan Mueller, 170–71.

Zaha Hadid Architects: Patrik Schumacher and Ludovico Lombardi, 172–75: drawings, text, and photos courtesy of Zaha Hadid Architects, London; photos by Roland Halbe (Vienna) and, Iwan Baan, 174–75.

Diller Scofidio + Renfro, Charles Renfro; Jelena Loncar, Christine Noblejas, and Adele Charlebois, 176–79: drawings, text, and photos courtesy of Diller Scofidio + Renfro, New York; photos courtesy of Iwan Baan, 178–79.

Steven Holl Architects: Steven Holl; Olivia Ryder, Julia van den Hout, 180–183: drawings, text, and photos courtesy of Steven Holl Architects; Iwan Baan, 183. Watercolors and text courtesy of Steven Holl, New York: 180.

Foster + Partners: Gerard Evenden, Tom Wright, and Hiba Alobaydi; photos Berlin Brain: Nigel Young/Foster + Partners and Reinhard Gorner, 88–89; photos Sharjah House of Wisdom: Chris Goldstraw, 184–85.

Dominique Coulon & Associates, 186: drawing, and photo courtesy of Dominique Coulon and Marine Joli, Dominique Coulon & Asociés, Strasbourg, France.

Antoine Predock; Amy Lawrence and Paul Fehlau, 187–88: drawings and text courtesy of Antoine Predock Architects, Albuquerque, New Mexico, USA.

Alberto Kalach Taller Architects and TAX, Alberto Kalach and Andrea Ruiz, 189–192: drawings and photos courtesy of Alberto Kalach Taller & TAX, Mexico City, Mexico; and Cida de Aragon, 190–91.

MVRDV: Winy Maas, Jacob van Rijs, Nathalie de Vries; Rory Stott, Irene Start, Nadya Domanitskaya; ARS, Marcel van de Graaf: 51; 193–96: drawings, text, and photos courtesy of MVRDV, Rotterdam; and Ossip van Duivenbode.

University of Chicago Library, 204: courtesy of Helmut Jahn Architects, Chicago, USA.

Lina Bo Bardi - SESC Pompéia Cultural Centre, 205: photos courtesy of Leonardo Finotti, São Paulo; and Federico Calabrese, Salvador de Bahia, Brazil.

Biblioteca del Mediterraneo, Alghero, 207: photos courtesy of Cida de Aragon, Las Vegas; and Davide Virdis, Giovanni Maciocco and Antonello Marotta, Alghero, Italy.

BIG - Bjarke Ingels Group: Kai-Uwe Bergmann, 209: photo courtesy of BIG Architects, New York/Copenhagen.

BookWorm, Nudes Architects, Mumbai, 230: photos courtesy of Nudes Architects, Mumbai, India.

Micro-Library, Shau Architects, Jakarta, 231: drawing and photo courtesy of Shau Architects, Jakarta, Indonesia.

The library of the future should be an optimistic beacon, unlimited with an amazing balance of digital information and a love of books. It should be an environmental example of high technology, achieving ecological excellence. The future library serves an important role as a community-building institution. It is a place where a child can find optimism for the future of our planet and the human condition.
— **Steven Holl, 2021**

The new library spaces, like the Rolex Center in Lausanne or the Oodi library in Helsinki, clearly show how we could embrace a "Post-Functionalist" condition: spaces do not generate behaviours, but rather welcome or embrace and host them. Supported by the means of information technology, we are able to find intimacy in wide, busy spaces and communication in intimate ones.
— **Cino Zucchi, 2021**

A library in the twenty-first century should embrace a digital future while playing a crucial role as a community hub for learning, underpinned by innovation and technology.
— **Gerard Evenden, Foster + Partners, 2021**

Foreword

The Future of Libraries: Adapting to Demographic Growth and Change

Kelvin Watson

America is changing. We have always been a melting pot of nationalities, religions, ethnicities and gender identities, but historically, many of these segments have been blocked from realising their full potential. Part of the change we have witnessed of late is that of diverse voices, raised to assert their rightful share of the American Dream.

The 2020 Census has brought into sharp relief the demographic shifts behind these voices. An in-depth report by the *New York Times* found that while the total population is growing at a slower pace, the share of people who identify as white has decreased over the past 10 years for the first time. The population growth that did take place, some 23 million people, was comprised of those who identify as Hispanic, Asian, Black, or more than one race. Nearly 1 in 4 US residents identify as Hispanic or Asian; and Black residents increased by 6%.

Contributing to slower growth is a lower birth rate in the US, which demonstrates the economic pressure on young families, from the lack of living wage jobs and the need for technical training and quality childcare, to high student loan debt, an unstable housing market, and the ongoing uncertainty brought on by the pandemic.

By 2030, one in every five Americans will be 65 or older, as the outsised Baby Boom generation continues to influence the country's demographics. The US Census Bureau (2020) predicts that because such a large percentage of the population will be aging, immigration will become the primary source of growth and will expand the number of non-English-speaking residents. Racial and ethnic diversity will also increase, with the total population expected to cross the 400 million mark by 2060 — an additional 76 million people.

This is the future reality that libraries must plan for but I see only endless opportunities to create new relevance in American society. The majority of the population will either have never entered a library (even as children), or will have an outdated view of what libraries are. Establishing and promoting a dynamic and positive perception of the "Library Brand" is critical as digital information options compete for our customers. However, we cannot do it alone. It will take commitment and investment on multiple levels:

- Elected officials, philanthropists, and educators must partner with library systems to invest public and private dollars in designing new building models and retrofitting existing structures, to adapt as technology continues to evolve. These infrastructure investments will become catalysts for urban revitalisation, creating civic pride in these new community centers, which will uplift lives through free educational support, and access to free services such as job training, after school nutrition, legal advice, and public displays of art, music, dance and theatre performances.

- By creating the library workforce of the future to work in our libraries, we must broaden our library science degrees. This includes courses in business, technology, social work and public policy that broaden the knowledge base we have and create advocates from a variety of perspectives. We also need more scholarships aimed at recruitment and training a more diverse workforce in the field. This pivot toward *Diversity, Equity, Inclusion and Accessibility* (DEIA) among librarians is critical in making our spaces more welcoming for future customers who will be more ethnically, racially, and gender-diverse than ever before. In order to build trust and engagement, our diverse audiences need to see themselves reflected in our library staff members.

- The importance of expanding and exploring new partnerships cannot be overstated. Beyond the traditional community groups, we must think outside the norms to deliver our services in new ways while developing advocates who know our value first-hand. Meeting people where they are introduces and enlightens new audiences on the revolution taking place for our libraries. I have personally seen the positive results of providing library access in parks, prisons, hospitals, airports, sea ports, and, most importantly, within school districts. As the population grows and diversifies, our educational systems will be stretched beyond the breaking point, and making the library experience a fundamental part of a child's education should begin in pre-K level and will help to ease this burden. By providing free homework help, tactile STEAM learning and access to computers and broadband internet. Libraries in low-income and rural areas can also work to extend their broadband access reach into the neighbourhoods that they serve.

- We must continually search for non-traditional ideas and unique programming that will reach those who feel disenfranchised in our communities and libraries. We must "invite the uninvited," which is how I refer to those who do not frequent libraries. They perceive themselves as outsiders and view our buildings as being for "other people" who look differently from them, are educated, or enjoy a higher standard of living. They are intimidated by libraries due to the barriers of access, and so, they exclude themselves. We could be describing veterans, unguided children and teens, previously incarcerated, those with low incomes or education levels, people experiencing homelessness, and people with disabilities. These people might be foreign-born, BIPOC, LGBTQIA+, and others who are perhaps unsure of how they will be received when they walk through our doors. As we design, build and programme our future buildings, we must study the surrounding neighbourhoods and incorporate the cultural vibe and sense of place.

These are not lofty goals for a remote future. They are critical steps that must begin today in planning for the need that is already here, which will surely impact the future.

As we look toward the future of our buildings and our collections, we can borrow inspiration from the visionaries who helped to create our grand American library system. While there have been many contributors to this legacy, certainly Andrew Carnegie (1835–1919) was the principal architect, both literally and figuratively. As a boy, he arrived penniless from Scotland, worked in a Pennsylvania factory, and dreamed of a better life. He fought for and won free access to the local public library and ever after it was open to the working people of the city. He became one of the wealthiest men in the US, but never forgot how the library contributed to his education. His vision was to provide this same access to all US residents and in the early 1900s, he donated $60 million of his fortune to build 1,689 libraries across the nation. Many of those buildings are still the most admired and patronized in their communities. For example, the Carnegie Library in Washington, D.C. is a beautiful Beaux Arts building that cost $300,000 and opened in 1903 to women, children, and people of all races. In fact, Black residents still remember that it was the only public restroom available to them downtown.

Carnegie made libraries community anchors for all Americans rather than luxuries for the wealthy. Another of his buildings became a home for me in St. Louis, Missouri. Aside from my church, as a young boy, the Central Library was the grandest, most sacred space that I had ever seen. I felt like a king every time walking those hallowed halls.

Nearly all of Andrew Carnegie's libraries were built using the "Carnegie formula," which continues to be a model of public/private partnerships. We must continue to design awe-inspiring spaces in this model that honour and welcome people from all walks of life and make room for activities, conversation, discovery, maker spaces, and hands-on learning for all ages.

I am also inspired by Augusta Braxton Baker, a remarkable woman who began her career in 1937 at what is now known as the New York Public Library's Countee Cullen Branch in Harlem. She led the way in DEIA even then, creating one of the first collections that ignored the racist stereotypes of the time, and portrayed the real life experiences of Black children. Her collection demonstrated to publishers the need to expand their titles for children of color. Ms. Baker was also an author, a consultant on Sesame Street, and the first Black woman to serve as New York Public Library's coordinator of children's services. Her advocacy that children need to see positive representations of themselves in literature and culture helped to jumpstart this movement, which is more important than ever for children of all racial, ethnic and gender identities.

As Ms. Baker knew well, inclusion and diversity are concepts that must be paired with education. Even in the twenty-first century, not everyone has embraced an enlightened way of thinking and sadly, we are witnessing a surge of intolerance and racism that for a long time was latent. To counter this negativity, our role is to be educators. We are guided by public policies that underscore our values of DEIA, and we must seek out programming for our library spaces that create enlightenment and empathy.

I also believe that as librarians, we are key community influencers and that we must create the conversations we want to have, not only with our local and state leaders, but also with grassroots groups that are affecting change. These discussions are what make our libraries true community forums and civic centers. As a library director, I am in our community libraries as a presence and a participant. I don't just monitor community developments, I create what I want to see and initiate the discussions that I want to hear. Since I represent my institution, I want the public to know who I am, what my vision is for the future of our Library District, and in return, I want to listen to their hopes and dreams so that my staff and I can provide the pathways to their goals.

I applaud this book's deep dive analysis into the library of the future and, frankly, the timing of it could not be better. The 2020 Census projects a demographic sea of change in the US, so as our democracy becomes more diverse, our buildings are ideally poised to become community service delivery centers. And once again, we will be called upon to reinvent our role as the great equalisers of society.

Reference

US Census Bureau (2020). *2020 US Census Data Report: Local Population Changes and Nation's Racial Ethnic Diversity,* Washington, D.C., available online at: www.census.gov

Kelvin Watson is executive director of the Las Vegas-Clark County Library District, Nevada's largest library system. Kelvin believes in the transformative power of libraries for the diverse communities that they serve. He oversees 25 library branches spanning 8,000 square miles, a budget of $77 million, 700 employees, and a collection of 3.2 million items. The Las Vegas-Clark County Library District includes 13 urban libraries, 11 outlying libraries and one outreach library. The district is a vibrant and vital member of the community offering limitless learning; business and career advancement; and government and social services support. Kelvin Watson joined the Library District in 2020 from his previous role as the director of the Broward County Libraries Division in Florida. Regarded as one of the most highly respected thought leaders in the library industry, he is credited with expanding the customer base in past library management roles, through outreach efforts to underserved and diverse populations. His deep experience in technology, partnerships and programme development, plus his demonstrated success in addressing the digital divide, will help the Library District to further expand its role as a free educational resource for all residents, with initiatives targeting non-traditional library users. Mr. Watson earned a Bachelor of Science degree in Business Administration and a minor in Military Science from Lincoln University in Missouri; and a Masters of Library Science degree from North Carolina Central University.

For more information, please visit: www.lvccld.org

Housing the world's collective knowledge, within which reside the milestones of human intellectual achievement, libraries are perhaps the richest of all cultural institutions.

— Jacques Bosser, 2003

Prologue

Michelle Jeffrey Delk

What is a Library

The notion of the library has had many manifestations, from public venues and enclosed buildings to expressions of nature. If we consider one of the most fundamental aspects of the library as a place to collect and to share knowledge, we might push beyond perceived boundaries and understand the library as a landscape and an ecosystem of connections.

The library as a public venue, one providing access to resources and a place to convene, is evident in varying degrees across time. This provides a lens through which we might reflect upon the library of the past and imagine the library of the future. Some of the earliest libraries were known as *mouseion*; as places filled with music, poetry, texts, debate and the oral traditions of storytelling, these became ecosystems for knowledge sharing rather than a singular physical structure. This history is evident in, yet also distinct from, the libraries we know today.

Outdoor public spaces have long been primary components of the *académie*, connoting places of wisdom. In ancient Greece, *stoa* were integral to the architecture as outdoor spaces lined with columns creating safe, protected space for dialogue. All were welcome here, and such a variety of spaces provided areas of respite, learning and discourse; embodying the notion of library as a place to share and to gain knowledge.

As libraries continued to evolve, documentation technologies offered increased opportunity to create printed, secure information. Libraries shifted to become the home for collections; typically closed to the public to protect and preserve resources. Such restrictions established a basis for political, social and cultural power while also shaping the physical characteristics of the library buildings through closed rooms or quiet spaces; often limiting access to sustenance, light and social interaction.

Over time, educational and ecclesiastical institutions were able to gradually open greater access to the knowledge maintained in libraries, thus supporting and magnifying societal and political transformation. The internet and the conversion of physically embedded knowledge into digital formats completely changed the value proposition of the library as the primary place to access knowledge for many individuals. Previously print-only material became more easily and digitally reproduced, increasing volumes of documentation, and as such, broad public access to texts not only reemerge.

This evolution, along with recognising the increasing importance in today's society for convening and contextualising culture, sharing values and providing social connectivity within an ever-increasing domain and understanding of knowledge has initiated a radical rethinking of the library. Libraries today have been liberated from the idea of "a building as a container" for valuable objects. This ongoing evolution of the understanding of knowledge and its vessel begs the question, "what is the future ecosystem of a library?" The promise for exterior public spaces to reemerge as integral to the library, engaging and shaping the ecosystem of our communities, has not only been unlocked, but the key has been placed in our hands.

Nature and the Library

The human relationship to nature also shaped our libraries. We may not always recognise our connection to nature and to the landscape, because, as with all relationships, there is complexity.

At one end of a spectrum, my colleague and partner at Snøhetta, Craig Dykers, sometimes shares the stories of *Theseus and Academus* in connection to the history of libraries. Greek mythology puts forward that Academus was honored after saving Athens and liberating young Helen of Troy from Theseus. A sacred grove of olive and oriental plane trees were planted to recognise Academus's wisdom. After his death, Academus was buried near Athens under a grove of trees that Plato later used for his academy, lending new meaning to the name "the Grove of the Academe." This lineage provided the root of the word *academia*, used similarly today to suggest a place of wisdom.

Such mythology is just one example of how humans have long been drawn to landscapes defined by groupings of trees as places to convene and to share ideas. Honoring our relationship to nature can be seen across many times and cultures, expressed in different ways. In some cases, through the building of religious structures in sacred spaces, and in others, the preservation of the spaces and the trees. Throughout history, people have traveled great distances to gather under sacred oak trees, listening for unknowable knowledge or simply the sound of the leaves as they shivered in the breeze.

At another end of this spectrum there are many cultures where buildings and landscapes are not the only repositories for knowledge. Oral tradition, amongst these communities, including the Indigenous populations across North America, travels with the individual knowledge keepers and is passed along through many generations. Here, transcription plays little role in how knowledge is shared, and the library may be seen as an action rather than a specific built location.

We can consider this history and our connection to nature as a platform of learning and sharing, and could easily ask; is a grove of trees also a library? From the grove of the Academe to the oral traditions across generations; there are landscapes that respond to different social and cultural conditions of place. Each formed a place of gathering and knowledge sharing, offering similar roles, just as the libraries that were built structures and housed within the *mouseion*.

Landscape as Library

Recently, I've been thinking of libraries similarly to how I consider parks; at times serving as places to be alone to contemplate or observe, or conversely, somewhere to congress with others. Parks and green spaces can often provide a sense of comfort, of connection to something larger where seasonality, ephemerality and vegetation are evidence of time and life lived. We learn through observation, conversation and through the activities we participate in when we spend time outdoors. There is a correlation to this experience that you can relate to: just as within a library, you might absorb yourself in a book, spend time alone, or engage socially in conversation with others.

As a young person, the quiet and intense isolation of my rural community could, at times, deplete my energy. Yet the town library held endless explorations to discover. I remember so clearly the atmosphere, the smell of the books, and the meditative solitude that also provided a gateway to the world. The library and its charmed whisperings drew me into this world. Getting lost in the library meant a welcome immersion into stories, characters and many far-away places and ideas, just as much as it was a place that provided the tools and resources allowing me to chart my own paths to new destinations and new opportunities.

Looking back, I recognise two distinct manifestations of libraries and their vastness of held knowledge. The landscape as a library provides a place of invitation and exploration just as the constructed physical library can offer the same. I realise now that the library itself is an opening, a portal for our minds to expand, to learn and to discover. For me, the "wild" of the forests, rivers, fields, and even the abandoned stone quarry behind my home were as much my library as the collection of books in that small-town building. This landscape embodied both body and mind, inviting me to shape the land, create shelters, be artistic, uncover picnic spots, or float a canoe in the lazy river current as I imagined myself an explorer about to discover something unknown. Didn't these experiences allow me to chart my own future journey by drawing both upon my own imagination as well as the stories I had read and the adventures I had dreamed of from the books I found in my local library?

Landscapes can be "read" if one spends time learning the language. Landscapes can tell the stories of past and present, of cause and effect, and of the complex and symbiotic relationships that we are intertwined within, yet are so easily overlooked. This understanding helps me see the landscape around us as a library, one that's lighter and physically more expansive, but not so different in spirit from the buildings we construct. The library is a landscape and the landscape a library: all full of ideas, information, and possibilities for each of us. In our minds and with our bodies, we recompose, observe, listen and contribute to our shared libraries from our own experiences and ideas.

We've long explored libraries to follow our curiosities, as places housing the mechanisms that bring information to our fingertips or that suspend us in a story. Yet, by expanding our understanding of the library to envelope the landscape, we can open access to more people while ideally recognising that many cultures and people experience the landscape and environment as a base of knowledge and experience—vis-à-vis their "library". We can both redefine the library and expand the ideas behind the design of libraries to be inclusive of different cultures, contexts and interpretations of how relevant knowledge and ideas are kept alive, expanded and disseminated.

Library as Ecosystem
Increasing equitable access to public spaces is an ongoing need. We live much of our lives in these spaces, in which we learn by creating connections between ideas and places, and through which, over time, we grow to recognise these relationships. It is easy to acknowledge that public space networks, including libraries, are part of the urban infrastructure of our communities. Providing access to knowledge and opportunities for people to come together allows us to create, deepen and explore connections crucial to a healthy society.

As explained in Andrea Wulf's (2015) *The Invention of Nature: Alexander von Humboldt's New World*, a Prussian polymath, geographer, naturalist, and explorer born in 1769, Humboldt discovered how climate, geography, nature and human societies are all interconnected. These are issues that we all are quite aware of today. Recognising, over 250 years ago, the interconnected web of life across this planet and the earth itself as a living organism, Humboldt's ideas about how we are all bound by an intricate "net-like" fabric were revolutionary for the nineteenth century and perhaps still quite relevant today.

Today, scientists studying forests, such as biologist David George Haskell and ecologist Suzanne Simard, recognise that building community and working together for the betterment of the whole can be found in even more surprising ways across the natural world. They remind us that there is a breadth of small and imperceptible biological pathways that connect trees to each other. This allows them to communicate and behave as though an entire forest is a single organism. Hub trees, or "Mother Trees", as Simard (2018) calls them, are the largest trees in forests and act as central hubs for below-ground mycorrhizal networks. They support young trees or seedlings by infecting them with fungi and ferrying them the nutrients they need to grow. So much so that studies even show how a dying tree will send its reserves and energy to a different species altogether, one that is thriving in the current condition. Such behavior acts for the betterment of the whole more so than that of the lone individual.

As designers, every project we engage with is set within a network of cause and effect. The decisions we make are not only about the project at hand but have an impact on a breadth of social and environmental outcomes that are not always easy to see or fully understand. Consider any direct corollary between nature and human health and how this is present in our communities: urban and rural; human, plant and animal. In many ways, this is how our social infrastructure contributes to the social, environmental and physical health of the people, plants and animals both near and far. Is the sharing of resources, this interconnected web of life, not also a library?

Fully considering the health of our communities is to question more deeply who these spaces are for and why. As we share all space with other biological life, not only our human counterparts, how might we expand the notion of public realm to be more inclusive? We are not the only organisms to communicate, build connections and thrive on relationships with each other. The landscape as a library holds and actively demonstrates this knowledge while offering the potential for us to interact and learn with our counterparts in nature.

What can we learn from the world around us and looking back to the *academie* in the tree grove? We can understand how sharing knowledge helps everyone, and how unseen connections may be as impactful as those we recognise. Libraries can be not only places for debate and access to information, filled with energy and the exchange of ideas, but a landscape of gathering and building connections.

Boundless Library

While ancient libraries certainly influenced the libraries of today, we've not yet drawn forth all that we can from these past examples. From the Library of Alexandria, to the Greek stoa to the Grove of the Academe, to the virtual access now so (relatively) broadly provided, and the many wonderful libraries you will find within this book; we continue to engage with each other while simultaneously connecting with people, places and knowledge across the globe. Our constructed, virtual and natural environments are inextricably linked. We should minimise the walls or boundaries that can limit us — this is how we make connections.

Humans by nature are social creatures. The places we spend time are the places where we observe, collaborate and engage with the world around us. As designers of physical spaces, our work does not stand alone or context-free. Our projects are opportunities to promote community and to influence the relationships that weave this world together.

Libraries continue to grow as a critical part of the social infrastructure of our communities and our cities, places for people to come together, to share and to debate. As we intuitively look back while also looking ahead, we might reimagine libraries as expanded places more than as repositories of resources. And while we continue to rely on the library to access information and resources, the library offers the opportunity for anyone to dream, to discover new places and to explore ideas that extend far beyond the walls of any building. This is not about any specific technology, but about how people interact with technology or access resources. We learn and explore with our bodies as well as our minds.

Our future libraries can become places that reflect the diversity, beauty and mystery of the world we all share. What this looks like is not a question of a building versus a landscape, or inside versus outside, but a question of how a library can eliminate borders, inspire us and expand connections to each other as a part of nature.

References

Goldfarb, Ben (2018). *Eager: The Surprising, Secret Life of Beavers and Why They Matter,* available online: https://www.washingtonpost.com/outlook/how-beavers-can-save-the-world-from-environmental-ruin/2018/07/26/7d7f9caa-53c9-11e8-a551-5b648abe29ef_story.html

Haskell, David George (2020). *The Songs of Trees: Stories from Nature's Great Connectors*. New York: Penguin Publishing Group.

Murray, S. (2009). *The library: an illustrated history.* New York: Skyhorse Publications.

Simard, Suzanne. TED Talk (2016), available online: https://www.ted.com/speakers/suzanne_simard

Wohlleben, Peter (2016). *The Hidden Life of Trees: What They Feel, How They Communicate—Discoveries from A Secret World* (The Mysteries of Nature, Book 1), available online: https://www.brainpickings.org/2016/09/26/the-hidden-life-of-trees-peter-wohlleben/

Wulf, Andrea (2015). *The Invention of Nature: Alexander von Humboldt's New World.* New York: A. Knopf.

Michelle Jeffrey Delk is a partner and discipline director of Landscape Architecture at Snøhetta. Fascinated by the urban environment and its influence on people's lives, Michelle has designed public spaces throughout North America. She cultivates trans-disciplinary collaboration while providing insightful vision for the creative advancement of the public environment. Since 2001, Michelle has lead diverse urban projects at a variety of scales with emphatic community and client groups. This has included the realisation of small downtown plazas, conceptual and construction plans for hundreds of acres of parks, streetscape revitalisations, the development of open spaces for campuses and the creation of new civic public spaces. Snøhetta is an international architecture, landscape architecture, interior and brand design office based in Oslo, Norway and New York City. The firm has designed and built several award-winning libraries. Snøhetta practices a self-defined trans-disciplinary process in which different professionals exchange roles in order to explore differing perspectives without the prejudice of convention. Snøhetta emphasizes an open exchange between roles and disciplines: architects, landscape architects, interior architects and graphic designers collaborate in an integrated process, ensuring multiple voices are represented from the onset of every project. When working with clients, this approach creates a place to mutually understand each other's objectives and interests. Snøhetta believes that trans-positioning promotes the positive benefits of moving out of one's comfort zone, defies narrow-minded thinking and encourages holistic approaches.

For more information, please visit: www.snohetta.com

"Forest of Knowledge" Library, Beijing, China (Snøhetta), 2018–22.
A forest-inspired large roof covers the entire library and each tree column is also a building technology component.

Photo Series

The Library as Public Space

Photos by Cida de Aragon, 2021

Mexico City

Stuttgart

Alghero

Las Vegas

San Diego

Commissioned photo series for this study: Cida de Aragon is a media artist and photographer. She researches and teaches analog and digital photography at the University of Nevada Las Vegas. Cida holds a Master's degree from Middlesex University (UK) and a Master's degree from Goldsmiths' College, University of London. The photo series shows aspects of libraries in Mexico City, Stuttgart, Alghero, Las Vegas and San Diego.

For more information, please visit: www.cidadearagon.com

Reimaging the Library of the Future

Part I. Introduction

More than Access to Knowledge: On the Changing Shape of Tomorrow's Urban Library

The Evolution of a Building Typology as Public Space
In Part 1, I will introduce the wider theme, discuss why this book is necessary, mention the publication's aims and explain its focus and limitations.

In the first decades of the twenty-first century, with a surge in the global urban population, the rising interest in the transformation of urban public space has become noticeable. During this period, the public sector has been slowly disappearing, and the private sector has increasingly taken over. This shift in the notion of public versus private has led to an increase of the public realm's privatisation and commercialisation. The present study hopes to add to a new understanding of concepts and transformation of public space by which designing for the knowledge society (which includes libraries) has recalibrated the city — a phenomenon that is increasingly resulting in an unstable urban condition, replacing the public, civic character of urban spaces.

As a consequence, today, we are not only witnessing the continuing commercialisation and privatisation of public space, but also the disappearance of the "civic" that was previously unknown. The public as commissioner of new architecture is retreating at a time when we need new ideas for public buildings and community more than ever. Futurists have speculated that, by 2050, the storing, expanding and sharing of knowledge (data) could be the last remaining form of public activity. The period of reflection that the economic circumstances at the beginning of the present century provoked (i.e., triggered by the 2008 global financial crisis) has reconnected architects with their leadership in the development of cities. This is especially relevant when the growing world population and the noticeable migration to urban areas are considered. According to UN-Habitat, every year until 2030 another 30 million people will move from rural locations to cities; and the share of the world's population living in urban areas is expected to increase from 55% in 2020 to 60% in 2030, putting additional pressure on infrastructure, public space, housing and civic facilities (UN-Habitat, 2020).

Unfortunately, in recent years, the quality of life in many cities has declined. The reasons for this decline include worsening air pollution, degraded public space, lack of green spaces, ever-increasing traffic—comprising mostly private cars—and housing that has become unaffordable. Therefore, we must plan better—including planning for the further growth of urban populations—so that we do not lose the liveability of our cities and the quality of their public spaces, which we currently still enjoy. This means that cities must provide suitable and shared, non-commercialised public space, facilities and civic amenities to accommodate the growth of these urban populations. Part of this will be the construction and renovation of libraries.

Unique Typologies of the Library

Traditionally, there are four major categories of libraries depending on their main user groups: public libraries that serve cities and towns of all types; academic libraries that serve colleges and universities; school libraries serving students from kindergarten through to the end of high school; and special libraries which are in specialised environments such as in hospitals or the government, the military, corporations, law firms, museums and so on.

Reimagining the Library of the Future reveals the current state of design of public and academic libraries, and recalls the ideals of this community-inspired typology and its wider legacy. The book features over 40 selected contemporary case studies from 12 countries and illustrates the diversity and expressive architectural potential of this unique and important building type that became public in the seventeenth century. Through comparative precedence study, the publication explores the historical stages, from the library at Trinity College in Dublin and the Bodleian Libraries in Oxford, to Stockholm Public Library, the History Faculty Library in Cambridge, as well as contemporary key precedents — including the development of libraries to create an urban place and destination. The selection of projects includes some of the most distinctive new library designs and covers all three categories: new construction, remodelling and expanding of existing buildings, and conversion (adaptive reuse) of non-library structures to libraries.

As gateways to knowledge and culture, libraries have always played a fundamental role in society. The resources and services they offer create opportunities for learning, support literacy and education, and help shape the new ideas and perspectives that are central to any creative and forward-thinking society. How will the emergence of new social factors, changes in demography, technological shifts and a change in cultural values continue to influence and transform the library? Is the current digital revolution the origin of a new crisis for the library or, on the contrary, can it drive and contribute to its renewal?

Are libraries dying? Since 2000, with the expansion of digital media, the rise of e-books and cuts to operational budgets, the end of libraries has been predicted many times over. While it is true that library budgets have been slashed, causing cuts in operating hours and even branch closures, libraries are not exactly dying. In fact, libraries are evolving. However, the overall use of many libraries has been declining. In the US, for example, there has generally been a fall of 31% in public library building use over eight years up to 2018 (Freckle Report, 2021). But at the same time, there are popular libraries where user numbers are growing; as the present study will show, this depends, to a large degree, on the mix of offerings and the design of the library. Many new urban libraries experience record visitor numbers.

As Pickles noted, "the often announced decline of the library is not the case, despite hundreds of millions of books, articles and manuscripts freely available online to anyone with access to a computer" (Pickles, 2015). Most rare books, fragile manuscripts and historical maps are now digitised, and digitisation has changed the relationship between a scholar and their library. So it first comes as a surprise when at some libraries the opposite happens: despite the internet, visitor numbers are going up, the reading rooms of libraries are the busiest ever, and there is a strong attraction to visit and see the original books or enjoy the quietness of library spaces. The absence of distractions makes it easier for users to concentrate, and being in a serious historic library environment reminds them that they are part of a long academic tradition; in addition, libraries encourage concentration because they are a way of separating home from work life. It even seems that the more material is getting digitised and available online, the more people are drawn into the library to see the authentic physical manuscripts. Now that so many people use the library again as a place to carry out their own work and research, libraries are thinking about how to best react to and accommodate the varying needs of their users.

This study shows that the library is a very unique typology that is undergoing — and will continue, even more so in the future, to undergo – great transformation. The series of presented library case studies touches on Louis Kahn's notion of "spaces which serve versus spaces which are served", as well as Rem Koolhaas's "stable versus unstable spaces" in relation to library design (as demonstrated so well in Louis Kahn's Phillips Exeter Academy Library and in OMA's Seattle Central Library) in order to query the potential of the library's typical programme. In doing so, the study projects the continuing evolution of the library as the backbone of the community: few other typologies express an equally strong idea of civic society, the collective, and the concept of sharing.

As the world continues to face economic, political, health and environmental crises and is forced to deal with uncertainty and rapid change, the aim is to examine the validity and continuity of one of our most accepted and trusted of public institutions. The contemporary public and academic library is not only defined by its collection of books or architecture, but also by something more, which this book aims to uncover. The widely accepted historical (but conceptually limited) function of the library as a "storehouse for collecting and storing manuscripts and books" has clearly expanded: the contemporary library building has evolved as an important extension of public space, a place for community meetings, and even as a catalyst for urban revitalisation.

Through the lens of the library, a new idea of public space emerges. This well overdue analysis examines how the typology of the library has always been a testing ground of public interest and shared civic space, evolving in interesting new directions today. As Kelvin Watson speculates in the Foreword, over the next decade the library will continue to expand its role as a free educational resource for lifelong-learners and all residents, with initiatives targeting non-traditional library users. Advocating the dissemination of knowledge while empowering the public, libraries continue to celebrate access to ideas, curiosity and empathy, supporting the urban ambition for the library to become a new civic hub for social support and community.

Consequently, libraries are not just places to study and read books for free. They are one of the very few public places left in our society where one is allowed to exist without any expectation of consuming and spending money. "Libraries really do change lives", Richard Francis-Jones of FJMT Studio told me (2021). Good libraries can be contemplative quiet places, offering free access to corners for privacy and large reading rooms with plenty of daylight and high ceilings. This publication not only examines the shifting role of library design that started in the post-war US and European construction boom (including some more recent examples from Asia), but also explores new ways of thinking about libraries through the genre-breaking concept of the learning centre and médiathèque — a public multimedia institution that contains not only manuscripts and books, newspapers and magazines, but also electronic multimedia materials such as videos, podcasts and sound recordings.

The Future of Library Design

Today, libraries are many things — ranging from research centres, gathering places, idea factories and repositories of cultural memory, to places where the internet can be used for free. Besides offering access to knowledge, most good libraries now have a popular coffee shop and breakout spaces for those who want to chat. An Oxford University professor of literature recently commented: "In the past, libraries were a little like supermarkets. Now they are more like laboratories — you can go in there with students to research and teach from the special collections" (Pickles, 2015). So, what are the trends and how does the typical library typology need to be reimagined and reorganised in order to remain viable and useful in the twenty-first century? Joshua Ramus (2004) stated that "our ambition for Seattle Central Library was to redefine the library as an institution no longer exclusively dedicated to the book". Part 2 of this study takes a closer look at the latest trends and ideas in library design.

The flexibility to accommodate change in function is important. Will Bruder organised the Phoenix Central Library as a "Flexible Warehouse of Knowledge" across five levels. He noted that "the uses of libraries, worldwide, have of course evolved substantially over the past 25 years. The Phoenix Central Library has proven highly adaptable to these changes and serves its purpose as well today as the day it opened. After years of heavy use and necessary small adaptions in functionality, the library still bears its architectural identity and reflects the need for libraries that can accommodate change" (2021).

The present book uses case study analysis to reveal general patterns that emerge, and introduces in Part 3 multiple design strategies relevant for the future of public buildings. It argues that public buildings and public spaces, which are termed "the collective", constitute the most significant aspect of cities today. Or, as library architect Francine Houben of Mecanoo added, "The library is always a social landmark in the city. Libraries are the most important public buildings" (2021). As with every public building, to achieve successful library architecture depends to a large degree on the engagement of the client. Herbert Muschamp noted: "What libraries need most of all are strong clients. A strong client is a librarian client who knows exactly what she wants", noting that, "In the history of the world, there has never been a great building without a strong client" (Muschamp, 2004). Outcomes of public building projects are largely dependent on the project engagement of their stakeholders, trustees and community leaders — a group likely to be less interested in issues of form and aesthetics, and more interested in the user experience, functionality and daily operation.

In Library as Stoa, Wingert-Playdon (2019) argued that a library "strongly demonstrates the role of public space and innovation in architecture". She added that a library today is increasingly becoming a hybrid that could be a studio and creative commons, a place for discovery, creation and preservation and sharing of knowledge. It is obvious that today's library is about creating a transformative and easily accessible place where people can come together. However, with so many roles to take on, its valuable communal spirit at the core could also be in danger of being lost. In light of recent developments —such as the 2020–21 pandemic— and people's ever-increasing screen time, mostly spent isolated alone at home, the future evolution of the library has emerged as an even more relevant topic.

There are twentieth-century architects who have become experts in the design of libraries and the particularities of this unique typology, including Alvar Aalto, Hans Scharoun, James Stirling, Arata Isozaki, Fumihiko Maki, Alvaro Siza and Norman Foster. More recently, the most remarkable and award-winning libraries of the first two decades of the twenty-first century have been designed by the firms Steven Holl Architects, Snøhetta, Mecanoo, Bolles-Wilson and FJMT Studio. They have worked on dozens of library projects across the world and developed a reputation for creating engaging buildings with bold civic spaces that respond sensitively to their specific brief and geographic location. Francine Houben argued that: "Libraries are the most important public buildings. It is not only about the design, it is the programme that needs to be tailored to the context and to the communities that it serves. Each library has its own challenges and our task is to prepare them for unpredictable change" (2021).

The selected cases in Part 2 show that some of these next-generation libraries offer dramatic, multi-storey walls of bookshelves, creating the interior space by the design of the book stacks or the specific layout of the circulation. The library programmes are now expanded to include exhibition spaces, child care and employment training centres that provide job-search help, skills and small-business support. The new libraries include large areas dedicated to children and a separate section for teenagers. Numerous new libraries offer public roof terraces with cafés, outdoor reading areas and a dramatic viewing platform to look at the city. The integration of greenery in gardens, rooftops and courtyards is a frequent design approach.

This study argues that the architecture of libraries is now at the intersection of many interdependent and contradictory forces, and the negotiations that must take place during their design phase. A selection of leading architectural practices has contributed short provocative statements on the library of the future accompanying the relevant case studies, including Steven Holl, Snøhetta, Mecanoo, Foster + Partners, Diller Scofidio + Renfro, MVRDV, Antoine Predock, Will Bruder, Zaha Hadid Architects and FJMT Studio, among others. Michelle Jeffrey Delk noted in the *Prologue* to this book that "it is not about any specific technology, but about how people interact with technology or access resources" (Delk, 2021), arguing that a library could also be read as a "landscape of knowledge" similar to a garden or vineyard. Jacques Herzog contended that "making intelligent and functional use of space is one of the traditional tasks of the architect and still of fundamental importance in library design" (Herzog, 2020). The various cases presented are libraries where the spaces are logically organised according to their use and function, reassuring us that digital technology has still not rendered books obsolete. However, the exact use, logic and function of this typology continue to shift, hereby advancing the typology and creating new inventive designs that can be so functionally specific that the resulting library offers distinct aesthetic and spatial experiences.

The notion of a "hybrid typology" is hereby of particular interest. Richard Francis-Jones of FJMT noted that

"the Bunjil Place project in Australia is an example of a new form of community and civic building that also includes a library. It is not a single-use facility that tends to divide and separate the community by interest, education or culture, but an inclusive hybrid form of public building, reflecting and embracing our diversity. This hybrid is a library, a cultural centre, a performance theatre, a public gathering space, a place of exhibition, gallery and display, a flexible and experimental space for events, lectures, debate and celebration. It is a help point, a service centre and a place of work and collaboration. Above all, perhaps, it is a place where all of this overlaps and interconnects and at the centre is the interconnecting fluid form of the foyer gathering space, a non-hierarchical space that unifies the complex" (FJMT, 2020).

Part 2 of this study returns to the notion of the "hybrid" in more detail.

The Wider Theme

There is already a large number of books on technical standards and planning guidelines for libraries. The focus of this interdisciplinary study is elsewhere: it starts by rethinking the role and meaning of civic space and public buildings, and offers fresh insight into the increasingly complex relationship between urban space, the design of libraries and everyday life. The book discusses the critical characteristics that shape new urban spaces by drawing on urban studies, considering urban planning, landscape architecture and architecture beyond the usual categories of street, plaza, park and arcade.

A reinvented library has become a central ingredient of any revitalisation of a downtown area or university campus through what urban planners call place-making, by establishing the library as the "third place" (as the in-between space, outside home and outside the workplace) for all segments of a community. New types of such hybrid public spaces include greenery, produce energy and food, collect and clean water, are socially inclusive, activated by 24/7 programmes, and are not necessarily on ground-level but might also be at heights three floors above ground. However, sustainability is now a driving factor in the urban design of public space and all urban development, and the library of the future will need to be a super-green, high-performing and energy-efficient building (see Part 3 for more on this). Public urban space has not only become a precious commodity but also one of the key vehicles for achieving sustainable urban development. The publication provides a range of relevant case studies of libraries with public spaces from Europe, Asia, Latin America and North America to address important questions about inclusiveness, processes of transformation and change, as well as the role of public space in a warming climate, urban design theory, and attitudes towards civic space expressed through urban life.

The Purpose and Limitations of this Study

This interdisciplinary study challenges the conventional idea of the library as "a building to store books" and aims to make a meaningful contribution to the discourse on the future of this particular building type by speculating on the next-generation library. It uses a critical case study approach to identify and discuss alternative and hybrid models of the public and academic library. The discussion touches on the future of civic space and public buildings in general, as well as how communal places are likely to change.

For the last 150 years, libraries have had a limited view of themselves as information-centred storehouses, but have recently evolved as a vibrant and vital member of community development, and as a basis for outreach efforts aimed at underserved and diverse populations.

Today, the library is not considered elitist anymore. But there is still a lack of systematic understanding of how public buildings and the collective civic space weave cities together through their interconnected spatial network. The research study wishes to examine this subject and the role of the library in advancing knowledge, enriching lives and building community. Hence, the question central to the study relates to the knowledge gap regarding how this role has changed. For example, libraries' community support plays an increasingly important role in a society that is more split and individualistic than ever. Therefore, the book's hypothesis is that the library of the future is about creating "a public place" — a destination. As the selected designs well illustrate, it is a reimagined place that creates a lasting civic value and a destination in the new digital society framework. Or, as Tigran Haas argued (2021), "the next generation of libraries in the network society are creating a new mission well beyond the storage of knowledge".

Since Étienne-Louis Boullée's unbuilt proposal for the French National Library (1785), new library spaces have become arenas for innovative concepts and utopian views of social place-making in the urban landscape. Recently, new institutional typologies have emerged, some of them using the "stacking" of functions as design principle that directly expresses the organisation of their different sections (Seattle Central Library by OMA is a good example of this). In the future, the typological boundaries will blur even further, making the library an important place for many. In the exploration and analysis of these speculative futures, our knowledge about the library as a public institution, place and social landmark is still developing, yet we seem further away than ever from imagining the definite type of building for it.

It seems that the library of the future is a phenomenon that has yet to be defined in terms of its performance, role and architectural appearance. It seems that, until now, the design drivers of urban spaces and public buildings, and the changing patterns in how they are used, have not been sufficiently explored. The publication presents different approaches and addresses questions concerning the design process, the idea of place-making, and the integration of ecological systems in the design of future-ready urbanscapes.

Today, cities are in a competition with each other to attract investment and talent, and to be seen as significant centres of culture and education. Every city or town dreams of a new library that is also a public magnet and a cultural signature building that will create a unique point of difference for city marketing and a touristic attraction. Libraries always exist in this multidimensional relationship within the larger urban, cultural and societal context and the wider knowledge systems they create. *Reimagining the Library of the Future* explores this transformation of an established typology from the traditional format to a communal incubator of ideas and place for new knowledge generation, exchange and sharing. It explores the opportunities and challenges for new hybrid types of libraries and the transformation of civic urban spaces previously known as *public*.

The 40 selected case studies presented in this publication (all with their different ambitions) do not reflect a complete list, but merely the author's preferences. Whether modest reuses or shiny newbies, these libraries all contribute to the search for the future of this reimagined typology. Therefore, the selected cases render visible a broad array of design strategies that partially build on the historical evolution of a unique typology: the library of the future.

Only thirty years after Johannes Gutenberg (c. 1400–1468) printed his first Bible using moveable type in 1445, Antonello da Messina (1430–1479) painted *Saint Jerome in his Study*. The work is exhibited in the National Gallery in London and shows Saint Jerome surrounded by books, an example of quiet individual study. St. Jerome had around twenty-five volumes within reach on the shelves with room for more; an obvious consideration was the security of these books since they were items of great rarity. Brawne (1970) suggests that this painting is the quintessential expression of the problem and solution to library design, as it encapsulates the relationship between the scholar and the tools of the trade—a relationship that dominated library planning throughout history.

The Library of Celsus in ancient Ephesus, modern day Turkey, was built around 135 CE in honour of a Roman senator, one of the most compelling libraries and façades. It stored over 12,000 scrolls and those who wished to read them would travel long distances to visit. They would stay until their work was complete, sometimes for weeks at a time, and were given a place to eat, sleep and do some sort of athletic activity. The Library of Celsus was the third-largest library in the Roman world behind only Alexandria and Pergamum.

A Short List of 100+ Relevant Libraries

Following is a list of relevant and distinctive libraries that have significantly contributed to the evolution of the typology, with the names of the designers in brackets. This is not a complete list; it's a list of my favorites, but there are many more. While it is impossible to list all important libraries worldwide, a closer study of these relevant buildings listed below will provide a very good overview of different models and approaches.

Historical cases (20):

Trinity College Library, Dublin (Thomas Burgh)
Bodleian Library, University of Oxford, UK (Thomas Holt; Giles Gilbert Scott)
Real Gabinete Royal Portuguese Reading Room, Rio de Janeiro, Brazil (Rafael da Silva)
Stiftsbibliothek Admont Abbey, Austria (Josef Hueber)
Maria Laach Abbey Library, Andernach, Germany (unknown Jesuits)
Oberlausitzische Bibliothek der Wissenschaften, Goerlitz, Germany (A. von Gersdorff)
Abbey Library of St. Gall, St. Gallen, Switzerland (Peter Thumb)
Laurentian Library, Florence, Italy (Michelangelo)
Royal Library at the El Escorial, near Madrid, Spain (Juan Bautista de Toledo)
Al-Qarawiyyin Library, Fez, Morocco (renovation: Aziza Chaouni)
French National Library, Paris, France – Unbuilt proposal (Etienne-Louis Boullée)
French National Library, Paris, France (Henri Labrouste)
Biblioteca Statale Oratoriana dei Girolamini, Naples, Italy (Giovanni Antonio Dosio)
British Museum Reading Room, London, UK (Robert Smirke)
Handelingenkamer Old Library, The Hague, The Netherlands (Cornelis H. Peters)
The Library of Parliament, Ottawa, Canada (Thomas Fuller)
George Peabody Library, Baltimore, USA (Edmund G. Lind)
State Library of South Australia, Adelaide, Australia (E. J. Woods)
Sterling Memorial Library, Yale University, New Haven, USA (James Gamble Rogers)
Stockholm Public Library, Stockholm, Sweden (Gunnar Asplund)

Modern cases (30):

Viipuri Central City Library, Vyborg, Finland (now Russia) (Alvar Aalto)
Wolfsburg City Library, Wolfsburg, Germany (Alvar Aalto)
Rovaniemi City Library, Finland (Alvar Aalto)
Mt. Angel Abbey Library, Portland, Orgeon, US (Alvar Aalto)
Phillips Exeter Academy Library, New Hampshire, US (Louis Kahn)
T. Fisher Rare Book Library, University of Toronto, Canada (Mathers and Haldenby)
Oita Prefectural Library, Oita, Japan (Arata Isozaki & Associates)
Kitakyushu Central Library, Fukuoka, Japan (Arata Isozaki & Associates)
Municipal Library Viana do Castelo, Portugal (Alvaro Siza Vieira)
University Main Library, University of Aveiro, Aveiro, Portugal (Alvaro Siza Vieira)
Berlin State Library, Berlin, Germany (Hans Scharoun)

History Faculty Library, Cambridge University, Cambridge, UK (James Stirling)
Science Library, University of California Irvine, CA, US (James Stirling Micahel Wilford & Associates)
Beinecke Rare Books & Manuscript Library, New Haven, US (Gordon Bunshaft, SOM)
Atlanta-Fulton Central Public Library, Atlanta, US (Marcel Breuer)
Basel University Library, Basel, Switzerland (Otto H. Senn)
The British Library, St. Pancras, London, UK (Colin St. John Wilson & Partners)
Geisel Library, University of California, San Diego, US (William Pereira)
Grand Bibliotheque Nationale de France, Paris, France (Dominique Perrault)
Cranfield Library, University of Cranfield, Bedfordshire, UK (Foster + Partners)
Carre d'Art, Nimes, France (Foster + Partners)
Peckham Library, Peckham, London, UK (Will Alsop)
The Hague City Library, The Hague, the Netherlands (Richard Meier & Partners)
Pedro Salinas Library, Puerto de Toledo, Madrid, Spain (Juan Navarro Baldeweg)
Public City Library Ana Maria Matute, Carabanchel, Madrid (RSP Architects)
State and University Library Goettingen, Lower Saxony, Germany (Gerber & Partner)
King Fahad National Library, Riyadh, Saudi Arabia (Gerber & Partner)
German National Library, Deutsche Nationalbibliothek expansion, Leipzig (Arat-Kaiser-Kaiser)
Saxon State and University Library, Dresden, Germany (Ortner & Ortner)
City Library Heidenheim, Germany (Max Dudler)
Jacob & Wilhelm Grimme Centre, Berlin (Max Dudler)
Central Public Library of Vancouver, Vancouver, BC, Canada (Moshe Safdie & Associates)
Salt Lake City Public Library, Salt Lake City, Utah, USA (Moshe Safdie & Associates)

Contemporary cases (60):

Muenster New City Library, Muenster, Germany (Bolles-Wilson + Partner)
Springdale Library, Brampton, Canada (RDH Architects)
Des Moines Public Library, Gateway Park Des Moines, US (David Chipperfield)
Darwin College Study Centre, Cambridge, UK (Jeremy Dixon & Edward Jones)
Sendai Mediatheque, Sendai, Miyagi, Japan (Toyo Ito & Associates)
Tama Art University Library, Hachioji, Tokyo, Japan (Toyo Ito & Associates)
Toyonokuni Libraries for Cultural Resources, Oita, Japan (Arata Isozaki & Associates)
Shenzhen Library and Cultural Center, Shenzhen, China (Arata Isozaki & Associates)
Bibliotheca Alexandrina, Alexandria, Egypt (Snøhetta)
Temple University Charles Library, Philadelphia, US (Snøhetta)
James Hunt Jr. Library, North Carolina State University, US (Snøhetta)
Ryerson University Student Learning Center, Toronto, Canada (Snøhetta)
Svalbard Global Seed Vault, Norway (Snøhetta)
Calgary New Central Library, Calgary, Canada (Snøhetta)
Theodore Roosevelt Presidential Library, North Dakota, US (Snøhetta)
Free University's Philology Faculty Library, Berlin, Germany (Foster + Partners)
University Library, Jussieu, Paris, France, unbuilt proposal (OMA, Rem Koolhaas)
Seattle Public Library, Seattle, Washington, US (OMA, Rem Koolhaas)

Queens Public Library, Hunters Point, New York, US (Steven Holl Architects)
Bibliotheca Vasconcelos Public Library, Mexico City, Mexico (Alberto Kalach & TAX)
Oodi-Helsinki Central Library, Helsinki, Finland (ALA Architects)
Vienna University of Economics Library, Vienna, Austria (Zaha Hadid Architects)
Rolex Learning Centre, Lausanne, Switzerland (SANAA)
House of Wisdom Library, Sharjah, UAE (Foster + Partners)
Mesa Public Library, Los Alamos, New Mexico, US (Antoine Predock)
Las Vegas Central Library and Children Museum, Las Vegas, US (Antoine Predock)
Burton Barr Central Library, Phoenix, Arizona, US (Will Bruder & DWL Architects)
Agave Library, Phoenix, Arizona, US (Will Bruder)
Billings Public Library, Montana, US (Will Bruder)
Hanoi Public Library, Hanoi, Vietnam (Farming Architects)
Virglio Barca Public Library, Bogota, Colombia (Rogelio Salmona)
Shenzhen SUST University Library, Shenzhen, China (Urbanus)
Pinghe Bibliotheater, Qingpu, Shanghai, China (Open Architects)
Tianjin Binhai New Area Library, Tianjin, China (MVRDV)
Bishan Public Library, Singapore (Look Architects)
Daegu Gosan Public Library, Daegu, South Korea (Jaja Architects)
Austin Central Library, Austin, Texas, US (Lake-Flato)
Mediatheque, Bordeaux, France (BIG)
Media Library, Bourg-la-Reine, France (Pascale Guedot)
Municipal Library, University of Sassari, Alghero, Sardinia, Italy (Giovanni Maciocco)
Stuttgart Municipal Library, Stuttgart, Germany (Eun Young Yi)
Delft University of Technology Library, Delft, the Netherlands (Mecanoo)
Birmingham Central Library, Birmingham, UK (Mecanoo)
LocHal Library, Tilburg, the Netherlands (Mecanoo)
Tainan Public Library, Tainan, Taiwan (Mecanoo)
Stavros Niarchos Foundation Library, expansion, New York, US (Mecanoo)
Martin Luther King Jr. Memorial Library, expansion, Washington, D.C. (Mecanoo)
Vagelos Education Center, Columbia U, New York, US (Diller Scofidio + Renfro, Gensler)
Cottbus BTU University Library, Cottbus, Germany (Herzog & de Meuron)
National Library of Israel, Jerusalem, Israel (Herzog & de Meuron)
Media Library, Thionville, France (Dominique Coulon & Associates)
Luis Martin Santos Public Library, Madrid, Spain (Mario San Juan Calle et al.)
Jose Hierro Public Library, Madrid, Spain (Juan Herreros & Inaki Abalos)
The Hive, University and County Library, Worcester, UK (Feilden Clegg Bradley)
Kanazawa Umimirai Library, Kanazawa, Japan (Kudo & Horiba with KHA)
Surry Hills Library and Neighbourhood Centre, Sydney, NSW, Australia (FJMT)
Max Webber Library, Blacktown, NSW, Australia (FJMT)
Craigieburn Library, Hume City, North Melbourne, VIC, Australia (FJMT)
Frank Bartlett Memorial Library and Moe Service Centre, Gippsland, VIC, Australia (FJMT)
Bankstown Library and Knowledge Centre, Bankstown, NSW, Australia (FJMT)
Bunjil Place Cultural Centre, Narre Warren, City of Casey, VIC, Australia (FJMT)
City of Perth Library and History Centre, Perth, WA, Australia (Kerry Hill Architects)

Libraries fulfill a special function in society. Library buildings are places of learning, gathering, and exploring. People often form strong emotional associations with the libraries in their lives. Architects approach library projects from multiple perspectives. Who will use the library and how will they use it? How will people get to the library? What collections will the library house? The municipal library of the twenty-first century is a mixed-use facility, a 24-hour library, meeting place, and community destination.

— Diego Grass, 2019

Bodleian Libraries, University of Oxford, UK (Thomas Holt; Giles Gilbert Scott), 1602
The Bodleian Library in Oxford was founded in 1602. With over 13 million printed items, it is the second-largest library in Britain after the British Library. The Bodleian Library is the main research library of the University of Oxford; it occupies a group of five buildings: the fifteenth-century Duke Humfrey's Library, the seventeenth-century Schools Quadrangle, the eighteenth-century Clarendon Building and Radcliffe Camera, and the twentieth- and twenty-first-century Weston Library. It was the Bodleian Library's innovation to store books on their ends rather than on their sides as had previously been the custom; this not only allowed more books to fit in a smaller space but also made them more easily accessible. The Bodleian Libraries lacked artificial lighting until 1929; reliance on the sun for light and heat kept the library's hours of operation quite short —as little as five hours per day during the winter. The Weston Library was designed by Sir Giles Gilbert Scott in 1934.

Maria Laach Abbey Library, Andernach, Germany, 1865
Founded in what was Belgium in 1093, this monastery library *Bibliotheca Sanctus* at Maria Laach Abbey is one of the best preserved and most beautiful libraries. It did undergo a traumatic transformation when the abbey of Maria Laach was abolished in 1802. The library was dismantled along with the existing book stock, about 3,700 volumes. In 1892, the Benedictine monks resettled the monastery and re-stocked the library. Today, the library has 260,000 volumes in the new reading room with about 9,000 manuscripts printed before 1800. The oldest section is in the Jesuit Library with rare books kept in a renovated cowshed with climate control. It is now one of the largest private libraries in Germany. The library also was entangled in controversy surrounding the Nazi regime as depicted in Heinrich Böll's *Billiards at Half-past Nine*.

Oberlausitzische Bibliothek der Wissenschaften, Goerlitz, Germany, 1806
The Upper Lusatian Library of Sciences includes 150,000 volumes and is a public scientific library located near Dresden, in the historic city of Görlitz. It was founded by historian and linguist Karl Gottlob Anton and landowner Adolph Traugott von Gersdorf to support the ideas of the Enlightenment. It holds materials ranging from legal texts to natural sciences to historical literature. Originally, only members of the their society could access the collection; today the collection is open to the public. Housed in a baroque building, the collection includes 14,000 years of regional history. For example, it holds historical maps, archives of the Upper Lusatian Society of Sciences, and an archaeological collection of ancient pottery.

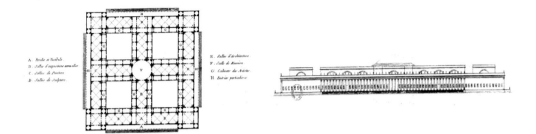

Design for a Public Library by Jean-Nicolas-Louis Durand, France, 1802–05

Jean-Nicolas-Louis Durand (1760-1834) regarded the Précis of the Lectures on Architecture (1802–1805) as both a basic course for future civil engineers and a treatise. Focusing the practice of architecture on utilitarian and economic values, he assailed the rationale behind classical architectural training: beauty, proportionality, and symbolism. The symmetrical floor plan of Durand's typology for a public building (such as a museum or library) is in the monumental spirit of the French Ecole des-Beaux-Arts emphasises its public character and significance of the building; it is a simply structured, systemised, and well ordered floor plan, where the exterior of the building directly indicated its particular use and functional performance.

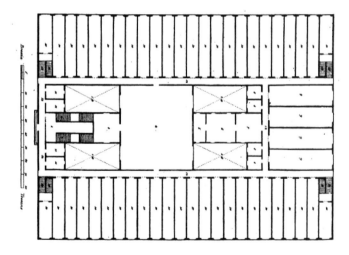

Design for a Library "Pubblica Universale Biblioteca" by Leopoldo della Santa, Italy, 1816

This floor plan is very different from Durand's earlier typology: it shows the three different areas of the central reading room, the narrow cabinets left and right for book stacks, and the small rooms for administration —an arrangement that was still common in the twentieth century (Schmitz, K.H., 2016). This typology changed again in the 1990s with the introduction of digital technologies and digitised material, which has not replaced the physical book and collection, leading to new spatial concepts. Today, as the selection of cases in this study demonstrates, the public and academic libraries have taken on several additional roles and functions, and do not always express externally what is going on inside.

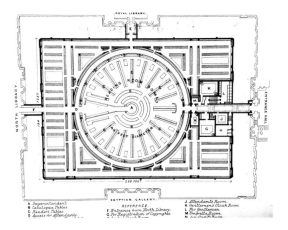

The Circular Reading Room in the central quadrangle courtyard of the British Museum, London, UK (Sydney Smirke), 1857 (renovated 1995–2000 by Foster + Partners)

In 1852, work commenced on the famous domed Reading Room and the surrounding 'Iron Library' (due to its iron book stack) and opened in 1857. The collection of close to a million books was held in revolutionary space-saving arrangements that surrounded the central reading room. The b/w photo above was taken in 1924. Inspired by the Pantheon and work by Claude Nicolas Ledoux, the rotunda form enjoyed some popularity in the 18th and 19th centuries as seen at James Gibbs' Radcliffe Camera in Oxford. Such a circular design was thereafter adopted by many other great libraries, such as Maughan Library at King's College in London and by the Stockholm Public Library in form of a simple cylinder within a box (Asplund, 1928). The relationship between pure geometry and intellectualism is a recurrent theme in many more library designs such as Isozaki's libraries, Mecanoo's library in Delft and Snøhetta at Alexandria. The dome at the Reading Room, inspired by the Pantheon in Rome, has a diameter of 43 metres (140 feet). The Reading Room was used regularly by a large number of researchers and writers, including notably Sun Yat-sen, Oscar Wilde, George Orwell, Mark Twain, Vladimir Lenin, and Sir Arthur Conan Doyle. In 1867, Karl Marx wrote *Das Kapital*. But many users found the intensively centred space too controlling. In 1997, the function moved to the new British Library at St. Pancras, but the Reading Room remains in its original form at the British Museum, now used as exhibition space (Caygill, 2000). The reading rooms of the British Museum or at Bodleian Library are exemplary of academic and research libraries founded upon private collections of the 18th century.

The circular domed Reading Room of Maughan Library at King's College, London, UK (James Pennethorne), 1851

Designed by Sir James Pennethorne and constructed in 1851, with further extensions made between 1868 and 1900, the Maughan Library is a grade II-listed building. Inside the library is the dodecagonal (ten-sided) reading room, inspired by the Reading Room at the British Museum. In the twentieth century, The circular shape for reading rooms was rejected as too rigid and without any flexibility to adapt to future change.

A library is an indoor public space in which you do not have to buy anything in order to stay.
— **Zadie Smith, Novelist, 2012**

Trinity College Library, Dublin, Ireland (Thomas Burgh), 1712–32
Thomas Burgh's classical eighteenth-century building at Trinity College, famed for its 'Long Room', home to the largest collection of books in Ireland. The 65 metres (213 feet) long main room is covered in marble and dark wood pilasters. When it was first completed, the Long Room had a flat ceiling, but the roof was raised to accommodate more books. In the United Kingdom, university libraries were founded in the colleges of Oxford and Cambridge in the thirteenth century followed by those of the Scottish universities in St. Andrews, Glasgow, Aberdeen and Edinburgh in the fifteenth century, and then in Ireland by Trinity College in Dublin in 1591. McParland (2001) comments on Burgh's classical library: "So few people had previously access to the Library that the symbolical value of the building was unimpaired by its internal incompletion and total absence of books. The building was eventually occupied in 1732."

French National Library, unbuilt proposal by Étienne-Louis Boullée, 1785
Neoclassical Enlightenment architect Boullée promoted the idea of making architecture expressive of its purpose; he developed a distinctive abstract geometric style inspired by Classical forms. His work was characterised by the removal of all unnecessary ornamentation and inflating geometric forms to a huge scale and symmetry. His work mostly comprised designs for public buildings on a grand, monumental scale. His 1785 proposal for the main reading room of the French National Library features a vast, barrel-vaulted ceiling and a modern shelving arrangement: stacked galleries of books over flat wall-cases. These seemingly endless bookcases were open and easily browsable, in contrast to the earlier medieval system of chaining that bound both books, and readers, to a specific location. Visitors are free to wander about and converse in small groups, but there is no provision of study desks for research in this idealised environment.

Bibliothèque Sainte-Geneviève Library, Paris, France (Henri Labrouste), 1838–51
Henri Labrouste (1801-1875) was a French architect from the famous École des Beaux-Arts school of architecture. He designed the famous reading room for the Bibliothèque Sainte-Geneviève, a public and university library in Paris. The slender iron columns with arches and the large windows give an impression of space and lightness. In 1862, Labrouste went on to design the Salle Labrouste, the main reading room in the old Bibliothèque Nationale de France.

Boston Public Library, Bates Hall Reading Room, Boston, Massachusetts, US (Charles F. McKim), 1895
The Boston Public Library opened in 1854; it contains roughly 23 million items, making it the second-largest public library in the US. The library is known for its incredible courtyard, entrance atrium, and its quintessential library reading room: the Bates Hall Reading Room, which was completed in 1895. With its elegant emerald-green reading lamps and dramatic arched ceiling and windows, the Boston Public Library's grand Bates Hall has been welcoming Bostonians in need of a place to work or study for more than a century.

New York City Public Library on Fifth Avenue, Rose Main Reading Room, New York City, US (Carrere & Hastings), 1897
Founded in 1895, the library opened in 1911: at this time, a grand library that was free to the public was still a fresh, almost radical notion. The New York Public Library (NYPL) has nearly 53 million items, and is the third largest library in the world. The incredible Beaux-Arts landmark was one of the largest marble structures in the US when it was built. Its historic Rose Main Reading Room was renovated in 2016; it stretches nearly two city blocks, measuring 90 m in length and 26 m in width (297 feet long by 87 feet wide), and has 42 long oak tables for users to sit in. The collection includes Columbus's 1493 letter announcing his discovery of the New World.

George Peabody Library, Baltimore, Maryland, US (Edmund G. Lind), 1878
This library interior is often regarded as one of the most beautiful libraries in the world. Completed in 1878, it was designed by Baltimore architect Edmund G. Lind in collaboration with the first Peabody provost, Nathaniel H. Morison, that described it as a "cathedral of books." The visually stunning, monumental neo-Greco interior features an atrium that, over an alternating black and white slab marble floor, soars 19 metres (61 feet) high to a latticed skylight of frosted heavy glass, surrounded by five floors of ornamental cast-iron balconies. Today it is used as research library by the Johns Hopkins University.

The Grand Reading Room at the Bancroft Library, University of California at Berkeley, CA, US, 1905
The library has a collection on the history of California and the North American West, which the author has frequently visited, and which is far from old-fashioned.

Reimaging the Library of the Future

PART II. The Past and the Presence

Tianjin Library (MVRDV)

Reimaging the Library of the Future

PART II. The Past and the Presence

1. The Evolution of the Library: from Stockholm to Sendai to Seattle to Tianjin

civic
 adjective
 civ·ic | \ si-vik

civic — of or relating or belonging to a city or community affairs; benefitting citizens as
individuals. Latin: *civicus*

*If something is related to or benefits an individual citizen, it can be described as civic. The
adjective civic comes from the Latin word civis, which was the word for a citizen of Ancient
Rome. It is also a root word for 'city', so civic can also mean anything related to a city. First
known use of the word civic: 1655, in the meaning defined above.*

— Oxford Dictionary

The Relationship between the City and the Library: New Types of Public Spaces and Places?
The starting point for the study in Part 1 was a discussion of the evolution of civicspaces and public
building typologies. The different scales of urban landscapes, along with their internal and external
dynamics, offer interesting research scenarios that can be approached from multi- disciplinary
points of view. Among these contexts, urban fabric, civic space and public buildings constitute
a basis for research from morphological, social, cultural, economic and environmental perspectives.
In the future, the renewal of public spaces and their continuous upgrading and maintenance is likely
to constitute one of the largest aspects of an architect's engagement. Research is now increasingly
important to support design decisions through data, and we are witnessing the awakening
of a new generation of architects who are more and more focused on applied research and
research-informed design processes to improve the human built environment.

The character of a great city has always been shaped by its beautiful parks, gardens, squares
and public space network, the latter of which creates the framework for the integration of public
buildings. Therefore, the research for this publication focuses not only on single buildings, but also
on the city and its public spaces as one of the most relevant architectural issue of the twenty-first
century, placing the spotlight on the regeneration of the urban fabric, through public buildings and
the integration of green spaces as an indispensable part of sustainable progress in human habitats.

The study identifies the following dangerous trends: (a) the increasing privatisation and commercialisation
of spaces that were once more clearly in the public domain, (b) the increasing surveillance of
public spaces and the control of access to them to strengthen the security and control of citizens,
and (c) the increasing use of design themes that employ "theme park" simulations and disrupt the
continuity of local history, meaningful culture and geography to transform the public realm into a
controlled territory of consumption. In an era of globalisation and neoliberal capitalism, urban space
has become increasingly anonymous and interchangeable, losing its authenticity.

Deep and consequential changes are on the way, affecting our cities. Online shopping has diminished retail in traditional town centres; home offices have replaced some large structures of administrative headquarters. What stands out in this transformation process is the impotant role of the library and other public buildings for the knowledge society. Richard Rogers argues that "architecture is about public space held by buildings." Upgrading public space is now recognised as a key catalyst of any good development. Free access and use of public space was once the basic principle of all urbanism. But the commercial dimension has infiltrated urbanism on every level, allowing globalisation to shape sterile versions of public space everywhere. Now it will be important how future public buildings, such as libraries, re-introduce other ways of doing things and how such buildings are presenting themselves within the public realm. Therefore, this study aims to:

(a) Anticipate future conditions of public architecture, such as the transformation of the library towards a public community destination (frequently combined with some green space), and their influence on how we perceive and experience the city; and
(b) Examine possible answers to the following questions:

- Why is it always a special privilege to design a public building, and what will be the role of public buildings in times when the civic has become increasingly privatised?
- What will be the future notion of the "civic"?
- How are typologies, such as those of the library, art gallery or museum, changing?
- What does it mean to design the civic realm and public buildings in the twenty-first century in a post-pandemic world impacted by climate change, demographic shifts and uncertainty?
- What might be the evolving future needs of visitors and users of libraries?

Different Types of Libraries: Varying Spatial Concepts, Plan Configurations and Layouts
We can identify different types of libraries: most institutions make a distinction between a circulating or lending library, where materials are loaned to patrons, institutions, or other libraries; and a reference library, where material is not lent out. Modern libraries are often a mixture of both, containing a general collection for circulation and a reference collection, which has restricted access. The different types of libraries include the public library, academic library, national or state library, reference library, children's library, specialised research library, or the digital library. In the last twenty years, we have seen an increasing shift to digital libraries and mediatheques.

Users of a public library have different needs from students at an academic library that might focus on specific research areas, or users of a specialised library and archive. Libraries are organised and maintained by different public or private bodies. They are usually funded and organised by a government or municipality, an institution (e.g., a school or university), a corporation (e.g., a law firm), or a private individual. The services that a library offers are commonly described as library or information services. Today, libraries take on a range of additional functions and increasingly serve as community hubs, where programmes are delivered and people engage in lifelong learning. Many libraries have rebranded as civic centres, community hubs, play spaces, meeting rooms, internet access services or any combination of the above. Despite this, library buildings still need to provide quiet and conducive areas for studying, as well as common areas for group study and collaboration, while increasingly providing for other functions. Lamba (2019) observed that "today's libraries have become increasingly multi-disciplinary, collaborative and networked".

Library buildings vary widely in size depending on the extent of the collection, and all collections are constantly growing. A local public library might have 100,000 volumes, university libraries possibly a million, and national libraries count their stock in tens of millions. Small libraries must specialise, e.g., such as a music library or photojournalism library, so that they can build decent collections. Most libraries have materials arranged in a specified order according to a standardised library classification system, so that items may be located quickly and collections can be browsed efficiently (e.g., the Dewey Decimal Classification system was introduced in the US in 1876). It is the responsibility of the architect to ensure that the library building is adequate for the many different needs that it must cater for, and numerous designers have made library buildings their specialty.

Early on, library designers need to make some fundamental decisions about the way books will be stored, how the circulation and day-lighting issues are resolved, and how the grand reading room or children's library section will be integrated. For instance, by using an Automated Storage and Retrieval System (ASRS) for the book storage of Temple University Library's entire collection (which includes two million books on site), the Charles Library, designed by Snøhetta and completed in 2019, was designed to balance the amount of space for books versus people, and significantly increase the number of social spaces to accommodate student and faculty research and facilitate collaboration. Snohetta's design approach took into account the diversity of the campus community, the site conditions and the university's strategic aspirations. The design process included intensive dialogue and collaboration with the campus community to fully understand the social aspects and future needs of the university before the design process was started. In this case, the library design is a direct reflection of the future strategic direction and ambition of the university.

The role of computers in the design, control and making of the public life [and space] is increasingly dominant, their presence pervasive, and their relationship with people characterised by a growing complexity.

— Michael Batty, UCL, 2017

Design Innovation: New Types of Public Spaces and Libraries Emerging
For centuries, cities were places of interpersonal interactions and random encounters. However, today, we observe the potential for technology and data to alter how we live and experience urban life and public space. The scenarios described in the above quote by Michael Batty include digital technology such as the Internet of Things, computer-controlled infrastructure, big data, AI and other digital developments that have turned our built environment into a site for the collection, processing and sharing of daily information data. This process results in complex interactions between people and place, excessive surveillance and the establishment of "smart technology- supported urbanism". Thus, two questions emerge: What kind of public space must a library be today and what will it be in twenty or thirty years? What do you want people to do in the library of tomorrow? Most dictionaries still offer a somewhat generic and outdated definition of a library as "a collection of books, or a room or a building where collections of books are stored. It is an institution which holds books and other forms of stored information for use by the public or qualified people" (Wikipedia, 2021).

Libraries are now of course much more than this; they are spaces where people of all ages can practise lifelong learning. The existence of libraries ensures that knowledge and technology are available to everyone, not just to those who can afford their own. This helps raise the education level of society as a whole. While libraries provide free acess to the internet, this can never be a substitute for the collection itself; the internet is an information and knowledge search tool to be used in addition to the traditional sources in the library. As gateways to knowledge and culture, libraries play a fundamental role in society. The resources and services they offer create opportunities for learning, support literacy and education, and help shape the new ideas and perspectives that are central to any creative and innovative society. Essentially, libraries provide equitable access to anyone in search of information, and in this way, they are still, and will remain, relevant.

In the Western world, most cities are already built, and the main focus is now on upgrading and enhancing the existing urban fabric. Unattractive urban space can lead to a situation where inhabitants are losing the future perspective for their hometown or neighbourhood. Urban regeneration of brownfields and empty buildings can contribute and heal, and an important part of this is to include the library as a public space and catalyst for urban renewal. At its essence, a library is a place to feed the mind and develop our community's intellectual capital. In Finland, for example, libraries have the ambition to be an indoor public space for everyone. There, it is common for larger libraries to offer access to multi-purpose events and meeting spaces; work stations for lifelong-learning activities; social spaces; children's story rooms and art galleries or temporary exhibition spaces; music-recording studios; and classrooms for training and up-skilling. Some libraries even offer a dedicated space for participatory democracy, debate and protest.

Historical Evolution of the Library: its Origins, its Transformations and its Prospects
The term "library" is based on the Latin word *liber*, for book or document, contained in Latin *libraria* (a collection of books) and *librarium* (a container for books). Also known as "bibliotheca", it refers to both the building and the collection. Beginning as a modest room for storing written scrolls and manuscripts, sometimes as part of a museum, it evolved into a place to study books, which would later turn into a central reading room. The history of libraries began with the first efforts to organise collections of documents, some dating back to 2600 BCE Private libraries made up of written manuscripts appeared in classical Greece in the fifth century BCE The great libraries of the Mediterranean world were in Constantinople and Alexandria, founded by Alexander the Great; the three largest libraries at this time were those at Alexandria, Pergamum and Celsus. These libraries drew scholars from across Greek, Roman, Jewish and Syrian cultures and were designed explicitly to manifest cultural grandeur. They featured a colonnaded walk (the Stoa), accommodation for scholars, as well as reading rooms.

In pre-fourteenth century medieval times, libraries were found in monasteries, abbeys or cathedrals, such as in Cluny, Maria Laach, the Vatican, or at Canterbury Cathedral. The library at Saint Catherine's Monastery located at the foot of the legendary Mount Sinai (today in Israel), is the oldest continually operating library in the world. In the Renaissance, with the emergence of universities (such as Bologna and Oxford University), the printing machine by Johannes Gutenberg (1445) led to a rapidly growing number of manuscripts that had to be stored, calling for more and larger libraries and for a new emphasis on the existing university libraries. This led to a call for new typologies and revised building designs. In fifteenth-century England, libraries became more common, such as in Gloucester, Canterbury, Salisbury and Cambridge. The Laurentian Library in Florence, designed by Michelangelo and commissioned in 1523, was the private library of the powerful House of Medici. Knowledge was locked away within closed monasteries and palaces, partly for safekeeping, and partly to maintain power. Over the next 200 years, the library evolved from a private "Schatzkammer" of the absolutistic monarchs and powerful aristocrats to become a showcase of Enlightenment and a bourgeois symbol for education. The age of Enlightenment, the European intellectual movement of the eighteenth century, emphasised reason and individualism rather than tradition, and it embraced the public library.

Over time, the accessibility of the collections changed, and they became open to the public. Liliane Wong (2016) noted that: "The great libraries of the ancient world were the property of kings; libraries of the Middle Ages were the realm of the church; Renaissance libraries the exclusive collection of wealthy aristocrats; and the great research and reference libraries the domain of private universities". Already in 1442, Leon Battista Alberti differentiated in his writings between public and private libraries, although his concept of "public" was still different from ours today. The concept of the library was dramatically altered by the invention of Gutenberg's move-able printing press. The resulting growth of printed matter in the sixteenth century led to increased literacy in a society in which the book was no longer the property of a few. Yet, access to a collection primarily benefitted an enlightened middle class of scholars, teachers and scientists rather than the general public. Only in the eighteenth century did the public library with accessibility for all emerge. Until then, the library had not yet evolved as a separate building typology with specific typical characteristics; for example, in the baroque period, libraries were still housed within a larger building complex such as a monastery, church, palace or castle.

During the early phase of library design, many libraries still shared their buildings with the museum, as both typologies were dedicated to collecting and storing precious artefacts. Nikolaus Pevsner noted that this had already been the case in ancient Greece, in Hellenistic Alexandria, where the whole group of buildings was called the *mouseion*, which is the origin of the term "museum" (Pevsner, 1979: 99). In the late seventeenth century, the largest and most thriving libraries were to be found in France, Germany and Russia, with new concepts for collecting and organising the manuscripts. One of the finest and largest seventeenth-century libraries was in St Petersburg, which was open to the public for free and held over 100,000 volumes and rolls of manuscripts, as well as a collection of maps and astronomical globes. The fact that museums and libraries became fully accessible to the public at the end of the eighteenth century was one aspect of the rise of the middle class into prosperity and into faith in education — the Humboldt ideal.

In the mid-nineteenth century, with the library moving into a separate dedicated building, even following Louis Sullivan's credo "Forms follows function" (1896), the question emerged of how the exterior could be a direct expression of the building's function. At this time, libraries were mostly designed in a neoclassical style. We can find that, in the eighteenth and nineteenth centuries, the circular rotunda form enjoyed some popularity for the design of reading rooms, as seen with Sydney Smirke's Reading Room of the British Museum and James Gibbs's Radcliffe Camera in Oxford, both inspired by the Pantheon in Rome and the work of Claude-Nicolas Ledoux. A circular design was thereafter adopted by many other great libraries, such as the Stockholm Public Library by Asplund (1928), which features a splendid cylinder within a box. The relationship between pure geometry and intellectualism also goes back to the abstract geometrical architecture of Andrea Palladio and Étienne-Louis Boullée, and it is again a recurrent theme in many more recent library designs, such as at Arata Isozaki's libraries in Japan, Mecanoo's library in Delft and Snøhetta's at Alexandria. In the nineteenth century, the now public libraries were no longer the exclusive realm of the privileged few. At this stage, libraries were split into three distinctive zones: reading rooms, service areas and book stacks, with much material still on closed access; however, the emphasis was beginning to shift from storing books to the needs of the readers (for a more detailed overview of the history of libraries, please see: Pevsner, 1979; Brawne, 1997; Edwards, 2009; Latimer, 2011; Campbell, 2013).

The first public libraries in the US were in Peterborough, New Hampshire (1833), while Boston Public Library opened in 1854. In the late nineteenth century, public libraries in larger cities were usually designed in the style of a neoclassical building, guided by the *City Beautiful* movement, with a monumental dome to light the entrance hall. Van Slyck (1995) noted that these tended to follow patterns set by the great public libraries, such as Sainte-Geneviève Library in Paris (1844–1850, Henri Labrouste), Boston Public Library (1888–1895, McKim, Mead & White), and New York Public Library (1897–1911, Carrere & Hastings), each of which made reference to the Renaissance palazzo: they featured closed book stacks and a monumental reading room on an upper floor. The book stacks were located at the back of the building, where long, narrow windows brought some limited daylight into the aisles. In the late nineteenth century, the library design sometimes emulated the characteristics of the department store, a new popular typology, with a sidewalk-level entrance into an atrium and large display windows.

The Continued Development of Library Design in the Twentieth and Twenty-first Century
The new philosophy in twentieth century library design included an emphasis on allowing readers free access to books stored on open shelves, providing children with particular reading areas, and establishing branch libraries in smaller towns. In 1800, the US registered only 64 public libraries with a total of 50,000 books; but the number of American public libraries more than quadrupled between 1896 and 1925, growing from 900 to 3,873. US philanthropist and industrialist Andrew Carnegie (1835–1919) directly financed a large number of public libraries across the country through his library building programme: over 1,600 public libraries as a means of encouraging self-improvement among the working poor.

The library interior of the second half of the twentieth century was equipped with standardised library furniture and modular shelving, which became the norm for public and academic libraries. Post-war construction included a boom of new libraries inspired by Bauhaus functionalism, suggesting that a library should look like a factory. Gone were the great spaces of reading rooms. Efficient but soulless, books were now mere tools, to be crammed into cheap shelving under eight-foot ceilings with strip fluorescent lighting. In the 1920s, the articulation of the building section of the library became an important way to drive new library designs. We can see this trend with the Stockholm Public Library (Erik Gunnar Asplund, 1924–1928) and at Viipuri City Library (Alvar Aalto, 1927–1935). Aalto took advantage of basement-level book storage to develop an innovative building section: visitors enter the library one level above the book storage area and walk up another level to the main lending room, which in turn became a gallery mezzanine level that allowed the librarians' desks to overlook the main reading room; skylights brought filtered daylighting into all the reading areas. Louis Kahn's Phillips Exeter Academy Library (1965–1972) has an equally unique section: it looks like a simple modest cube on the outside, but reveals a monumental atrium and a complex section on its inside. Today, we see a renewed appreciation for these early library buildings from the nineteenth and twentieth centuries.

The wave of new university campus projects in the 1960s and 1970s included numerous new libraries as part of campus masterplans, and these new libraries usually occupied prime sites at the centre of their campus. This was a trend in the US, UK, Germany and other coutries where new universities were founded. University libraries became the focal point, the intellectual centre of college life, and the heart of the campus, and often lead the way in the rethinking of building types. With numerous new projects built during this period, the large academic library design received much refinement. Here, in general, the noisier functions of the entrance area, circulation desk and exhibition space were acoustically separated from the reading rooms and stacks which were usually located on the upper levels.

The 1980s saw the construction of a large number of cultural precincts in North American, European and Japanese cities, and this boom of new art museums was frequently in combination with new library projects, where public buildings were discretely tied into the historic urban fabric. Norman Foster designed the Carre d'Art in Nimes, France, noting in 1984 that "the resulting interaction of the two cultures of the visual arts and the world of information within the same building created a richer totality". In the last decades of the twentieth century, there was again a concerted effort to make libraries delightful places to read, with a renewed focus on the provision of natural light (e.g., the libraries designed by Hans Scharoun in Germany and Alvaro Siza in Portugal since the mid-1970s). Another trend was the manipulation of the ceiling plane to create monumental reading spaces, as seen with the fifth-floor reading room of the Phoenix Central Library (by Will Bruder, 1990–1995). The use of irregular plans became more common, to give the various functions their own spatial articulation. Notable examples of this approach include the Berlin State Library (by Hans Scharoun, 1967–1978), the Muenster New City Library (by Bolles-Wilson, 1987–1993), and the more recent libraries by Antoine Predock, Snøhetta, Mecanoo and FJMT Studio. Since then, the book collections of all libraries have been growing constantly, and increasing student numbers at universities are putting additional pressure on available library space. The largest library in the world, for example, is the new British Library which was built during the period spanning 1978–1997 in London, and it contains more than 170 million items.

One could say that, in the last 300 years, the library has gone through a transformation from private collection and storehouse of knowledge, to a public forum, and then to a globally networked information administrator and community hub. The first libraries were multi-focused institutions, which included places to meet and exchange ideas, often as part of a museum. Today, the library offers users constantly advancing digital capacity combined with spaces for concentrated reading and lifelong learning.

In the end, the demise of the physical library, which was so frequently forecast to occur around the year 2000, never happened, as the library continues to evolve and take on expanded roles in the community. The library as a cultural and social facility, a place for community interaction and celebration of learning, remains hugely important. More recently, with these new functions of the building, the naming of libraries has become an issue: they are now sometimes called mediatheque, learning resource centre, discovery centre, or neighbourhood knowledge hub — reflecting the libraries' expanded roles in the community, their new specialisations, the change to electronic resources, and the shift from collection-based libraries to the user-focused, service-rich libraries of tomorrow.

The dictionary defines a library closely in connection with the services provided by librarians, as "a collection of materials, books or media that are easily accessible for use and not just for display purposes. A library is responsible for housing updated information in order to meet the user's needs on a daily basis. ...In addition to providing materials, libraries also provide the services of librarians who are trained and experts at finding, selecting, circulating and organising information and at interpreting information needs, navigating and analysing very large amounts of information with a variety of resources" (Oxford Dictionary, 2021). Thinking about the interesting relationship between public space (e.g., the Greek Agora with the Stoa, or the early university campus) and the role of knowledge is here of particular relevance. Knowledge generation, dissemination, application and preservation are activities common to libraries: it is now about reinventing a forward-looking, future-proofed typology that can handle the ever-increasing knowledge accordingly.

As we see throughout history, from time to time, building typologies are evolving and are being redefined. For example, the Ferry Terminal in Yokohama (completed in 2001) reinvented the typology of a ferry terminal; in the same way, Toyo Ito's Sendai Mediatheque (which also opened in 2001) has made an important contribution and enabled us to think differently about libraries. It is obvious that the library of the future has much expressive architectural potential to achieve a certain visual uniqueness, but it will also change the way we use and experience the facility on the inside.

Today, contexts and narratives change at hyper speed, and, through this, different new roles are found for the library. The zeitgeist of the last decades claimed that "the library is dead". The rupture emerged with the introduction and rise of the computer and the internet, and the library had to find new ways of positioning itself and adapting to new media surroundings. Some people saw the ideas of "authenticity and originality" as myths (and renounced the library as a symbol of outdated bourgeois values) soon to be replaced by scanned and digital data. However, a steady process of "functional morphing" kept the library very much alive.

The European City Model and Libraries as Catalysts for Regenerating Urban Space
The benefits of a compact, walkable and mixed-use city have been much researched and dicussed; the glorification of the European compact city model is ongoing, but the aim cannot be to turn every city into this one model (for a more complete discussion on the compact, walkable city, please see: Whyte, 1980; Lynch, 1981; Kostof, 1999; Hall and Pfeiffer, 2000; Lehmann, 2019; Crawford and Davoudi, 2012). For example, Los Angeles presents a fundamentally different idea and model, as do the cities in Asia. It is time to rethink the way we look at every city in terms of a comparison with the European city. We have, for much too long, looked at things from an exclusive Western perspective. Because of our deep nostalgia for the European city and its compact urban form, composition and coherence, we have become obliged to reject almost every alternative.

The US city typology has cars everywhere, with high-rise towers in abundance downtown, and the urban core is surrounded by flat one- and two-storey suburbs, with cul-de-sacs ending at the doorstep. Los Angeles simulates at Rodeo Drive and at the Grove a European walkable city, imitating the density of Italian towns, while Las Vegas features a Venetian setting with canals and a replica of inner city Venice landmarks. Europe seems to always be a very suitable model to be replicated in Asia, where everybody loves the European townscape with its squares and boulevards. Asia celebrates European urbanism and uses it as an agenda to improve and remodel its cities. Asia has built numerous fake villages, replicas of romantic towns, and landmarks copied from Germany, Denmark, the Netherlands, the UK, France, and Italy, where entire reconstructions of parts of Amsterdam, Copenhagen, or Heidelberg can be found in Shanghai and Nanjing. How relevant is its fakeness if the copy is as good as the authentic original?

In the meantime, no longer tasked with designing monumental megaprojects, European architects have to find other, more modest ways to make an impact. The city of the twenty-first century is going to be one of climate crisis, which is also a crisis of public space. We know that a hold or decrease in urbanisation will not meet the demographic increase. We will not succeed in making a city habitable and sustainable just with standards and figures. We must make an urbanism of public space: walkable, green, resilient. This includes questions of urban density, e.g., how far apart to place two buildings? How much public space is required around the entry of a library? Depending on the place, the architect and urban designer must know the answers to these questions of spacing; a central question for making a city, which is also a social one. The question of urban density is physical, and public space is the medium in which we live together. If done well, the architecture of public space can make density happy and healthy.

Life in the contemporary city is unpredictable and full of random encounters. The movie *The Truman Show* (1998) displays a happy townscape that takes no risks; it is a secure, predictably comfortable, non-intellectual environment. More recently, the hype around the "smart city" trend turned out to be a technocratic dead end. However, at its best, the city is a system that is essentially unpredictable and full of surprises. Turning it into a city with less and less unpredictability, like a city controlled by sensors and complete surveillance, would mean the death of the quality of any public space. Too much control is detrimental to the quality of any public space and spontaneity. Libraries of the future will need to be similar to good public spaces: flexible, informal, full of possibilities, random encounters and a degree of surprise.

The Loss of the Public Sphere and the Democratic Role of Public Architecture
Driven and shaped by invisible (mostly commercial) forces, the new global cityscapes —such as in Dubai, Singapore or Shanghai —embody specific social, political and economic ideologies. During the first decade of the twenty-first century, the effects of the neoliberal market economy and globalisation on architecture and the production of the city were fundamental: firstly, the homogenising tendencies of globalisation led to sterile and exchangeable versions of public space; secondly, real estate developers and city leaders saw architects as people who could create a new identity through "icons", architectural objects, and who could deliver what the market economy thought it needed in terms of superficial city branding. Today, we are living in a time when the public as a client is disappearing and form is less and less connected to anything, such as meaning, logic, historical precedence, site specificity or a social-functional

programme. It is the beginning of a time when architects are given the exceptional opportunity to create random form or, in fact, any form. Beyond formal and aesthetic aspects, it is critical to understand the implications of form and the need for appropriate architectural solutions to ever-accelerating demands.

We live in a moment where architectural form is often made for its own sake, for novelty — and the design of libraries offers plenty of such potential for formal indulgence. Everywhere, the public sector is retreating and disappearing —including as a client of civic projects and an owner of public space —and the private sector is taking over. These are worrying developments, as we need strong end-user representation and cannot collectively sustain an environment that is based on complete randomness or arbitrariness. As with every public building, architecture depends, to a large degree, on the client; indeed, just as Herbert Muschamp put it: "What libraries need most of all are strong clients. This is a librarian client who knows exactly what she wants", noting that "In the history of the world, there has never been a great building without a strong client" (Muschamp, 2004). Sometimes it is impossible to know the difference between a library, an office building or a shopping mall, as these have all started to look generic and alike.

Our task is to prepare libraries for unpredictable change. Libraries are the most important public buildings. It's not only about the design, it's the programme that needs to be tailored to the context and to the communities that it serves; each library has its own challenges and our task is to prepare them for unpredictable change.

— **Francine Houben, Mecanoo, 2021**

The Dramatic Urban Changes Thrown up by the Forces of Globalisation and Digitisation
Rem Koolhaas (2018) argued for some time that there is evidence that good architecture is related to the public sector as the client, and to its historical stewardship of creating and maintaining inclusive non-commercial urban space. In a recent lecture, he noted that "For 5,000 years, architecture has been a public profession, a profession that works for the public interest as agent of change. The social mission of the public as client — which was also a cornerstone of early modernism — largely disappeared in the period of Neoliberalism and the free market economy, and in the face of reduced public budgets. More and more responsibility has been transferred from the public to the private sector. We are in the process of losing an architecture of good intentions that was never in question during the twentieth century" (Koolhaas, 2018).

With the loss of the public client, has much of the architect's work lost its authenticity and innocence? In her book *The Value of Everything* (2018), economist Mariana Mazzucato outlined the crucial role that the public sector (government, municipalities) plays in generating broad value in the economy and in the community. "Government is not just a facilitator of private sector value creation, but an active creator of public value. This is twenty-first century economics". A library is always a direct expression of this kind of public investment and a non-commercialised public realm.

Public urban space and public facilities not only constitute a precious commodity, but also one of the key vehicles for achieving sustainable urban development. However, the public sphere has shrunk, is in risk of losing its meaning, and much of the public architecture is in danger of losing its nobility in the era of Neoliberalism. From 1990 to 2010, we saw the acceptance of globalisation as the dominating shaping force; and, more recently, we have almost the reverse situation —more and more people are becoming critical of, and disappointed with, globalisation and its related economic systems, such as excessive capitalism, over-consumption and outdated concepts of infinite growth.

Consequently, the position of architecture and urbanism has been compromised, with a disconnection from the public sector and an increasingly intense relationship with the private sector, which has led to the dissatisfaction of stakeholders concerning the increasingly disappointing outcomes of large urban developments in regard to their public spaces and buildings. Commonly, developers instruct architects to pioneer "something exciting" —to create an icon that people will notice as exceptional and memorable. The concept of rapid instant urbanism and place branding emerged and was exported all over the world, operating along similar lines, from Las Vegas to Singapore, Dubai, Shanghai or Macau.

It has now become obvious that a rebalancing of these excessive development trends is necessary, and one of the key questions is: How can public space become public again?

In all likelihood, the answer to this question requires new models of urbanism that are more community-based, less profit-driven, respect and protect the ecosystem, and are more socially inclusive, thus meaning that they do not exclude large numbers of people in society from participation or use of facilities and urban space. Architecture, including the library of tomorrow, needs to redefine a new position to again become public and to regain a degree of credibility; based on an urbanism that does not create "quasi-public" spaces or facilities that are in fact privatised. As mentioned earlier, we are living in a time when architectural form is less and less connected to anything, such as logic, programme, historical precedence, or site specificity. Thus, the question must be asked, what is appropriate and meaningful in the architectural design of a library for tomorrow? David Chipperfield argued that "architectural quality no longer depends on the skill of the craftsman, or on a commonly shared architectural language that is based on a shared understanding of established typologies" (Chippperfield, 2020). This new "freedom of any shape" exposes new responsibilities of the designer, beyond typological explorations; numerous architects are now critically examining how far architecture still has to express "the local" in its material, scale, and tectonics (Hashim Sarkis, 2021). What might be these new limits of architecture (and library design)?

The Reimagined Public Library: New Hybrid Programmes
Programming the next-generation library will be crucial. Writing a building's programme (brief) is three-dimensional strategising. An architectural programme is, in its most basic form, is a table of requirements that initiates a project. It is a list of functional measurements (e.g., the amount of books required to be shelved; or aisle width and minimum ceiling heights), determined by building and safety codes, access and standards. However, any great work of architecture adds to the programme and transcends the simple data of functional requirements, challenging convention.

It is timely to examine the development of the design of library spaces over the last 20 years, including the move from the collection-dominated library buildings of the nineteenth and twentieth centuries to the "service- rich, user-focused ones of the twenty-first century" (Latimer, 2011). This evolution was influenced by changing methods of research, the forms in which information is provided, and the way knowledge is delivered to the end-users, which has evolved in new directions. This development had a significant impact on the evolution of library spaces, and one of the indicators of this change is that numerous libraries have turned their periodical reading areas into café areas with wireless networking. Described as a "cultural department store", the Forum in Groningen, in the Netherlands (designed by NL Architects) is another multi-functional library building that includes exhibition spaces, movie halls, assembly rooms, restaurants and also some books.

More than any other building typology, the library reflects the values of a particular society. Therefore, one hypothesis of the book is: our times of uncertainty and rapid change —caused by growing economic and social inequalities, the climate crisis, collapse of biodiversity, massive population displacements, demographic shifts and political polarisation —demand new design approaches and typologies for public space and public buildings based on recalibrated values of social equity and environmental sustainability. This includes rethinking public buildings for times of unpredictable change. Like the "market", you don't need a ticket to enter the library. It has been helpful to extend the notion of public building beyond the view of a "single typology", as a library of tomorrow will also function as a health centre, kindergarten, café and exhibition space or hot-desking workplace. The hybrid library can be redefined as a new, multi-programmatic meeting place for underserved surroundings and impoverished neighbourhoods.

The size of any book collection is constantly growing, and large libraries count their stock in tens of millions of items. The British Library, for example, contains more than 170 million items and its 750 kilometres of shelves lengthen by eight kilometres a year. Library historian Ken Worpole noted that "A city with a great library is a great city" (2013). The library of the future will be heavily influenced by the way we look at the world. Today, a new urban library is also a key element of urban regeneration and public place making, in order to engage with the complexity of the city more effectively, shifting towards more communal and informal models (Nevarez, 2021). The recent rediscovery of the value of urban context and adaptive reuse has led to an end of the "architectural object", with a shift away from the design of autonomous, isolated and self-referential objects with a singular programme, towards developing deep-green buildings with hybrid programmes and the ability to support catalytic spatial programming to strengthen the public space. The plurality of sources and diversity of answers addressing the future vision of the library, as a new prototype or public hybrid, is appropriate because there is not one single source from which these answers can come.

With the emergence of e-books, will there be fewer reasons to visit a library? Interestingly, the trend shows that the opposite is the case: there is a renewed interest in the authentic book or original manuscript, with the number of library visitors interested in rare manuscripts increasing at libraries worldwide. While digitised material has had an enormous impact on society and workplaces (e.g., a vast amount of information is available online 24/7, and the gradual disappearance of bookstores is a result of this), it has not replaced the physical collection of books. Quite the opposite: libraries have expanded and broadened the provision of knowledge. Libraries now focus their services more strongly on the needs and desires of the users, and new programmes are incorporated into the library, ranging from retail, entertainment, education and healthcare, to the arts – constantly creating new hybrid types with names such as learning centre, mediatheque, or community hub. With such flexibility and adaptation of its physical environment, it seems that the library has secured its future relevance in society (and its own future). In *The Library of Babel,* Jorge Luis Borges (1941) describes a fictional library as an infinite labyrinth of hexagonal rooms; he writes: "I suspect that the human species is about to be extinguished, but the Library will endure."

The architect is tasked with designing enduring, compelling and functional spaces for libraries and with developing new typologies. Architects are used to strategically ask and consider, "What if...?" and are able to imagine the future of library settings differently than a librarian would do, or the technical norms would dictate to them. Architects are well-placed to reimagine libraries, as they combine the work of the designer of new systems with the approach of the designer of new objects. Experiments can lead to desirable alternative answers to the question of tomorrow's library without necessarily dealing with the complete picture, with all evidence, or the full solution to the problem. Furthermore, the answer to this question cannot be solely technological. It includes inviting a different audience that has never previously used libraries by offering expanded programmes. Hence, it might be a bold speculative project, or it might be a proposal that suggests slow, step-by-step improvements to the existing model to better integrate and reflect changes in society.

Seattle Central Library by OMA is a typological milestone. Here, architects first identified the programmatic components that are most likely to change soon (caused by technological or social change), and combined the more stable parts in areas (boxes) with highly traditional library planning. The unstable components were located in "voids" between the boxes where they can easily be transformed, reconfigured and adapted if necessary; and a circulation loop that connects all stable and unstable parts. The building resembles a built diagram. It became a radical solution for the combination of functionally different components that turns the public into participants. For tomorrow's library, the notion of the hybrid building typology is of particular interest. Richard Francis-Jones of FJMT Studio in Sydney (known for beautifully designed public libraries in various Australian towns) argued that his project, Bunjil Place Cultural Centre, is a programmatic hybrid, noting that "It is an example of a new form of community and civic building. It is not a single use facility that tends to divide and separate the community by interest, education or culture, but an inclusive hybrid form of public building, reflecting and embracing our diversity. It is a library, a cultural centre, a performance theatre, a public gathering space, a place of exhibition, gallery and display, a flexible and experimental space for events, lectures, debate and celebration. It is a help point, a service centre, and a place of work and collaboration. Above all, perhaps, it is a place where all of this overlaps and interconnects and at the centre is the interconnecting fluid form of the foyer gathering space, a non-hierarchical space that unifies the complex" (FJMT Studio, 2020).

A Shared User Experience and Reconnection with Nature

A library poses questions about the relationship between books, knowledge and power. Architects and librarians are cognisant that the typology of the library needs to continue to change, including the public spaces around the library building. In addition, the urban presence of the library in the neighbourhood needs to be rethought: will the new type of library be a building without books? The known typology will evolve into something else that is closely connected to knowledge, but less and less connected to physical books. However, the future library should not aim to replace the role of the museum, art gallery or performance space. If we want to future-proof the typology, it is a good enough starting point to base the library of the future on the spatial qualities of the library of the past, some of which we seem to have forgotten. In the next-generation library, a large number of spaces will need to be devoted to gatherings for community meetings, expressing a public spirit. These spaces should be operational 24-hours, so as to support the development of the community. The library of the future will also offer more contact points and opportunities for greater engagement with a range of knowledge professionals.

Approaching the future of the library in a socially responsible way, rather than in a technological way, the next-generation library will offer a sense of arrival and provide easy access to knowledge in the heart of the neighbourhood (similar to the core idea of the Centre Pompidou, the radical cultural centre of 1970s Paris). On the ground floor, an auditorium will offer a place for discussion, and other parts of the library might be organised around it, because tomorrow's library will need to be about social connectivity and a shared experience. "The library of the future will need to be an incredible place to read and meet, where it will be a pleasure to read as a shared experience", predicted Sergio Lopez-Pinheiro (2021).

To draw people to the library, it will offer adequate spaces for civic purposes that were traditionally not part of a library. For example, the library of the future might offer a space for assembly and protest (similar to Lina Bo Bardi's open plaza at the Museum of Art in Sao Paulo). It will also bring nature and greenery into the building, in the form of green walls, vegetated screens, rooftop gardens and other greenery to reconnect people with nature. The library will also be much better integrated into its surrounding urban context, as suggested by Snøhetta's Michelle Delk — a firm that has established itself as designers of academic libraries.

Numerous library experts agree that tomorrow's library will be a place for networking and lifelong learning, active 24 hours a day. It will offer maximum flexibility for future changes that are still uncertain and somewhat unpredictable, with spaces for increased collaboration (as suggested by Mecanoo's Francine Houben, 2021). However, some designers do not support the call for maximum flexibility. Joshua Ramus (formerly at OMA, responsible for Seattle Central Library), for instance, argued against flexibility and generic neutrality in the design of library spaces. He prefers architecture to advance a building's typology and produce inventive designs that "are not flexible, but functionally so specific that they offer very specific and distinct aesthetic experiences" (2004).

The "social condenser" concept that Steven Holl refers to in his statement on the future of the library (page 176) was originally coined by the Soviet Constructivists in the 1920s to describe the sociological thrust underpinning their collectivist housing blocks. Steven Holl (2021) notes that "The library of the future should be an optimistic beacon, unlimited with an amazing balance of digital information and a love of books. It should be an environmental example of high technology, achieving ecological excellence. ...The library of the future is for tomorrow, much more than its past, book-filled ancestor. It is a place where a child can find optimism for the future of our planet and the human condition". Most recently, Steven Holl has come close to building this model at Queens Public Library (2015), but not without controversy: library experts have critised its overcomplicated section for what could have been a much more simple and easily accessible branch library.

The Library as an "Idea Factory" and Creative Commons
For any city, a new library can be a smart strategic investment, tied to urban, economic and cultural outcomes of equitability, liveability, knowledge, sustainability and vibrancy. As a repository of books and all kinds of other media, libraries of the twenty-first century can serve as an idea factory and a type of community and exhibition centre with an educational programme and access to a digital maker space with 3D-printers, visualisation tools and other creative resources, as a way to train and empower people with interest and skills in digital technology. It can be an idea factory with programmes for self-improvement and continuing education; a meeting place with free public facilities and meeting rooms; with spaces for adult learning and child care; a cultural hub that displays and conveys the culture of the area; and a kind of public resource and government services centre with outreach to elderly, immigrants and people with limited resources.

To do something transformational and regenerate a city centre, one must always be bold and have a long-term vision. Today, an urban vision includes a more pedestrianised and denser city comprised of a mix of residential buildings, healthcare, office spaces and green space. The library at the heart of an urban regeneration development can be a catalyst and hub that connects all these other developments together. This is a model that we can frequently find on the university campus, where the library is at the heart of the campus plan. The more we put multiple functions into the library, the more possible it will be to resuscitate the economy and enhance the overall liveability of a city. A reinvented library is the ideal catalyst for urban regeneration and social inclusion.

Accessibility of the Collection: Maintaining a Close Relationship between Book and Reader
While technology is becoming increasingly important, the solution to the above-mentioned problem cannot be based purely on technology, as there is always the need for the integration of any technology into the societal context. The importance of a well-defined design brief (this is, a detailed programme of all spaces and their requirements and relationship to each other) is essential for the successful design of a new library, as well as the reflection on the success or failure of building projects following completion, through post-occupancy evaluation (POE). The library programme should include an opening statement defining the vision for the library that reflects the ethos, aspirations and aims of the parent institution (i.e., the city, the university, the corporation), which can directly be used to guide the design process. It must be a living document that is updated and expanded during the process of design, as new insights are gained, combining the experience of architects, librarians, facility managers and others.

Two primary functions occur in libraries: the storage of the information source and the opportunity of having access to that information by individuals at a time of their choosing. That this is a matter of a direct and individual relationship is crucial, and of primary design significance. The library (and the museum) allows for individuals to decide when they need access and equally to determine what information they want. This freedom of choice, within the constraints of availability, is of paramount importance to any concept of the freedom of information and the library of the future.

— **Michael Brawne, London, 2000**

In every library, there are two different, opposing components that need to be balanced and reconciled: the library as a public forum for dialogue and community activities (these are best located close to the entry level); and the library as a quiet, scholarly sanctuary (these quiet spaces are usually best located on the upper level). At the same time, a close relationship between books and readers is still essential. Concerning the romanticised relationship between library user and the book, Dutch architects MVRDV (2021), the designers of the radical and spectacular Tianjin Library, noted: "The heart of the building is its expansive atrium of cascading bookcases, which form a kind of landscape of stairs and seating that curves upwards to merge with the ceiling. The popularity of Tianjin Library as a social media spectacle and as an entertainment destination is as much a result of symbolism and a certain aesthetic sensibility as it is a response to the library's collection of actual books. What does it mean that physical libraries –and especially the aesthetic sensation of being surrounded by books –are romanticised in this way?"

So, what constitutes good design for a contemporary library? The answer to this question is relevant when it comes to redefining the transformation of this long-time established typology. As the case studies in this book illustrate, libraries increasingly integrate other functions and are designed to be able to grow in the future, for expansion and with flexibility for as-yet-undetermined needs, e.g., as communication technologies evolve. Hence, one hypothesis is that the library of the future is about creating a flexible place and community destination, preferably in consultation with its future users.

Citizens around the world want to participate in shaping the public spaces and libraries that they inhabit. *Participatory design* means that there is a process and protocol for the engagement of citizens, to ensure community members are consulted, actively involved and able to contribute to the library design. This dialogue with future users is critical. Brigitte Shim (2019) notes that "Citizens and designers alike need to work together to determine factors such as why we build, what we build, and how we build, so that our civic spaces can accurately reflect our shared values and aspirations."

To adapt to our current world, libraries will need to become almost as ubiquitous as the internet itself: our libraries will become hang-out destinations, and our hang-out spots will become libraries.

— Winy Maas, MVRDV, 2021

Some Practical Issues: the Functional Needs of a Library that should be Considered
There are existing library design manuals that focus exclusively on the practical and technical questions. However, this is not the purpose of the current study. Nevertheless, below are some general recommendations for avoiding common problems in library design or dysfunctional spaces. The designer must visit numerous libraries and gain deep experience of the functional and technical needs, internal organisational concepts and the latest trends in library design. To this end, the designer should be aware of the role of each key element of library architecture and consult with as many librarians as possible, since they are a valuable source of information. As mentioned, there are ever-advancing cultural demands, social changes and technological requirements, including the knowledge of requirements for collection storage, service desks and user circulation, reading room seating, study areas, staff workspaces and the children's library section. This also includes knowledge of security systems, public accessibility, stock-holding, back-office functions,

learning centres, spaces for concentrated reading, archive requirements, and the inclusion of other services such as community meeting spaces. The following is an incomplete list of the drivers and the functional needs of a library that should be considered in the design process:

- The three major components of a traditional library are: the readers, the books and the staff, all in purposive contact with each other.
- Facility operations and space utilisation and practicalities, e.g., open plan transparency vs closed spaces are to be considered.
- Organisational goals, specific user-occupant needs (the head librarian and other staff are always a good source of information on this).
- The general expectations of visitors, the community and of library staff might differ; collect feedback, conduct a survey.
- Library standards, design and planning guidelines: these standards are available online (e.g., by the IFLA) and are important for the adequate size of spaces.
- Arrival and entry zones; parking, landscaping; vertical circulation (stairs, ramps, elevators, fire escapes and compartments); it does not need to be over-complicated.
- Accommodating the various basic library functions: catalogue with terminals, reference area, special collections area, shelving, staff work spaces, etc.
- Define in the plans and section: where are the distinctively different areas for (1) the library as an active public forum for dialogue and activities, versus (2) the library as a quiet, scholarly sanctuary. It is beneficial to define these areas early, e.g., by identifying them on the different levels.
- At least one upper floor should provide for quiet, independent and private places to read and study.
- How does the library integrate new additional functions (e.g., an adult learning centre with classrooms), and how does it deal with the need to be able to grow (dealing with the later expansion and flexibility for as-yet-undetermined future needs as technology evolves)?
- Think about what the most likely changing needs of visitors will be in the next five to ten years.
- Conduct a post-occupancy evaluation (POE) a year after completion.

What might be the Architectural Goals for the Library of the Future?

Once the library is completed, there is always the question concerning the overall success of the project in meeting the goals that were defined at the outset, as well as offering a functional, environmentally-sustainable and energy-efficient operation. At that point, however, it is usually too late for correcting major mistakes. Therefore, it is necessary to clearly define the project goals early in the design phase and it is critical to update these throughout the design process. The following is an incomplete list of "10 basic architectural design goals for a successful library", which could be considered for any new library:

- Establish an identity and uplifting, civic presence for the public building, with easy way-finding: the building needs to project the "proper image of a library" —as a landmark and community place.
- Can the project provide an "urban room" in the form of a public plaza or garden space (e.g., a roof garden; there might be possible security issues to be resolved), and as a buffer to the street noise from traffic?
- Create an environmentally conscious building with low operating costs.
- Design an airy, spacious library with high ceilings and filtered, controlled natural light. Maximise day to most parts of the library, especially to the circulation areas and staircases (with control for glare and overheating, most likely using shades and louvers, to avoid damage to book collections).
- Create an outdoor reading area with adequate seating, possibly in combination with a café.
- Segregate the children's area from the adult areas (due to different noise levels).
- Design the public access computer area so that it can easily grow (flexibility); it is best located close

to the entry so that it is easily accessible.

- Ensure that the front circulation desk and reference desk areas are easy to be found, and offer direct surveillance of the entrance/exit areas, controlling access and possibly the children's area, for security and sight lines.
- Book stacks: place shelving and storage adjacent to reading and study areas to avoid long distances.
- In general, placement and number of public bathrooms and elevators needs to be carefully considered.

Responding to societal change, the library of the future will be devoted to strengthening the ideals of open access to knowledge, democracy through civic engagement and discourse. As mentioned earlier, there are many different ways people use libraries. Wandering the book shelves is now considered by some as a nostalgic activity, yet it is one way of broadening the horizon and looking beyond a simple online search. Architectural design is important, as it prescribes how we research, collaborate or socialise — these activities are always impacted by the built environment. A colleague has recently told me that he has gone to libraries at universities to check whether he wanted to work at that institution. "Good library: good place," he concludes.

One could say that an ideal library enables the imagination and sharing of knowledge. It serves as an agent of change, with confidence but without control, offering comfort and headspace.

Note: Besides the important library discussion, more background on the current socio-political urban condition including the threat of climate change and a critical reflection on twenty-first century public space, can be found in the recommended writings of Richard Sennett (1977), Anthony Giddens (1999), Ulrich Beck (2000), Richard Florida (2002), David Harvey (2005), John Urry (2011), and Mariana Mazzucato (2018).

The Prussian geographer, naturalist and explorer Alexander von Humboldt (1769–1859) in his library and study in Berlin; paintng by Eduard Hildebrandt, 1856. Humboldt's extensive library suggests the wide range of his interests and knowledge, shaped by the educational ideals of German classicism. The painting shows the ageing explorer surrounded by the trappings and symbols of his long and accomplished life. He was arguably the most important naturalist of the nineteenth century, published more than 36 books, traveled over 4,000 miles across four continents, and wrote well over 25,000 letters to an international network of colleagues and admirers. In his library, Humboldt was surrounded by over 11,000 books, countless stacks of correspondence with a global network of peers, forty years' worth of travel diaries and field notes, maps, globes, paintings, sculptures, stuffed specimens, rocks and even a fragment of a meteorite.

General Case Studies: from the Twentieth to the Twentieth-first Century

We have long explored libraries to follow our curiosities. We have many tools at our fingertips to access information or fall into a story, yet by expanding our understanding of the library to include reading the landscape, we may recognize that many cultures and people experience the landscape and the environment as their "library".

— Michelle Jeffrey Delk, Snøhetta, 2021

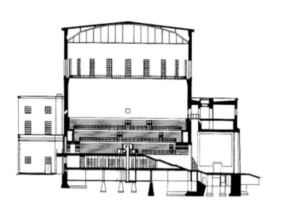 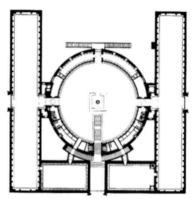

Stockholm Public Library, Stockholm, Sweden (Erik Gunnar Asplund), 1924-28

Stockholm Public Library, Stockholm, Sweden (Erik Gunnar Asplund), 1924–28
Inspired by the work of Claude-Nicolas Ledoux, Asplund's extremely influential library design marks the finale to a neo-classical architectural era. It is based on the geometric shape of a cube encompassing a 24m-high cylinder (rotunda). Stockholm Public Library was Sweden's first public library to apply the principle of open shelves where visitors could access books without the need to ask library staff for assistance, a concept Asplund explored in the United States during the design of the library, and the design was influenced by Asplund's study tour of US public libraries. The main lending library is housed in a cylinder in the middle of the building, accessed via a grand staircase, and is surrounded by three wings with flat roofs. The staircase has treads which are quite long and deep, giving the impression of a wide ramp rather than a flight of steps. The rotunda is the library's central book hall with a diameter of 26m; it has two galleries and accommodates about 40,000 books on the shelves. The library includes more than 2 million volumes. All the furnishings in all the rooms were designed for their specific positions and purposes. It is Asplund's most important works and illustrates his gradual shift from Nordic Classicism to functionalism.

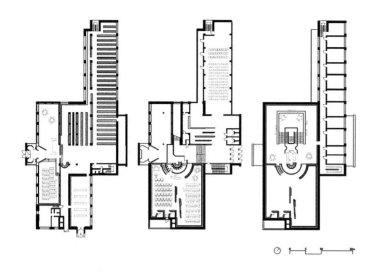

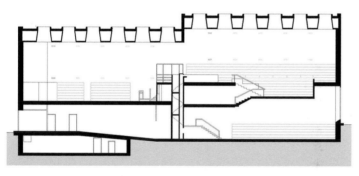

Central City Library, Vyborg, Russia, at the time of construction in Viipuri, Finland (Alvar Aalto), 1927–35
Viipuri Library is one of the major examples of 1920s functionalist architectural design. It features two simple rectangular blocks, and inside, a wave-shaped ceiling in the main auditorium, the shape of which was based on acoustic studies. Such architectural solutions as a sunken reading-well, free-flowing ceilings and cylindrical skylights, first tested in Viipuri, would regularly reappear in Aalto's later works. The framework of the library plan comprises several reading and lending areas stepped at different levels, with the circulation desk for supervision in its centre. It has a rectangular plan accommodating all small-scale spaces and offices in a side wing; and the other part with the reading room, which is the main space. Aiming to fill the reading rooms with diffuse light, Aalto invented a conical skylight that would funnel in natural daylight without allowing direct, shadow-producing solar rays: a series of 55 circular skylights provide soft daylight to the interior —an element frequently reused by Aalto. It's appropriate to the Scandinavian/Nordic climate and brightens up the interior spaces. The richness in detailing and materials for the interiors is in contrast to the rough brick exterior of the "shell", again a reflection of this country's environment and regional traditions, where people spend more time indoors. Over his long career, Alvar Aalto designed numerous other libraries in the following years, in the US and Germany. The b/w photo above was taken around 1938.

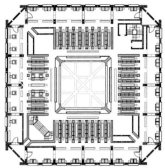

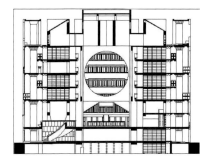

Phillips Exeter Academy Library, New Hampshire, USA (Louis I. Kahn), 1965–72

The building is the composite of two distinct elements of a library: the storage of books—with their great weight and need to be kept from daylight—and the user being alone with a book close to where the daylight is. The plan illustrates Kahn's notion of "spaces which serve versus spaces which are served". Reading is understood as a private activity and this is reflected in the plan: the periphery of the building consists of a series of small reading areas along large windows. This outer ring is made of brick masonry construction; it surrounds the inner ring and central atrium which is made of concrete, where books are stored away from strong sunlight. The entire building is made of only three materials which are left exposed: brick and concrete with wood for doors and windows.

74

When asked about the heroic, monumental atrium void at the centre of his otherwise relatively modest Phillips Exeter Academy Library, Louis Kahn explained, "Nobody has ever paid the price of a book; they pay only for the printing!" In other words, it was the intangible knowledge, rather than the physical medium by which it was disseminated, that was priceless.

Kahn spoke frequently about the idea of the library as a "sanctuary of books and ideas". At Phillips Exeter Academy Library, he used half-enclosed desks placed near windows that have a small glass area related to the desk. Each reader is able to adjust a wooden sliding window shutter to control the amount of light falling on the page, a simple but effective idea. Yet every reader is part of the larger space and also in contact with the outside world. Kahn's meticulous attention to detail in the use of materials and natural lighting provides high quality user spaces.

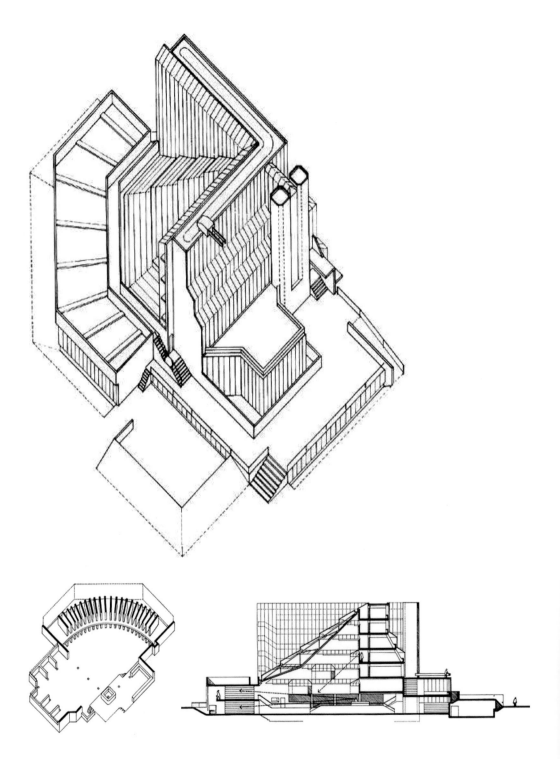

76

History Faculty Library, Cambridge, UK (James Stirling), 1964–67

The Cambridge University History Faculty Building, of which the library was a key component, was the subject of a design competition in 1964, which was won by James Stirling. The building married high-tech architecture with contextual sensitivity through the use of glass and steel detailing alongside brick walls and platforms. The L-shaped volume contains a large glass roof with a single-volume atrium space, which covers the reading room designed to accommodate 360 workplaces, surrounded by book stacks arranged on two floor levels. As a library, it owed more to the great reading rooms of the nineteenth century with their emphasis on security and supervision than to the more liberal approach of the new universities. The industrial glass roof was also a reference to other British masterpieces such as the glass roofs at Kew Gardens and the Crystal Palace (the basis of a high-tech style that evolved in Britain). The circulation followed the security driven concept of the Panoptikum: the glazed corridors running round the upper parts of the library ensured that people moving around the building were always in visual contact with the librarians. The librarian seated at a centrally located desk, and the radial arrangement of bookshelves allowed a single staff member to survey several aisles of bookshelves.

Other library architects of these decades of rapid university growth were Denis Lasdun, Ahrends-Burton-Koralek, and Basil Spence —all of them designers of significant 1970s UK libraries. James Stirling was among the first post-war British architects to achieve widespread international standing.

Basel University Library, Basel, Switzerland (Otto H. Senn), 1962–65
Basel University Library, officially the Public Library of the University of Basel, is the central library of the University of Basel. Founded in 1471, it is also one of the oldest in Europe. It serves as the Cantonal Public Library for the city of Basel. With over 3 million items in its collections, the library is one of the largest in Switzerland. Its distinctive "Lesesaal" reading room is covered by a hyperbolic paraboloid (double curvature) concrete shell, creating a unique space with filtered daylight. The library was designed by Otto Heinrich Senn and opened in 1965.

Grand Bibliotheque Nationale de France, Paris, France (Dominique Perrault), 1989–95
Architect Dominique Perrault describes the French National Library as:

- *A place, not a building*
- *A symbolic and magic place*
- *A place for concentrated reading*
- *A place capable of growing*

The Bibliotheque de France was built on a stretch of industrial wasteland on the banks of the river Seine, and became the starting point for a complete restructuring of this entire district. The horizontal volume has four corner towers at the scale of the city that resemble open books, all facing one another. The national library is seen as an accumulation of learning and of knowledge that is never complete. At nighttime, the four glass towers shimmer like four lighthouse beacons. The towers house the book stacks and the administrative departments. In its center is a sunken garden. The general reception area is situated between the Seine and this garden. The specialised thematic libraries (current affairs, audio-visual, study, and research) are arranged on several mezzanine levels within a tall volumetric space. Their reading areas are entirely glazed on the garden side, and on the outer side equipped with a range of facilities and technical services. The message of the design is clear: at the core of the project—and perhaps at the center of human knowledge—is nature, not humans or urbanism.

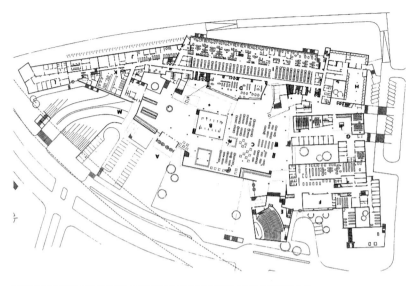

Berlin State Library, Berlin, Germany (Hans Scharoun), 1967–78
The site of the State Library is part of the Kulturforum, facing Mies van der Rohe's New National Gallery, as well as Scharoun's own masterpiece, the Berlin Philharmonic Hall (completed in 1963). Before the fall of the Wall, it was located on the Western side in close proximity to the Wall, crossing the historical Potsdamer Strasse. The building is over 300 metres (over 1,000 feet) in length and it is a true "People's Palace". Two entrances offer access from the plaza on the western side: the north entrance serves as the library's public main entrance, while the one on south provides direct access to a lecture hall. The ground floor forms a huge open area with a ceiling height of 6 metres (19 feet); the main space is the reading room located on the third floor with a triple floor height of 9 metres; its ceiling is perforated by circular skylights with diffusers that filters the sunlight. Books are stored in the basement and in the four top levels of the book tower. The library uses a closed-stack system in which books are delivered to the users upon request. The exterior of the building is clad with golden-coloured aluminum panels, the same panels Scharoun used for the Philharmonic Hall across the street. The design was with participation by Edgar Wisniewski, and the aim was to express lightness and transparency in post-war Germany, following a historically heavy and dark period.

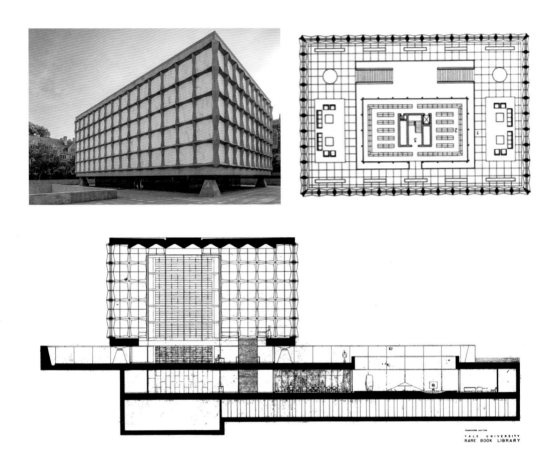

Beinecke Rare Books & Manuscript Library, Yale University Campus, New Haven, US (SOM, Gordon Bunshaft), 1960–63

The Beinecke Rare Book & Manuscript Library is the literary archive of the Yale University Library, and is the largest building in the world devoted to the preservation of rare books and documents, including a rare 1455 Gutenberg Bible. The entire library is a windowless, monolithic, abstract cube shaped around the massive display in the center. The monumental rectangular volume is clad in marble, supported by four large pilotis and seems to float over the plaza. The book stacks are placed underground, rising up inside the volume of the large exhibition hall as glass book tower: the six-storey glass-enclosed tower of book stacks holds 180,000 volumes. The façade's marble cladding is thin and translucent, introducing filtered natural daylight so that rare materials can be displayed without damage. From the outside, the building appears as if it is completely solid. The exterior framework gestures to the golden ratio: fifteen marble blocks run across the face of the building, five run vertically, and ten run along its depth, representing the ratio of 3:1:2.

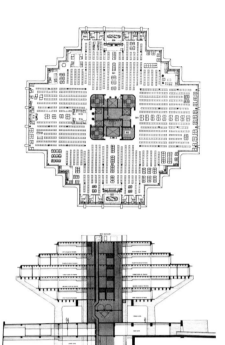

Geisel Library, University of California, San Diego, US (William Pereira), 1968–70
Geisel Library is the main library building of the University of California, San Diego. The building is partially submerged; it displays a nexus between brutalism and futurism that its architect, William Pereira, pursued throughout his career. With its strong, expressive concrete piers and hovering glassy enclosures, the library balances massiveness and levitation, giving the library an unusual, otherworldly appearance. The building is an eight-storey brutalist structure with two submerged floors and six floors of varying sizes above ground level, optimising daylight in the stacks, the ability to browse the shelves and the potential for future expansion. The lower two stories form a pedestal for the six-storey, stepped tower. The interior spaces are less spectacular, rather ordinary, but with good views from the top floors.

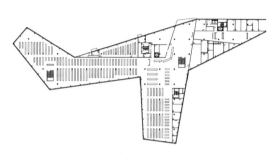

Des Moines Public Library, Gateway Park, Des Moines, Iowa, US (David Chipperfield), 2001–06
The public library forms an integral part and centerpiece of the new Des Moines Western Gateway Park. This area of the city has undergone extensive redevelopment and the new library and park have become the main catalyst for its urban renewal. As well as library facilities, the elegant building contains a flexible activity space, education facilities, children's play areas, a conference wing and a cafeteria, reinforcing the civic nature of the building. The 13,000 sqm (130,000 sqft) library is a two-storey building with a consistent uniform red-coloured, glass-metal skin giving the building its distinctive appearance. The unusual form of the building creates external spaces of differing character within the park while, facing the city, and together with the historic Masonic Temple building, it frames a new entrance courtyard. Internally, the bookshelves are arranged in such a way that visitors are always facing the park, giving a sense of openness and transparency.

Saxon State and University Library, Dresden, Germany (Ortner & Ortner Baukunst), 1996–2002
The Sächsische Landesbibliothek –Staats- und Universitätsbibliothek, SLUB) Dresden is both the regional library for the German State of Saxony as well as the academic library for the Dresden University of Technology. The collection has over 5 million volumes and includes the Deutsche Fotothek, holding some 5 million photographs. The library was first established in 1556. With over 40,000 sqm (400,000 sqft), the building provides 1,000 study desks, of which 200 are located in the main reading room. The library itself consists of two stone blocks of identical size placed opposite one another on a lawn. Between them, a glass surface set flush with the lawn, is the skylight of the central reading room. This reading room is at the heart of the three-storey library base, which extends beneath the lawn across the entire area of the former sports field. Dark wood was chosen for the paneling in the underground reading room, creating a dark atmosphere. The paneling is set out in the same punch card pattern reiterated on the outer façades of the two cubes, where local travertine was used.

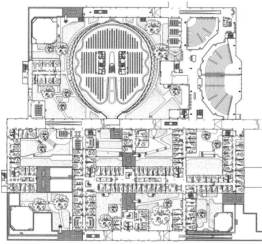

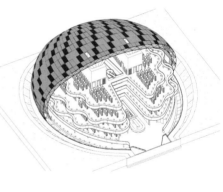

Free University of Berlin, Philology Faculty Library, Berlin, Germany (Foster + Partners), 1997–2005
Occupying a site created by uniting six of the University's courtyards, the redevelopment scheme
involved the restoration of the original modernist buildings and creation of a new library for the Faculty
of Philology. The Free University of Berlin's latest addition houses four floors that are contained within a
naturally ventilated bubble-like enclosure clad in aluminium and glazed panels on a tubular steel frame
with a radial geometry. Glass panels filter daylight penetrating the interior and create an atmosphere of
concentration while granting views of the sky above. The library's distinctive cranial form, characterised
by a translucent inner membrane, has earned it the nickname –The Brain. Foster + Partners' design
places an emphasis on sustainable principles, particularly with regards to the potential for buildings to
adopt passive and active technologies to radically increase energy efficiency.

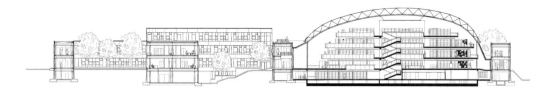

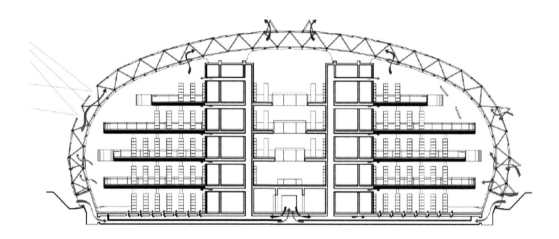

The 'Brain' is a high-performance structure that invites an abundance of natural light and fresh air into its spaces. In direct response to Berlin's varying climate, the mass of the structure's concrete slabs acts as passive thermal storage. The building is further heated and cooled by piped water concealed within the blocks. Remarkably, the library can be entirely naturally ventilated for 60% of the year through the clever incorporation of openable panels and introducing controlled fresh air drawn in through an undercroft. This means that the building consumes 35% less energy to a comparable structure.

Münster City Library, Münster, Germany (Bolles-Wilson + Partner), 1986–93

The new City Library was inserted into an inner-city carpark. The library is often a visual landmark and focal point for the surrounding area. Large openings in the façade reveal the library activities inside to the city's passers-by. The building is cut in two parts by a new pedestrian laneway that presents an urban axis of a nearby church. Connection between the two parts is via the first-floor bridge and in the basement (where the two buildings become one). Two large sloping copper walls form the pedestrian laneway. One building part is a ship-like solitaire that forms an outer perimetre of the project with its curved wall. The library wants to tackle the question of the changing status of information by creating three zones: near, middle and far. The far zone is long-term storage with no public access. The middle zone is the familiar lending library, the realm of the book; the plan registers this as a clear form, a segment of a circle. This zone is quiet, books line its large curved wall and reading is done. The near zone is pure information, the library's catalogue and information desk as a supermarket of information. The café, exhibition area and newspaper reading salon are in the uncontrolled area close to the entrance. The "Kinderbusen" is the children's library, projecting into the rear courtyard.

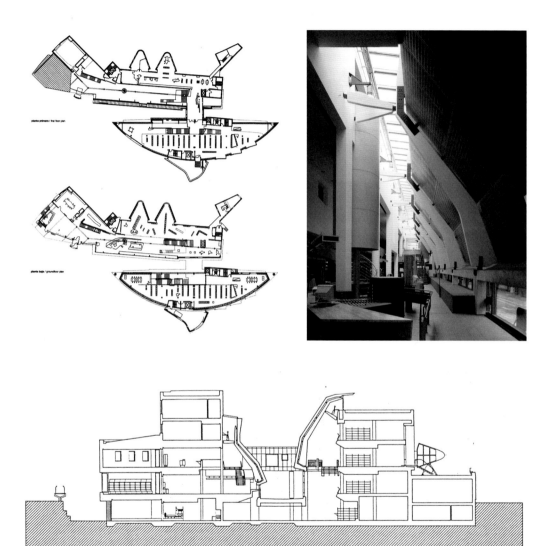

After almost thirty years, this key building, heavily influenced by Aalto, Scharoun and the playful Architectural Association background of the designers remains near the top of the ranking list of more than seventy public libraries in Germany. The complexities of the overall building form are derived from internal organization and a careful re-constitution of the fragmented context. Since Münster, the architects have designed several other libraries, however, none with the same spatial intensity and inventiveness.

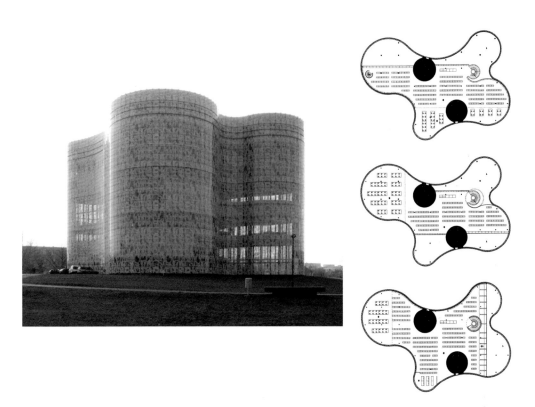

Cottbus BTU University Library, Cottbus, Germany (Herzog & de Meuron), 1994–2004

Public access to the library was a requirement of the Brandenburg University of Technology (BTU) when a competition was held in 1993 for the modernisation and development of the campus; the BTU is a young university founded in 1991. The architects Herzog & de Meuron were commissioned to design a new library for BTU, which was to create a new image for the university: an information, communications and media centre that would also be used by the local population. HdM concluded that "what was required was a landmark, a solitaire within the surrounding urban architecture that would communicate the new spirit of the university and relate to the environs in many different ways" (HdM, 1994).

The amoeba-like plan is a purposeful configuration and the result of different flows and movement. Its unusual continuous single form allows the creation of reading rooms in many different sizes. Located at the main entrance to the campus, curved pathways lead to the glazed library building, and once inside, the library user is led through a variety of different-sized reading rooms and open-access areas. Some reading rooms are two or three storeys high, giving a very spacious feeling, while others are more intimate with lower ceilings. A sculptural spiral staircase cuts through the entire structure and links all the storeys. Colour is a major factor at Cottbus and six intense colour bands run throughout the building with grey and white predominating in the reading rooms to aid concentration and avoid distraction for the reader; while information counters have bright colours. A trend in university library design has been the use of fritted or printed glass. At Cottbus a white veil with texts and alphabets in different languages is printed on both sides of the building's glazed shell. The printed pattern breaks up the reflection and softens the glass exterior. During the day, the interior of the building is concealed behind the façade; at night all is revealed. The architects' idea was to create an identity for the library that looks exciting and entices people (including tourists) to come inside to find out what is going on.

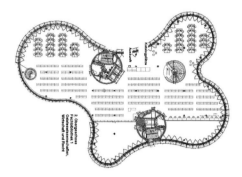

National Library of Israel, Jerusalem, Israel (Herzog & de Meuron), 2013–22
Below: Computer rendering of the library currently under construction at the time of writing. "Our design responds to the context and reflects the ambitions of the National Library of Israel," say the architects. "It is open and transparent but grounded in the traditions of great libraries and the city itself. As in the past, books will remain at the center. They form a foundation and necessary balance against constant technological change. Books root the building to the ground and are visible to all in a central void" (Jacques Herzog, 2019). This more traditional library combines on six floors (34,000 sqm) a central research centre, venue for indoor and outdoor cultural activities, a hall for digital experience and a climate-controlled underground storehouse for its treasures. The book well, a punch of offset concentric circles passing through each floor of the building, culminates in a skylight.

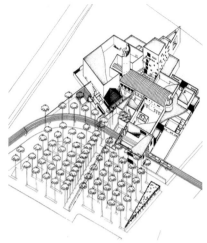

**Las Vegas Central Library and Children's Discovery Museum, Las Vegas, Nevada, US
(Antoine Predock Architects), 1987–90**
The Las Vegas Central Library and Children's Discovery Museum is a desert building and civic monument located in the downtown area. It combines the museum to the west and the library to the east, with the Children's Discovery Museum bridging both parts conceptually and architecturally. Antoine Predock speaks about how the design acknowledges both the future technical requirements of evolving library system technologies and the importance of a personal relationship with books. Future growth of workplaces, intimate reading alcoves and layouts of staff workstations to maximise public supervision all influenced the design strategies. The sandstone wedge houses the administrative areas.

Lied Library — Main library for UNLV, Las Vegas, Nevada, US
(Welles-Pugsley, Leo Daly and Simpson Coulter), 1994–2000

Established in 1957, the Lied Library building, at five stories, 30,000 sqm (300,000 sqft) and over 1.8 million volumes on a total 45 km (28 miles) of shelving, opened in 2000. It is the largest on the University of Nevada, Las Vegas campus, featuring an impressive atrium space with escalators bring users up to the second floor. While the library isn't great architecture, it is a popular building with a welcoming entrance area, an effective wayfinding system, and a new Makers' Space' for digital fabrication. Its vision statement says: "Graduate lifelong learners, inspire transformative research, and connect diverse communities."

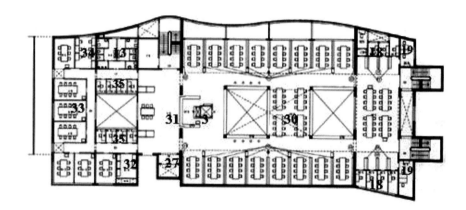

New Academic Library, University of Aveiro, Aveiro, Portugal (Alvaro Siza Vieira), 1988-95
The library (approximately 6,200 sqm; 62,000 sqft on four floors) is located at the heart of the campus masterplan, and it is organised in three zones: the zone of utilization (including offices and study rooms); the zone for storage (including air-conditioned spaces and the book storage on the ground floor); and the zone of service (including spaces for the maintenance and support of the library's functioning). It was decided early on that the users should have free access to the books, and that the "basic unit" of the user is the reading table with two shelves forming a semi-autonomous space. The main entry is on the second floor, while the lower ground floor is destined to technical services and book storage. The upper three floors accommodate the visitors with the central part occupied by various reading rooms. The library holds over 300,000 volumes and utilizes filtered natural daylight for the reading rooms: indirect and diffuse daylight penetrates through large windows and Aalto-like skylights. Alvaro Siza's philosophy is often compared to Alvar Aalto's approach to maximise daylight filtering.

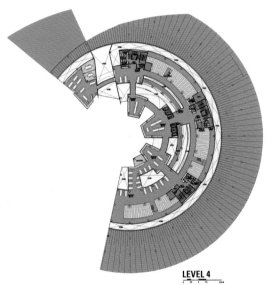

LEVEL 4

Central Library, University of Indonesia, Depok, Indonesia (Denton Corker Marshall), 2008–11
The architects' statement says that the new library conceptually bridges the ancient and the contemporary knowledge in a form inspired by the ancient stone steles and light play. The five-storey building is conceived as a new social and knowledge hub for 30,000 students; it is located on the waterfront of the campus lake. Its circular form follows the circular patterns of the campus masterplan. A series of stone-like towers project from a mound landform, seen as abstracted stone tablets rising from the earth mound. These towers are clad in granite and have varying heights. The part of the library that faces the lake is "eroded", forming an opening and allowing daylight to enter. The layout of the reading room on the ground floor is designed as an open space for interaction. It houses bookshops, offices, an exhibition space, retail and an internet reading room; the upper floors offer additional meeting rooms and an auditorium. Continuous curvilinear pedestrian ramps link the different floors to encourage visitors to explore the space around the central void, between the bookcases and the reading rooms. The space programming aims to avoid having sectional departmental libraries, which would fragment student activities. The library promotes interaction between different activities and is a place of gathering.

OMA, Rem Koolhaas: two unbuilt library projects for Paris, France, 1989 and 1992
Dutch firm Office for Metropolitan Architecture (OMA) has been at the forefront of rethinking and redefining the library. While their recent work tackles the predictability and conventions of the hospital and shopping centre typologies, their earlier work entailed a deep rethink of the library. OMA has a 20-year history of exploring and testing ideas for the library of the future that illustrate how the library has finally outgrown its traditional role as a stable storehouse for knowledge, embracing the dynamic nature of the institution itself.

OMA's earlier competition proposals for two libraries in Paris (the competition for the Grande Bibliothèque Nationale in 1989; and the Jussieu University Library Competition in 1992 —both remained unbuilt) foreshadowed the concept and design of Seattle Public Library, which was completed in 2004. Both provocative designs that have never been built show Rem Koolhaas's aversion to "the whole idea of a typology" (Zaera Polo, 1992); dealing with the question: How to house information and knowledge in the digital age? Koolhaas has chosen an abstract, almost industrial language and structural expression that turns the visit to the library into an urban experience.

The circulation for the unbuilt projects establishes a continuous circuit, a loop in form of a double helix (similar to the structure of DNA) inside a simple large cube; the loop is formed like a ramp, a "book spiral" along which all the accessible book storage facilities and other functional elements are lined up. The ramp winds through the entire building like a meandering boulevard lined with all the parts of a library, where the visitor becomes a flaneur seduced by the world of books and information, enjoying the continuity of knowledge on a scripted way of movement through the building's voids. Here, the circulation pattern drives the design in plan and section, as well as the information gathering of the library visitor, introducing a new relationship between the library's different components. Zaera Polo (1992) argues that more information-rich environments suitable for a mediatheque are those with relatively open, flexible floor plans and easily accessible resources, using removable partition walls rather than fixed walls. Koolhaas (1995) has argued that these differentiated spaces serve not as a collection of rooms, but as a series of incidents; "it's no longer simply a library but rather a system with many different components." He describes this as a design method "aiming not for stable configurations but for the creation of enabling fields that accommodate processes that refuse to be crystallized into definitive form; a method not about separating and identifying identities, but about discovering unnamable hybrids."

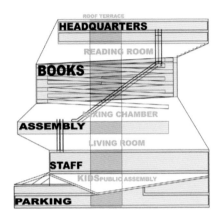

Seattle Central Library, Seattle, Washington, US (OMA with LMN Architects), 1999–2004

The new Seattle Central Library can be seen as a milestone in the design of the library of the future. The building is set into a hill and takes up a full city block. Paul Goldberger (2004) called it "the most important new library to be built in a generation, and the most exhilarating." Koolhaas and Ramus started out by investigating how libraries actually work, and how they are likely to change. At a moment when libraries were perceived to be under threat of a shrinking public realm and mass digitisation, this project combines these two seemingly opposing forces to create a flexible civic space. It introduced a new approach to the way how people and information are brought together and that has had a huge impact on the way architects and library managers look at designing libraries, especially public libraries. The library is an eleven-storey building, interconnected by a public circulation loop. The concept was to provide an information store giving equal priority to both new and old media through the provision of a four-tier book spiral with stacked and overlapping platforms, in between which are what are described as "trading floors" with a "living room entrance" (Futagawa, 2006). The book spiral idea that first emerged in the 1989 competition for Paris was finally realised ten years later in Seattle. The core of OMA's design strategy was to redefine the library as an institution that was no longer exclusively dedicated to the book, but rather as an information warehouse where all potent forms of media, new and old, are presented equally and legibly. The users are surrounded by information sources, and there is maximum interaction between them and the librarians who can provide expert help in exploiting all resources whether printed or electronic. The architects divided the programme in stable and unstable parts. The stable functions included the administrative part of the library, the book storage, meeting rooms, staff offices and the carpark—all contained in fixed boxes. The unstable functions, which imply a greater amount of movement of people across them, were stacked in the section of the building, placed above and below the floating boxes. "Unstable" refers here to the speed in which certain programmatic components are likely to change, technologically or socially.

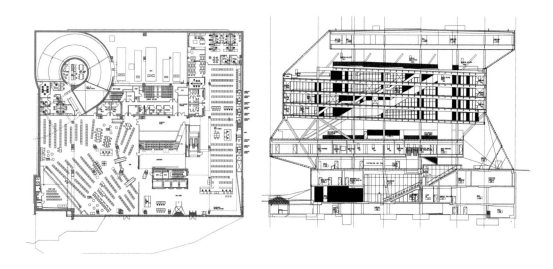

Seattle Central Library, Seattle, Washington, US (OMA), 1999–2004

The stacking diagram emphasises the programme and creates enclosed void spaces that can generate unexpected new programmatic uses. Joshua Ramus, who was the partner in charge of the Seattle project for OMA, argues that the biggest threat to the contemporary library is actually the excessive requirement for flexibility, as he wrote in 2004:

"As new media emerged and gained currency, the library seemed threatened, a fortress ready to be taken by a marauding hoard of technologies. In this fairy-tale, the electronic becomes barbaric. Its intangible, ominous ubiquity, its uncontrollable accessibility seems to represent a loss of order, tradition and civilization. In response, the language of the library has become moralistic and defensive. Its rhetoric proclaims a sense of superiority in mission, social responsibility and value. The last decade has revealed an accelerated erosion of the Public domain —replaced by increasingly sophisticated and entertaining forms of the Private. The essence of the Public is that it is free. Increasingly, public space has been replaced by accommodations of quasi-public substance that, while suggesting an open invite, actually make you pay. The library stands exposed as outdated and moralistic that it has become the last repository of the free and the public.

Our ambition was to redefine the library as an institution no longer exclusively dedicated to the book. In an age where information can be accessed anywhere, it is the simultaneity of all media and (more importantly) the curatorship of their contents that will make the library vital. Flexibility in contemporary libraries is conceived as the creation of generic floors on which almost any activity can happen. Programmes are not separated, rooms or individual spaces not given unique characters. In practice, this means that bookcases define generous (though non-descript) reading areas on opening day, but, through the collection's relentless expansion, inevitably come to encroach on the public space. Ultimately, in this form of flexibility, the library strangles the very attractions that differentiate it from other information resources. Instead of its current ambiguous flexibility, the library could cultivate a more refined approach by organizing itself into spatial compartments, each dedicated to, and equipped for, specific duties. Tailored flexibility remains possible within each compartment, but without the threat of one section hindering the others.

Our first operation was to consolidate the library's apparently ungovernable proliferation of programmes and media. By combining like with like, we identified programmatic clusters —five of stability, and four of instability. Each platform is a programmatic cluster that is architecturally defined and equipped for maximum dedicated performance. Because each platform is designed for a unique purpose, their size, flexibility, circulation, palette, structure and MEP vary. The spaces in between the platforms function as "trading floors" where librarians inform and stimulate, where the interface between the different platforms is organized— spaces for work, interaction and play. By genetically modifying the superposition of floors, a building emerges that is at the same time sensitive (the geometry provides shade or unusual quantities of daylight where desirable), contextual (each side reacts differently to specific urban conditions or desired views), and iconic. The problem of traditional library organization is flatness. ...As collections unpredictably swell, materials are dissociated from their categories. Excess materials are put in the basement, moved to off-site storage, or become squatters of another totally unrelated department. The Book Spiral implies a reclamation of the much-compromised Dewey Decimal System. By arranging the collection in a continuous ribbon — running from '000' to '999' —the subjects form a coexistence that approaches the organic; each evolves relative to the others, occupying more or less space on the ribbon, but never forcing a rupture. For Seattle, the Spiral's 6,230 bookcases are guaranteed to house 780,000 books upon opening, with flexibility to grow to 1,450,000 books in the future (without adding another bookcase). The traditional library presents the visitor with an internal matrix of materials, technologies, and specialists. ...The Book Spiral liberates the librarians from the burden of managing ever-increasing masses of material."

— Joshua Ramus, 2004

For me, Seattle Library is a building that is at the same time old-fashioned in terms of resurrecting the public realm, and contemporary in terms of addressing the key issue whether the book is still relevant. What was fascinating is that when we started looking at the programme, we divided it into only two activities –those programmatic components that we assumed would remain stable over time, and those where we assumed they would start to mutate and change their character fairly quickly.

— Rem Koolhaas, OMA, 2005

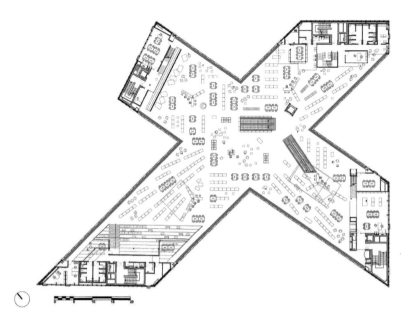

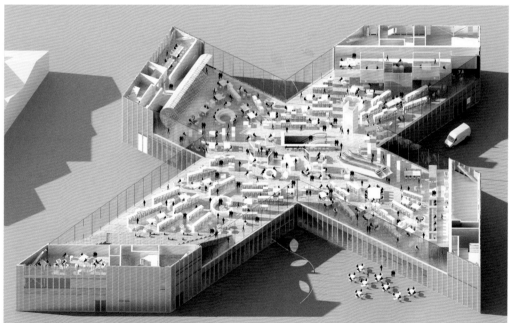

Careu Regional Library, Caen, France (OMA with Barcode Architects), 2010–17
Bibliothèque Alexis de Tocqueville is a public library for the metropolitan region Caen la Mer in Normandy. The unusual cross-shaped plan of this four-storey library supports the city's ambition for the library to become a new civic center. Much of the library's organisation is driven by its powerful cross-shaped figure plan.

Unlike a traditional library, the client wanted to create a new type of space where many different fields of study exchange knowledge freely and easily. In our first study, the library, multipurpose hall, café, and many other different programme parts were stacked to make a tall multi-storey tower. But finally, as the programme defined a meeting place for students we felt that everything on one floor and in one room was best. We did not make a normal one-room space but incorporated patios and topography to organise the programme such that each is separated and connected at the same time. The large space undulates up and down creating an open space under the building so that people can walk to the entry at the centre of the building.
— Kazuyo Sejima, SANAA, 2010

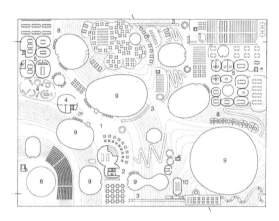 

Rolex Learning Center, Lausanne, Switzerland (SANAA), 2004–10

The Rolex Learning Center functions as a radical laboratory for interdisciplinary learning and international cultural hub for EPFL. The main library, containing 500,000 volumes, is one of the largest scientific collection in Europe. Four large study areas can accommodate 860 students and offices for over 100 employees. Influenced by Toyo Ito's concept of the Sendai Mediatheque, the various sections are not separated by any walls, forming a continuous open space and landscape with few glass partitions. A multimedia library offers access to 10,000 online journals. Ten teaching areas for seminars, group work and meetings are integrated in the continuous landscape interior in separate glass bubbles. Spread over one single fluid space of 20,000 sqm (200,000 sqft), it provides a seamless network of services, libraries, information gathering, social spaces and rooms to study, restaurants, cafés and outdoor spaces. It is a highly innovative building, with gentle slopes and terraces, undulating around a series of internal "patios", with almost invisible supports for its complex curving roof, which required completely new methods of construction. The concrete —in some areas almost one metre (3 feet) thick— was poured over a precise formwork of sloping geometries created from 1,400 individual molds.

Reimaging the Library of the Future

Selected Case Studies with Statements from Library Designers

Arata Isozaki

Thoughts on the Library of the Future

In 2006, Arata Isozaki wrote about the way he changed his design method around 1973, moving away from functionalism towards an architecture of pure geometrical configurations. He compares the two different conceptual approaches that he applied to Oita Prefectural Library (1962–66) and to Toyonokuni Libraries for Cultural Resources (1991–95). Both libraries are located in Oita, in the south of Japan, and are 30 years apart. Isozaki wrote:

"I changed the way I design in the early 1970s, around the time when I published an essay entitled 'About my Method'. Earlier, I had designed the Oita Prefectural Library by means of what I called 'process planning'. In accordance with an orthodox, functionalist interpretation of modern architecture, I took the volumes required by the programme and determined their functional relationships. Next, taking into account the anticipated growth of those functions, I broke down the volumes into sets (clusters) of rooms, that is, containers. I assumed that there was a one-to-one correspondence between form (container) and content (function). I was searching for a form that was responsive to changes in function as time passed. However, as my theory of process planning had indicated, the process could not be entirely automatic. At some point, I had to deliberately intervene and terminate the process. In that sense, the process was not entirely impersonal.

Then came 1968 with all its philosophical implications. I came to realise that the idea of 'planning', which I had embraced and which I had thought applicable to everything —the state, the economy, society, architecture, the city— was bankrupt. I began to doubt the very idea of architectural planning. I became interested in the automatic generation of forms. That is, I came to believe that basic forms existed a priori and that 'planning' meant anticipating their self-generation. I sought determinants of form in pure geometrical configurations. One of those configurations was the cubical frame. In the Gunma Prefectural Museum of Fine Arts, I proposed arranging the frame in rows, and the voids generated inside them represented the 'art museum of the future'. Thirty years later, when the Oita Prefectural Library needed to be rebuilt on a larger scale, I arranged cubical frames on a square plan, creating a void measuring nine bays, or eighty-one cubical frames in total. This 'Hall of One Hundred Columns' became the new open-stack library.

This was very different from the way I had approached the design of the earlier library. The idea based on a superficial functionalism, that content (function) should correspond to form —the idea of honesty of expression— was turned on its head. Form (expression) was now allowed to generate content (function). The building type was still the same, but I took an entirely different approach to its design.

In both libraries the entrance hall (vestibule) and the main room are separated by an intermediate space that is very different in character. In the earlier work, light is introduced through slits in a folded-plate roof; in the second library, light enters through a gap between the square envelope of the space and a disc inscribed in the square. There is a difference in the design of the circulation spaces. In the earlier building, visitors go through a tunnel-like space painted green; and in the second, they climb up stairs. Each time, the arrangement is intended to prepare visitors psychologically by means of a distinctive spatial experience for a different space for reading."

— Arata Isozaki, 2006

Oita Prefectural Library, Oita, Japan (Arata Isozaki & Associates), 1962–66

Oita Prefectural Library is an icon of structuralism and brutalism in architecture. Its tubular concrete beams emphasize the weight of the building and the way light is introduced from above, through openings in a folded-plate roof. Isozaki wanted to give the building an open-ended character and reveal the structural elements in section. In the spirit of the time, this was an idea of architecture that was itself an organizational structure and system rather than an object: one could imagine the spatial and structural system to continue endlessly.

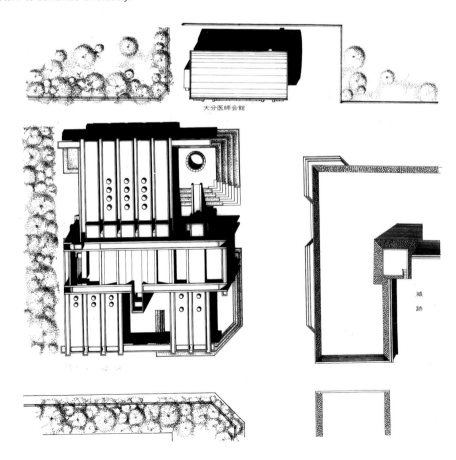

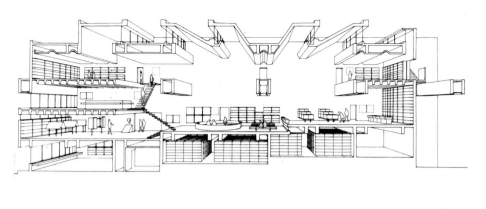

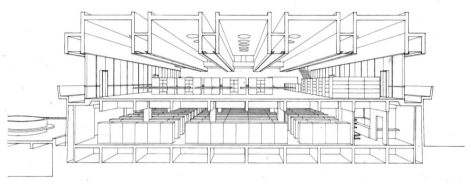

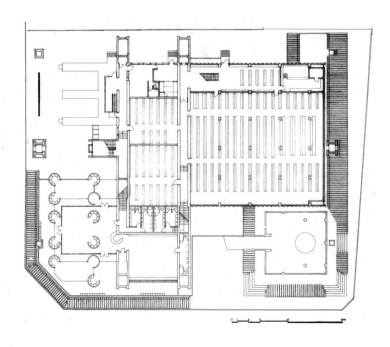

108

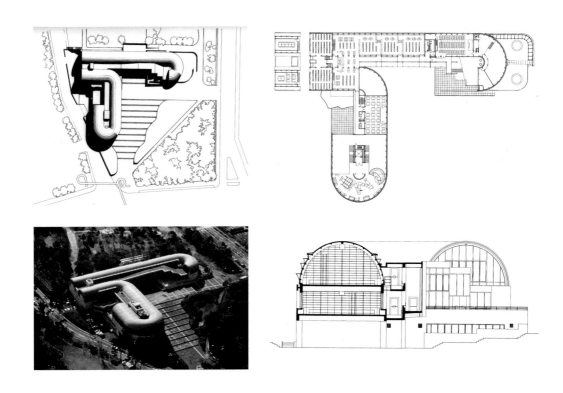

Kitakyushu Central Library, Fukuoka, Japan (Arata Isozaki & Associates), 1973–74

At the same time, Arata Isozaki designed Kitakyushu City Museum of Art, as the municipal government thought of the museum and library as a combined cultural manifesto. The unusual shape of the Central Library was conceived as a continuous and curving semi-circular vault. Two vaults start side-by-side but turn at different points. A split-level scheme was adopted in response to the sloping site. A ramp, visible on the outside front façade, links the different levels. The programme combines three different facilities: the central library (located in the middle), a historical museum and an audio-visual centre. The vault spans 11 metres (36 feet) and consists of precast concrete arcs.

The 1970s are frequently called the era that represents the "beginning of the contemporary". Arata Isozaki told the author in a conversation (2000) about his approach: "The vaulted space of the library immediately calls to mind the drawing for the French National Library by visionary French neoclassical architect Étienne-Louis Boullée. At this time, in 1973, I was well acquainted with the existence of Boullée's project, but did not quote it directly at first. However, it was from this time on that I consciously used quotations and historical references in my designs. This was the time when I also changed the way I designed, and published it in an essay entitled 'About my Method'." In the 1980s, with postmodernism, it became a common design strategy to include historical references and quotations from historical buildings.

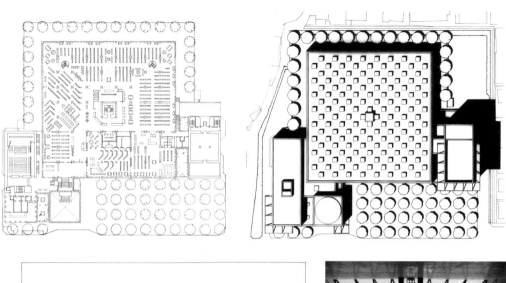

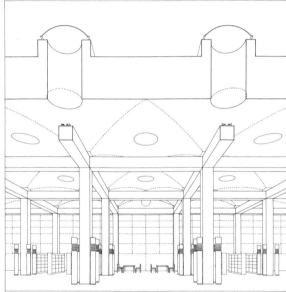

Toyonokuni Libraries for Cultural Resources, Oita, Japan (Arata Isozaki & Associates), 1991–95
This is the new 18,000 sqm prefectural library in Oita, replacing Isozaki's earlier building, from 30 years earlier, which became far too small to serve its community. He designed cubical frames on a square plan, creating a large uniform void measuring nine bays laid out in a 7.5m grid, or eighty-one cubical frames in total. The "Hall of One Hundred Columns" (a concept found in ancient Roman architecture: one large room supported by one hundred posts, giving a flexibility so that anything could occur) became the new open-stack library. All open shelves are installed in this single-level space, the grand reading room. The closed stack can take another 1.6 million volumes. The main entrance hall is a cube (15x15m in size), finished in exposed concrete in order to produce a neurtral space: an "anteroom" as in Michelangelo's Laurentian Library.

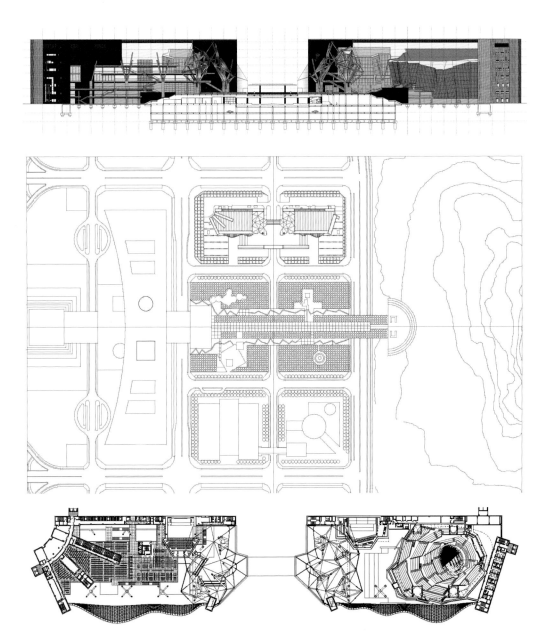

Shenzhen Library and Cultural Center, Shenzhen, China (Arata Isozaki & Associates), 1998–2007
Shenzhen Cultural Center includes Shenzhen Library and Shenzhen Concert Hall and is located in the Futian District of Shenzhen. It was the first of a series of cultural projects in China that Isozaki won by design competition. Both facilities, the library and concert hall, are connected into a unified whole through a large two-storey platform facing the city's central urban axis; it provides for a unique public space, the Cultural Square. The concert hall consists of an 1,800-seat vineyard typology hall with excellent acoustics and a small 400-seat theatre studio.

Toyo Ito & Associates

Sendai Mediatheque, Sendai, Japan (Toyo Ito & Associates), 1995–2001

A key milestone in library design, with an innovative structural system and a non-hierarchical organisation of spaces to establish continuity between the various programmes. Toyo Ito wrote about this radically innovative hybrid building:

"Sendai Mediatheque is a suggestion for an architecture embodying new types of programmes. It is a facility combining an art gallery, a library, a service center for persons with visual or auditory impairments, and a media center of visual images. From the original competition throughout the basic planning, our prime objective consisted of dismantling conventional archetypes such as museums or libraries, rearranging each of these programmes, and restructuring them into a 'mediatheque' complex. This involved a series of exchange of opinions with the local citizens as well as hearings with experts of various fields to take place along with the basic planning.

Since the nature of such discussions is endless, never reaching any conclusions, the hardware that is the architecture, requires a flexibility which makes it possible to develop all types of programmes. As opposed to an architecture as an example of formalism, an extremely simple yet conceptual building was composed of three elements: plate, tube, and skin. 'Plate' is a schematic presentation of various media's different forms of communication between humans and things or among humans, realized onto six sheets of square slabs. 'Tube' is a tree-shaped element of 13 pieces integrating the plates by piercing them in the perpendicular direction. Not only is it flexible as a structural body, but is also a space for flow of information, energies (light, air, water, sound), and lines of vertical motion. The tubes' effects account for the electronic and natural flows creating a field among the homogeneous state of the plates. 'Skin' is the outer layer that separates the indoors and outdoors of the building. Especially important is the double-skin glass façade facing the main street. The mediatheque, composed of these three simple elements, offers itself as a place where the body as an electronic fluid and the primitive body unite with nature, integrated into one. It is a symbol of public space for the people of Sendai: full of life like an urban plaza, it is now attracting over 2,000 users every day."

— Toyo Ito, 2001

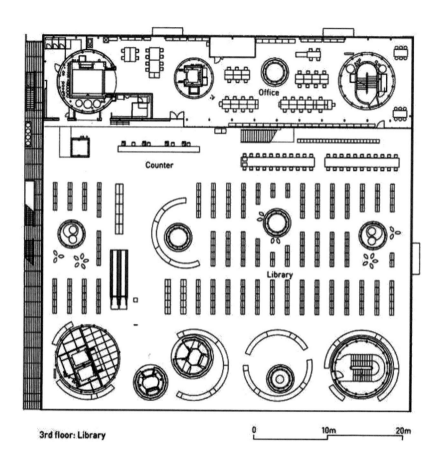

3rd floor: Library

0 10m 20m

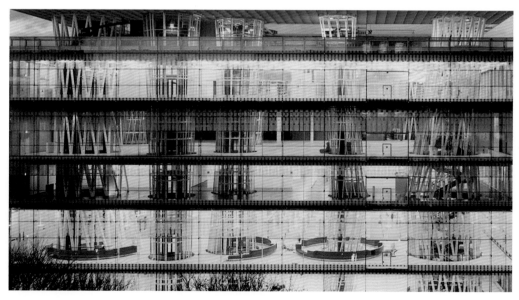

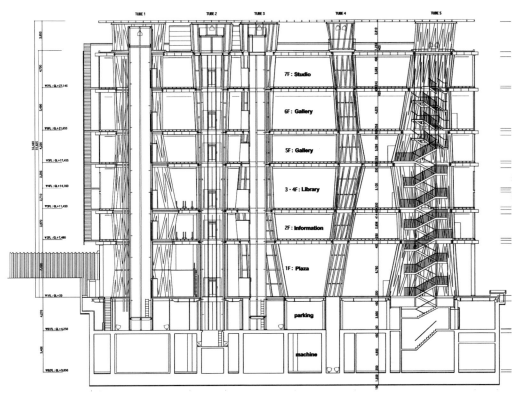

TUBE 1   TUBE 2   TUBE 3   TUBE 4   TUBE 5

7F : Studio

6F : Gallery

5F : Gallery

3 · 4F : Library

2F : Information

1F : Plaza

parking

machine

Tama Art University Library, Tokyo, Japan (Toyo Ito & Associates), 2006–08
Located in the suburbs of Tokyo, this 5,500-square-metre monastery-like library lies between Tama Art University's main gate and the center of campus. University libraries in general play a major role in their respective locations, but at an art university, the library must also reflect and inspire creativity. According to the architect, the library takes advantage of a gentle, three-degree slope of its ground floor, with colonnades providing simple, arch-like structural support. These 20-cm-thin arched walls are formed with plate steel reinforced with concrete, with a maximum span of more than 12 metres (39 feet). Rows of the colonnades are arranged in a configuration that produces a variety of interior spatial types and exterior views.

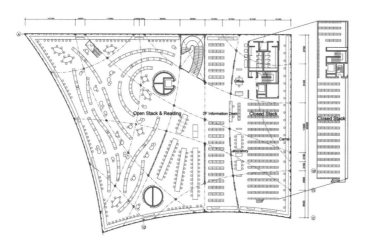

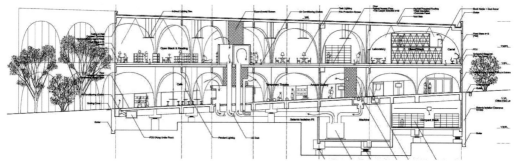

Minna No Mori Gifu Media Cosmos, Gifu City, Japan (Toyo Ito & Associates), 2010–15

There are many words that could describe Gifu's Media Cosmos: a library, art gallery and cultural hub, located between the railway station and Gifu Castle. Locally sourced cypress wood was used for the lattice ceiling. Minna No Mori, or "everyone's forest", was chosen as the official name to illustrate the library's ties to the community, with generations of carpentry and surrounding forests, connecting it to the use of wood. The extraordinary roof, supported by spillikin columns, is a lattice of 12 m length 120 x 20 timber laths, cold bent and screwed together on site as a multi-domed shell roof. Renewable, low-carbon, efficient and economically constructed without glue, the roof is simple to disassemble and reuse. Gifu Media Cosmos is divided into three different sections, each serving its own distinct purpose: the central library, an area for cultural events and art exhibits, and a community hub that houses the community activity center and multicultural plaza. Here, citizens can participate in a number of activities ranging from language classes and counseling, to seasonal activities that change every month. There is also in-house retail (Starbucks, Lawsons), a viewing platform to see nearby Gifu Castle and free Wi-Fi provided throughout the building. Lightweight textile domes define functional "neighbourhoods", like reading, resting or study areas, within one large library room.

Snøhetta

Thoughts on the Library of the Future

Libraries are places of connection, where people, information and resources come together in dynamic and diverse environments. While the vision of a library as a quiet book repository is an alluring one, this model represents only one of the many forms libraries have taken across history. In ancient times, libraries were social spaces full of life, with porous connections to the outdoors, in later centuries, they transformed into privileged places of rarefied knowledge.

At Snøhetta, we envision that the boundaries of the library will continue to spill out into their surroundings, and that in turn, libraries will begin to take on the qualities of the places they are located. As we invite urban and natural environments, new communities, and more varied forms of knowledge production and storage into library settings, their physical and experiential qualities will necessarily change. Just as no two neighbourhoods are exactly alike, no two libraries should be identical.

Additionally, the growing proliferation of library types – branch, regional and central libraries; research and archival libraries; and national libraries to name a few –show us that rather than being under threat, libraries have grown increasingly sophisticated and specific in recent decades. We envision this complexity to expand as the twenty-first century progresses. We also maintain that despite changes in technology, patronage or design, libraries will remain as they always have been: gathering places where different types of people and varied forms of knowledge come together through an inclusive and open exchange.

— Craig Dykers, Snøhetta, 2021

Bibliotheca Alexandrina, Alexandria, Egypt (Snøhetta), 1989–2001
Situated between the University of Alexandria, the Mediterranean Sea and the Alexandria's historic centre, the Bibliotheca Alexandrina creates a space where people, ideas and texts collect beside an ancient harbour. Egypt's Bibliotheca Alexandrina was completed in 2001 as a municipal library capable of containing 4 million books within its walls. Technically, it's a national library for the country of Egypt, the Bibliotheca also functions as a town square that fosters outlets for intellectual and social ideas that extend beyond the country's borders. The original library of Alexandria was established in the third century BCE, and was one of largest and most significant libraries of the ancient world. Meant to evoke this ancient library founded by Alexander the Great, the structure was designed as a tilted disk with a stone façade carved with letters from 120 different languages. Characterised by its circular, tilting form, the building spans 160 metres in diameter and reaches up to 32 metres in height, while also diving some 12 metres into the ground. With its vast reading areas cascading down seven terraces and its circular form echoing that of the harbour platform on which it sits, the library aims to bring together the printed and the electronic worlds of knowledge, as well as regenerate the seaport area of the city and act as a symbol of culture and national pride. While it took numerous years to get realised, it was a crucial project of urban regeneration and one that established Snøhetta as library designers.

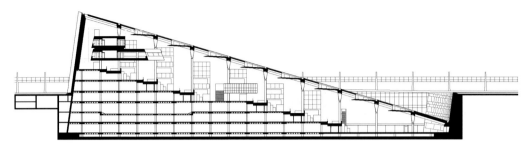

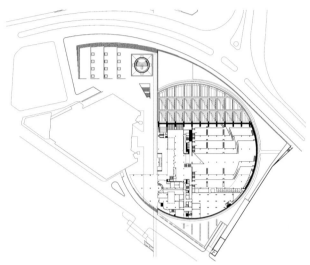

119

James B. Hunt, Jr. Library, North Carolina State University, Raleigh, NC, US (Snøhetta), 2008–13

The NCSU Library wants to set a new benchmark for technologically sophisticated collaborative learning spaces. The library is designed with an unexpectedly social focus. Generous open spaces connect all floors, and open stairs emphasise an interactive and social environment alongside more focused study areas. The building's design recognises the power of chance encounters and celebrates the role physical space plays in the intellectual stimulation of its users. Technology zones are integrated throughout the library: interactive digital surfaces, high definition video display screens and the Game Lab for the development of new video games. An automated book delivery system for the library's 2-million-volume collection is a highly effective cost and space saving measure that reduced the building area by 200,000 sqft, allowing more of the budget and library space to be allocated towards technology and collaborative learning spaces. With interiors lit by natural daylight and reading rooms facing out over a nearby lake, the library has become the intellectual and social heart of the university, challenging our conception of how research and learning take shape on campus.

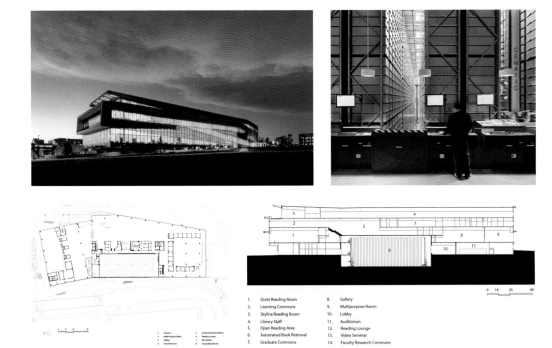

1.	Quiet Reading Room	8.	Gallery
2.	Learning Commons	9.	Multipurpose Room
3.	Skyline Reading Room	10.	Lobby
4.	Library Staff	11.	Auditorium
5.	Open Reading Area	12.	Reading Lounge
6.	Automated Book Retrieval	13.	Video Seminar
7.	Graduate Commons	14.	Faculty Research Commons

Charles Library at Temple University, Philadelphia, PA, US (Snøhetta), 2013–19

Sitting at the heart of campus, the Charles Library was developed in close collaboration with engineering firm Stantec. The layout rethinks conventional library tropes, introducing a wave of technologies and collaborative learning facilities to the large student body. Flowing wooden arches, elegant glass volumes and a striking three-storey domed atrium lobby are capped by a 4,700 sqm (47,000 sqft) green roof, one of the largest in Pennsylvania. This contributes to the stormwater management system, which relocates heavy rainwater to two underground catchment basins. An oculus carved into the expansive cedar-clad dome allows light to pour into the lobby. Access to the library collection is stored primarily in the high-density Automated Storage and Retrieval System (ASRS), affectionately termed the "BookBot", holding over 1.5 milion items.

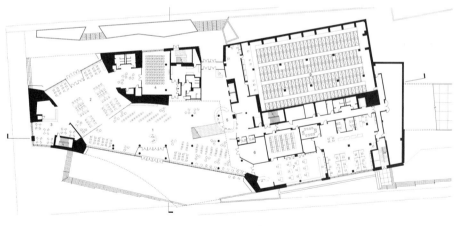

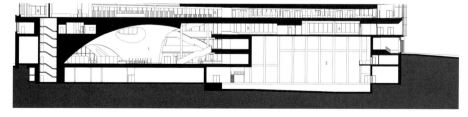

Ryerson University Student Learning Centre, Toronto, Canada (Snøhetta), 2009–15

Designed in collaboration with Zeidler, the Student Learning Centre (SLC) at Ryerson University, which includes library functions, has a façade of geometric panels of fritted glass and iridescent metal. The 14,000 sqm building is located next door to and connects with the main campus book repository; it features multipurpose spaces to accommodate study and student activities, and an eco-friendly green roof. The SLC gives students eight uniquely designed floors of generous space to meet, study and exchange ideas. Conceived as a "library without books," the design develops natural conditions for groups of people to interact while also offering areas for introspective study. It encourages students to make the space their own. The SLC is a library built for the digital age that encourages students to interact; its design approaches posit new possibilities for how user-driven forms of intellectual and social engagement can anchor a site, campus and community around knowledge. Organised as a collection of informal gathering and interactive spaces connected by staircases, the design of the SLC is inspired by ancient stoa, colonnaded hallways where philosophers of yore would come together to share ideas debate their methods.

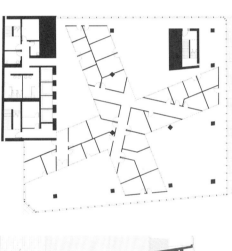
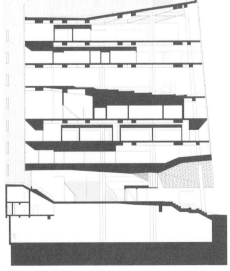

Calgary Central Library, Calgary, Canada (Snøhetta), 2013–19

Throughout history, the agora has represented a public space where people gather, debate and share information in ways that presage how knowledge is exchanged in the contemporary library. The Calgary Central Library is designed to symbolically replicate the historical function of the agora by using a building and the surrounding site to seamlessly connect a pair of neighbourhoods once divided by a light rail line. Snøhetta, in collaboration with Dialog, designed the façade of the 22,297 sqm (240,000 sqft) library by using inspiration from the province's arch-shaped Chinook cloud formations; it includes interlocking hexagonal patterns, allowing every side of the building to hold equal importance and look as though it could serve as the library's front. The building is sited within a complex urban condition, where a fully functional light rail line crosses the site from above to below ground on a curved half-moon path, dividing Downtown and East Village. In response, the design lifts the main entry over the encapsulated train line. The library uses simple gestures like a covered porch on the exterior and a central interior atrium to turn the site into a multi-level public space. Gently terraced slopes rise up to the heart of the building, allowing for people arriving from every direction to interact with the library. The unique design, which arches over the rail line, is filled inside with western red cedar, allowing the flowing forms to merge nature with modern design. Organised on a spectrum of "Fun" to "Serious," the library programme locates the livelier public activities on the lower floors, gradually transitioning to quieter study areas on the upper levels.

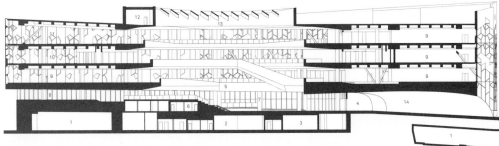

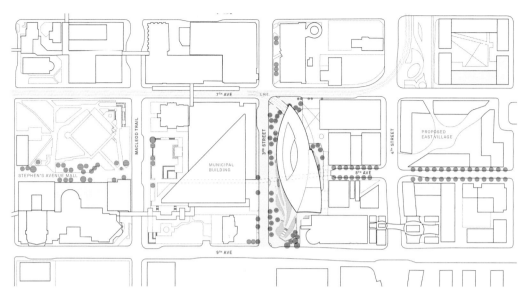

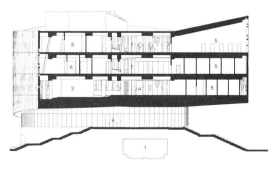

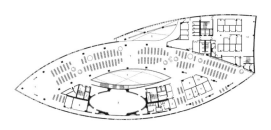

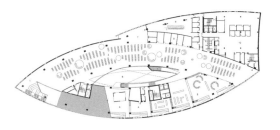

Theodore Roosevelt Presidential Library, North Dakota, US (Snøhetta), 2020–25

Landscape conservation, naturalism and civic values come together at the Theodore Roosevelt Presidential Library in Medora, North Dakota, where building and site unite to accentuate the ecological and cultural knowledge embedded within the region's diverse habitats and landscapes. This project understands the "landscape as the library" and its design is informed by the President's personal reflections on the landscape, his commitment to environmental stewardship and the periods of quiet introspection and civic engagement that marked his life. The design for the library is more than a building; it is a journey through a preserved landscape, punctuated with small pavilions providing spaces for reflection and activity. Inside the library, large windows highlight views to historically significant landscapes and complement the rhythm of the interactive exhibitions within. The library extends beyond its walls to encompass a collection of trails, scenic overlooks and pavilions that entice visitors to pay attention to the plants, animals and natural processes that define this uniquely American landscape. Its construction will use locally sourced and renewable materials.

Mecanoo

Thoughts on the Library of the Future

The library of the future must be for the people. It must offer everyone, whatever their age or background, the knowledge, skills and paths they need to find their own future.

At Mecanoo, we have been reimagining the library ever since the 1990s, when we designed the Library of Delft University of Technology. It opened libraries to a future of new forms, but we also work with historic forms, such as New York's world-famous library, the Stephen A. Schwarzman Building on Fifth Avenue. We are re-engineering this grand, glorious beaux-art building from 1911 for twenty-first century crowds and new forms of study. These are research libraries, but what about circulating libraries? In 2021 we created new central libraries in New York, Washington and in Tainan —people's libraries.

Mecanoo's architecture does not have a hallmark style. It is always driven by our philosophy of focussing on people, place, purpose and poetry. Our architecture has a humanist approach. When we designed the Library of Birmingham, we spent much time observing library users, and we learnt that the library must be for the whole community. Inclusivity must be built in. Washington's Martin Luther King Jr. Memorial Library (MLKL) and New York's Stavros Niarchos Foundation Library (SNFL) are designed to plug into the incredible energy, diversity and hopes that the people of those cities have.

Next, we come to the importance of place. I always say libraries are the cathedrals of our time. Cathedrals were once at the heart of city life, where people gathered, gossiped and traded. Libraries must be animated by civic life too. Lobbies, landings and even stairs can be social attractors. At Birmingham, Washington and New York, we have created new roof gardens open to all. And with dramatic shapes, such as the upside-down ziggurat shape of Tainan Library or SNFL's Wizard's Hat, we bring excitement to the whole city.

We need libraries because their purpose is to provide wisdom. Lifelong learning starts with children, so play is designed in for them. For teenagers, dedicated areas reflect their culture. To serve the whole community, we provide facilities like auditoria or studios or rehearsal spaces. It is not just by reading or watching that you learn. Workshops with equipment to learn skills are also part of the library of the future. The MLKL has a large Maker Space —somewhere where you can make noise! A library's purpose also extends to encouraging a healthy lifestyle. Why not make stairs visible and attractive to encourage people to use them instead of elevators? Why not bring nature to the people, for example with roof gardens?

Poetry in architecture is intangible, however, a building needs an emotional dimension beyond the programme it delivers. It must have a magic in the combined effect of all its design elements. Then, the library becomes pleasure —a pleasure that carries everyone's future.

— Francine Houben, Mecanoo, 2021

Delft University of Technology Library, Delft, Netherlands (Mecanoo), 1994–97

In 1994, the TU-Delft commissioned the architects to design a library that would become the heart of the remodelled university campus. Sited next to the much-revered, colossal Van den Broek & Bakema auditorium, the building had to be both a landmark and yet sympathetic to its surroundings. A campus atmosphere was missing where students and teachers could meet informally. The end result is a library tucked away under a vast expanse of grass roof on which students can, and do, walk and relax. The library's main features are the accessible roof and a cone, the symbol of technical engineering, which pierces the lawn and the library roof. The lawn is lifted to form the roof of the library, a roof that can be walked over. A gently ramped flight of steps below entices people up and into the building. A vast white cone over 40 metres (130 feet) high and floodlit at night pierces the grass roof and acts as a beacon at all hours. It is both spectacularly symbolic and functional as it lets in daylight into the middle of the building. Daylight enters the building through climate-controlled glass façades, as well as through the cone, whose base forms the focal point of a central space. The architects wanted a library that doesn't hide away the books in storerooms. Although many of the books are stored in the basement, many are also stored in full view in a vast bookcase, from ground floor to fourth-floor ceiling. The entrance area acts as reception space sending out a welcoming message. This was Mecanoo's first important library, and it's still evolving and changing.

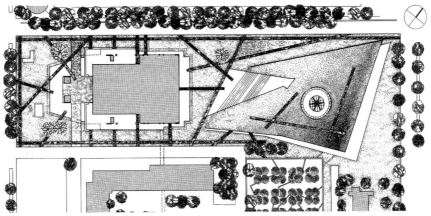

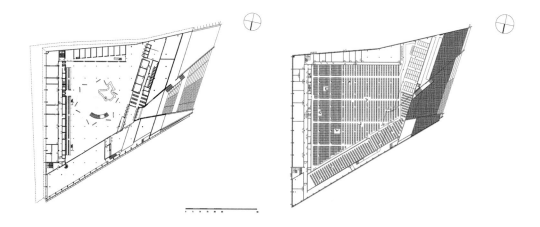

Birmingham Central Library, Birmingham, UK (Mecanoo), 2008–13

The Library of Birmingham was designed as a large "people's palace" for the UK's second biggest city. Four rectangular spaces stacked on each other in a staggered pattern to create terraces. A cantilevered volume not only provides shelter at the entrance, but also serves as a grand urban balcony and loggia with a discovery garden. The sunken circular courtyard cut out of the square in front of the library is a protected outdoor space that invites daylight deep into the building. The core of the design is the "book rotunda", where elevators move visitors across the openings between floors through interconnected and overlapping voids that provide also for natural light and ventilation. Ever-changing vistas unfold from the inside through the delicate filigree skin of interlocking rings, inspired by the city's proud tradition of its metal and steel industry.

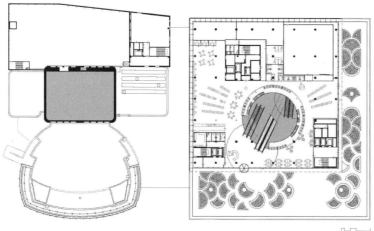

Birmingham Central Library is one of the largest public libraries in Europe, and it was partially by luck that it was built. Following severe cuts to public funding in 2012, the UK saw a fierce and passionate battle to save public libraries. British novelist and library campaigner Zadie Smith criticised the politicisation of the library debate. "When we were children, you'd never imagine that you'd get into a right versus left argument about the purpose and use of a library. It seems extraordinary to me," she wrote. "I really don't find it a political argument. It's about equality of opportunity. You know you don't expect everyone to be as educated as everyone else or have the same achievements but you expect at least to be offered at least some of the opportunities and libraries are the most simple and the most open way to give people access to books." She continued, "Libraries are vital to every society in every culture. They don't discriminate. They don't care if you are rich or poor, well read or can't read a word."

LocHal Library, Tilburg, Netherlands (Mecanoo), 2016–19

This is an adaptive reuse project of a converted locomotive hall that now houses the highly popular new public library of Tilburg. The project was a collaboration that involved Civic Architects (as lead architect), Braaksma & Roos architectenbureau (restoration), and InsideOutside/Petra Blaisse (interior concept and textiles). Mecanoo's playful and innovative interior design generates striking contrasts to the industrial structure of the shed by combining characteristic historical elements with new oak and steel additions. An industrial shed like the LocHal is anadaptable building that can accommodate multiple uses within its lifecycle through retrofit.

Tainan Public Library, Tainan City (Mecanoo), 2016–20
Mecanoo teamed up with Mayu Architects for the design and delivery of the public library in Tainan.
The design references the history of the region, which comprises remnants of maritime trade with Europe
since the seventeenth century, the Chinese Ming dynasty, and of Japanese settlements from the
beginning of the twentieth century. The library is now home to documents illustrating the city's cultural
heritage, modern art, music, films and over a million books —including more than 16,000 books from
the Japanese occupation period.

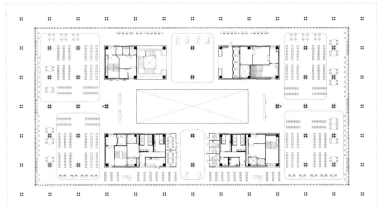

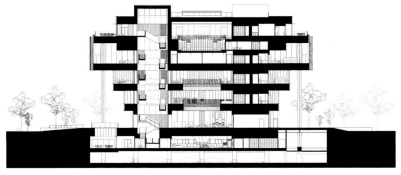

Stavros Niarchos Foundation Library renovation and expansion, New York, US (Mecanoo), 2015–21
The Stavros Niarchos Foundation Library (SNFL), built in 1914 in Manhattan and originally a department store, underwent a complete renovation by Mecanoo in collaboration with Beyer Blinder Belle. The building is now topped with a distinctive angular roof and contains a wide range of additional public amenities. Long tables recall the impressive scale of those in the former Rose Main reading room, and a new ceiling artwork in the "long room". The renovation uses traditional materials including natural stone, terrazzo and oak. SNFL's ground floor is arranged around an internal street (spine) that runs beneath a floating linear canopy of wood beams, from the Fifth Avenue entrance to the welcome desks. The heart of the library is the long room, a new space that truly brings the idea of a library into the old structure. A triple-height void has been cut out, 9 metres (30 ft) wide and rising 26 metres (85 ft) from the second storey, revealing a new abstract ceiling artwork by Hayal Pozanti.

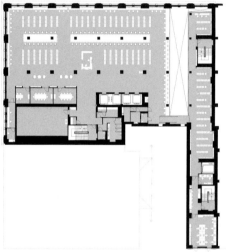

Balancing the amount of space for books vs people, the library programme was expanded and the fifth and sixth floors host now a business centre and learning centre facilities. SNFL's vertical arrangement of the programme improves the user experience and journey of learning. Elevators and stairs continue to the seventh floor, which is built at the original building's roof level. This new floor has pitched wood slat ceilings and contains a flexible 268-occupant conference and event center. Externally, an L-shaped roof terrace includes a roof garden and café; it is Manhattan's only free, publicly accessible roof terrace and offers sweeping views of the surroundings. Above, a dramatic new roof slopes up to cover the mechanical equipment, reaching eye-catching 56 metres (185 ft) above street level. Its angled pitches and a patinated copper-coloured aluminum surface are inspired by Manhattan's beaux-arts copper-clad mansard roofs.

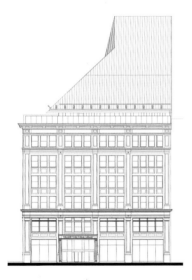

The library of the future must offer everyone, whatever their age or background, the knowledge, skills and paths they need to find their own future. A central circulating library must empower the community it serves. The Stavros Niarchos Foundation Library, for example, is a powerhouse of wisdom, and its street presence brings drama and magic to Manhattan, visibly expressed with its Wizard Hat roof.
— **Francine Houben, Mecanoo, 2021**

Perhaps no place in any community is so totally democratic as the town library. The only entrance requirement is interest.

— Claudia "Lady Bird" Johnson

Martin Luther King, Jr. Memorial Library renovation and expansion, Washington, D.C., US (Mecanoo), 2014–21

Working in collaboration with OTJ Architects, Mecanoo was responsible for renovating the Martin Luther King Jr. Memorial Library (MLKL) — a landmark building designed by Mies van der Rohe in 1970. The team transformed the main entrance and the two adjacent cores into focal points by making them more transparent and designing new spacious and daylit public stairwells. This creates a clear and welcoming entrance area, which makes the facility significantly more legible for visitors. The great hall, a centralised area designated for cultural performances and informal events, now forms the beating heart of the library. A central objective of the redesign was to highlight the library's social gathering purpose and its strong presence as a social landmark in the city, while balancing the very different legacies of Mies van der Rohe and Dr. King. The remodelled library features a new café and rooftop garden.

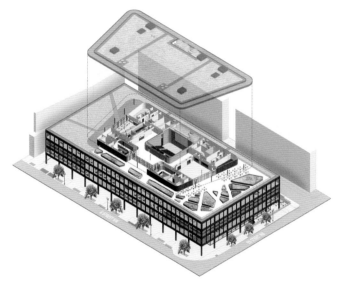

FJMT Studio

Thoughts on the Library of the Future

For a moment I want to look at one of the most structured spaces of shared data storage and shared access for over two thousand years: the public library. It is literally a giant storehouse of hardcopy data in an environment that gives us relatively easy access to this data.

It is now completely redundant. We don't need these endless shelves of books, papers and card indexes. We have it all on the cloud, in the ether, viewable through numerous personal portals like our phones. Our technology has made it obsolete, it should be long dead and gone. But the opposite is in fact true.

Ironically, the library is now the most important public building of the twenty-first century. Why isn't it dead? And why does it still have books in it? The Library itself has been transformed from a storehouse of the collection and quiet individual study into a true community meeting place. It is now made up of a diverse interlocking series of spaces for study, casual reading, interaction, collaboration, children's spaces, community spaces, café environments, lounges and outdoor terraces and gardens. It is a place where guidance and assistance is available offered without obligation, where we can meet by arrangement or informally bump into our neighbours.

It is, paradoxically, the most grounded and localised community environment that at the same time facilitates and supports our global community interconnection. And the books themselves with the tight narrow spaces between the shelves, it is important we do not overlook the multivalent nature of these spaces, they were not just about access to hardcopy data, they frame and connected us in very particular ways.

And beyond its spaces and facilities, the public library embodies the culture and the social values. More than any other contemporary building typology, the contemporary library has become a "place" within our urban environment. It has become a shared and socially inclusive place for the whole community facilitating lifelong learning and social interconnection.

— Richard Francis-Jones, FJMT Studio, 2021

Surry Hills Library and Neighbourhood Centre, Sydney, New South Wales, Australia (FJMT), 2005–09
This library for the City of Sydney is proof that libraries build capacity and resilience in communities. With its tall internal gardens, double height timber louvres, tranquil reading nooks, smart community rooms, childcare facilities and bustling street views, it has become a highly popular place. Collins Street road closure was converted into a modest public park with a raised grass platform. This new space extends the function of the building and reasserts it as a public place. The brief was developed in close consultation with the local multi-ethnic community, and the key approach emerging was that the community wanted a single facility where everyone could share and meet. The library is over two levels (ground and lower-ground levels); the community centre on level 1 comprises meeting rooms, a teaching kitchen and offices. On level 2, the childcare centre accommodates 25 children and includes an outdoor landscaped play area. Transparency became an architectural theme, creating an inviting and welcoming building. The tapered glass atrium is a response to the ambitious sustainability objectives: a series of glass prisms create an open, transparent façade, akin to a doll's house, and addresses the new open space, making all the different activities of the centre visible, encouraging participation. The resulting public building expresses a certain "monumentality", significance and dignity.

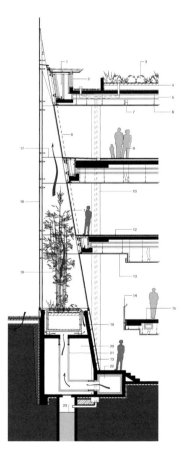

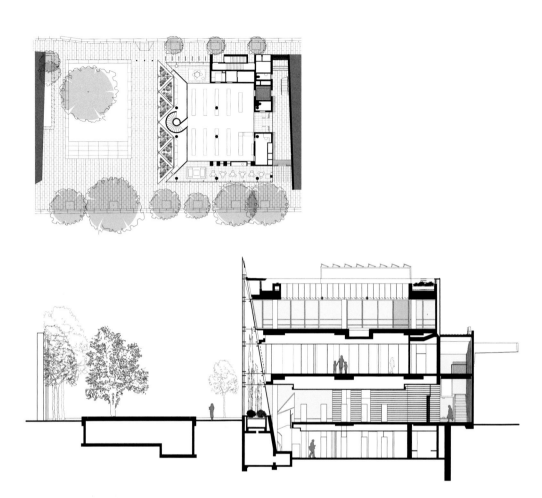

Max Webber Library, Blacktown, Sydney, New South Wales, Australia (FJMT), completed in 2006
This library seeks to express its civic function despite its location in a typically underresourced outer suburb, such as Blacktown. Tom Heneghan (2006) notes that "certainly, the meaning of the contemporary library is very different from that of its historic predecessors. At Henri Labrouste's Bibliotheque St Genevieve in Paris (1851), for example, the entrance was through a thick wall inscribed with the names of the great authors (with very little room left for post-1850 writers to be added) —a beaux-arts billboard announcing the culture that reposed within. It told exactly where we stood: outside its portals, regarding it with awe! As with most libraries, it was an entirely introverted building, focusing on itself and its distinguished contents. The Blacktown library is entirely of another ideology. If it aims to venerate anything, it is the concept of community access to knowledge. This is effectively a build-ing without walls —more akin to a pavilion open on all sides to invite in the life of the streets." On the three sides that address the surrounding streets, the library's transparent floor levels effectively give the sense of being an active part of the public life. Such welcoming transparency is possible because archived materials are housed in the upper, fully sun-shaded room, with most of the borrowable books in a windowless side wing. This allows the reading room to be fully glazed, open, casual, unobtrusively supervised and centred on a grand stairway, which serves as something of a visual lure: it directs attention through an elliptical void to the upper level, while the roof lights spill controlled daylight throughout both levels. The result is a generously scaled, thoughtfully detailed and brightly lit public living room.

Craigieburn Library, Hume City, North Melbourne, Victoria, Australia (FJMT), completed in 2012
Incorporated in 1994, Hume City is a fast-growing municipality that required a library, learning centre and gathering space. The selected site is surrounded by an expanding series of new housing projects and retail developments. The native vegetation and indigenous landscape was rapidly replaced with imported brick, concrete and tiles that characterise such new housing developments. In contrast, the library uses locally sourced rammed earth as the primary building material, establishing a green agenda and setting a new benchmark for the growing township. The building was conceived as a series of interlocking pavilions of varying height and scale that step down from the entrance, accommodating a two-storey central reading space and the lower scale of the children's library. Each pavilion extends into the landscape through a louvered roof that creates a series of northern verandahs. The primary reading room consists of a double-height volume with excellent access to natural light and reading areas positioned along the glazed northern façade. Within the shade of the verandahs, community activities such as markets and music functions occur, as well as the natural spill of activity from within the library. In addition to the core library services, the project includes an art gallery, café, childcare, computer training centre and meeting and function spaces.

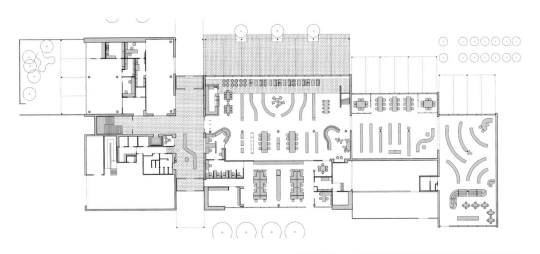

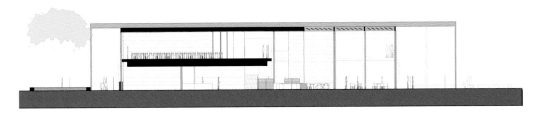

Frank Bartlett Memorial Library and Moe Service Centre, Gippsland, Victoria, Australia (FJMT), completed in 2016

Situated in a sweeping valley surrounded by mountain ranges, the small regional town of Moe was viewed as the poor cousin of its neighbours. Unemployment was high, and there has been little investment in the public realm, with residents having to travel far for services. The new library changed the place. It creates a gently curved and stepped platform of landscape and walls that follows the line of the railway, shielding the noise from the trains while opening up to the town centre to offer a new sunlit public square. Suspended above this curved podium and dramatically cantilevering over the pubic space are two timber-clad volumes oriented directly down the main street, and enforcing a civic vista. These wooden portals that frame views to the mountains, placed carefully on a landscaped platform, have created a new civic heart and identity for the town. It is truly a place for everyone to feel welcome and included, a place that brings the community together and that marks the shared aspirations of the town.

Bankstown Library and Knowledge Centre, Bankstown, New South Wales, Australia (FJMT), completed in 2014

The architects argue that, as a building type, the library is "the most meaningful twenty-first-century public building." The Bankstown Library and Knowledge Centre (BLaKC) is a public space designed to encourage intellectual, creative and social exchange. Located in the heart of Bankstown, the development revitalises a disused site and creates a rich spatial experience. Part of the design of the BLaKC is the adaptive reuse, renovation and integration of the existing Bankstown Town Hall. Salvaging high quality materials (i.e., timber, precast concrete, aluminum and stainless steel) from the existing structure enables the BLaKC to set a new benchmark for the reuse of recycled materials. Embodying sustainable design philosophies and environmental systems, it is a state-of-the-art community hub that includes a library wing over three levels, a theatre seating 300 people, IT lab and conference facilities, meeting rooms, café and public domain.

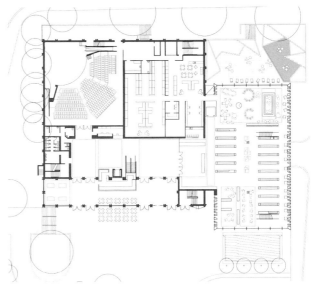

Life and Loss in the Library

From its beginning, perhaps in what is now Iraq over 2,500 year ago (Campbell, 2013), the library has evolved to become part of us and what it means to be a community with shared ambitions to know, learn and aspire to what knowledge can bring. The library building came to figure our towns and cities all over the world and over the many years of evolution and adjustment the library took on its own life.

A form, special structure and character of the library became its own, beyond the mere pragmatics of being a storehouse of documents and human knowledge, to have its own life almost independent of our fickle changes in taste and needs. Our life and that of the library took on an intimate symbiosis. We made great libraries from need and ambition which then began to shape and form our life and experience. In unique ways, they opened our minds and framed our lives joining us and connecting us in ways we never anticipated through the libraries' strength of independence and identity.

The library not only served our thirst for knowledge and longing for immortality, but also framed, in its unique way, our everyday moments of love found, love lost, introspection and discovery.

The narrow book-lined shelves framed spaces for our lonely searches, reassuring, holding us with broad arms, shelving generations of thoughts and dreams in the layers of books we will never read, but within which we feel the comfort and connection of a parents embrace. Or they will draw us in unaware and in our innocence we pull out a single book, to reveal a narrow window to another pair of like searching eyes, connecting strangers and perhaps possible future loves to be found or lost within the linear labyrinths of possibilities.

These are the unique poetic spaces of library shelves and stacks that offer us far more than mere access and convenience. These are alleys of promise and loss, within which we will always experience more than that for which we search and may never find.

Not so the grand space of the library reading room, which opens wide with grandeur and a generosity of invitation, bringing us together like a broad family of knowledge seekers longing for camaraderie. But this great gathering room paradoxically demands our silence, forcing us to reach out to each other with whispers, secret notes in plots against such demand. Here we are alone, buried in our singular purpose and focus, but also together, strengthened and supported by the company of strangers in joint purpose. There is a sense of shared intensity as we study and scribble at these great family tables, and can feel within this space both separation and connection.

The shared reading room and the rows of singular aisles of book-lined shelves are just two of the unique spaces and frames for our lives the library has given us, in many forms and variations.

In our own time, as the need for hard copy recedes and the information of the world seems available from every computer screen, we have begun to question the nature and future of the library. Yet we have seen no diminishment of purpose for the library, rather an important extension and transformation. The social equalising role has been maintained and enhanced through open access to information technology, a diversity of facilities and array of community spaces for all interests. The library has become the quintessential so-called "third space", between our home and our work.

But as these special differences, first, second and third merge through the mobility of our technology —as our homes become an extension of our workplace and the shopping centre lays claim to the third space of community —our libraries have become harder to distinguish, in both form and content, all filled with soft living room furniture, meeting rooms, computers and play areas; we can feel a certain sense of loss. In our enthusiasm to reform and extend the life of the library something essential to its nature, its unique composition, materiality, spatiality and perhaps even soul can slip through our good intentions.

The comfort, security and encouragement of being surrounded by the architecture of books and the surety of the knowledge they hold for you, even though you know you may never draw on it. The comfort of strangers framed generously within an architecture of shared purpose and camaraderie.

These uniquely reassuring spaces belong to the library alone and without them we may have a fine community living space with access to computers for all, and this is important, but it will not be a library, and will not give such deeply worn reassurances.

— **Richard Francis-Jones, FJMT Studio, 2021**

Reference
Campbell, James (2013). *The Library: A World History*, University of Chicago Press, Chicago.

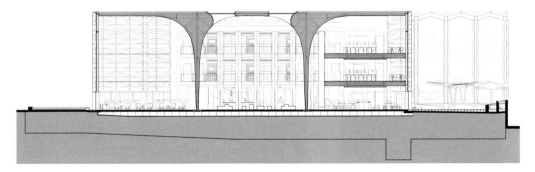

Bankstown Library and Knowledge Centre, Section

Bunjil Place Cultural Centre, Narre Warren, City of Casey, Victoria, Australia (FJMT), 2013–17
Bunjil Place is an example of a new form of community and civic building that includes a library. It is not a single-use facility that tends to divide and separate a community by interest, education or culture, but an inclusive hybrid form of public building, reflecting and embracing diversity. It combines a library with a performance theatre, public gathering space, exhibition gallerys and a flexible space for events, lectures, debate and celebration. The foyer gathering space is a non-hierarchical space that unifies the complex. A central theme was the interpretation of the land in the culture of Wurundjeri and Bunurong people, the traditional owners of this land, to conceive the project as an extended public ground plane and a broad sheltering roof. This dynamic roof provides a sheltered central civic space protected from the noise and pollution of the highway. It is an impressive glulam timber grid-shell and the grillage is a highly complex shape made of thousands of lamellas into the voluptuous structure. An extremely high level of precision was achieved by the German supplier and the whole structure was screw assembled on site in a kit of parts.

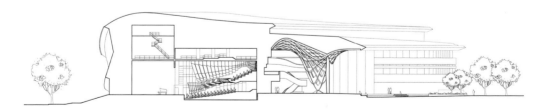

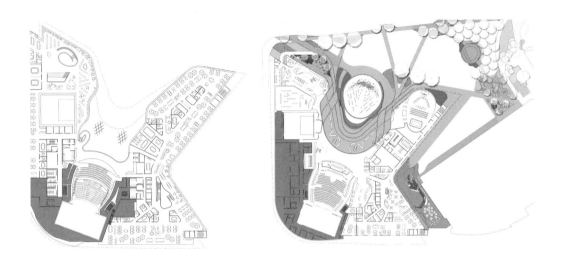

Will Bruder Architects

Libraries are like trees: place-based, rooted, long-storied. They have trunks and are resplendent with branches. They draw nourishment from their place and offer back seeds, fruit, leaves and needles that embody and nourish their place.

But, unlike trees, libraries are decidedly an invention of recorded time. They are built on the relatively recent ideas, materials, ambitions, philanthropy, and the backs of many. As repositories of deep human knowledge and experience, they have much to offer and inform our future. And, libraries are decidedly free, not mandatory. They take all comers from scholars to book lovers, to babysitters, to kids, to home schoolers, to teens, to makers, to hackers, to aspirant entrepreneurs, to ad-hoc gatherers, to those needing a stable internet connection, and/or a place to warm or chill. Inside, their spaces offer walking, wandering and serendipitous discovery at the trunk or at the branch. Libraries offer an area of temporary refuge as well as access to the world.

As to the future of libraries, one needs remember that librarians have always been architects' most challenging and rewarding clients. The stakes are high given the complexity of this very public building type, but hopefully library/architecture collaborations will continue to bear fruit well into the future. After all, architecture and libraries share a common tap root; they both strive to serve the public and to demonstrate the best creative efforts of their time and place.

— Will Bruder, 2021

Burton Barr Central Library, Phoenix, Arizona, US (Will Bruder Architects with DWL Architects), 1990–95

Phoenix Central Library is located in the city's vibrant downtown and cultural centre. It offers 28,000 sqm (280,000 sqft) of flexible floor area that will accommodate the collection's growth until 2040 and beyond (currently at one million volumes). It is a building for a desert setting. The entries to the library are accented by stainless steel plates that reflect the changing colours of the Arizona sky; the curved east and west façades are clad in weathered copper. The south elevation is 100% in glass with automated solar tracking devices that minimise heat gain and glare. Shading sails at the north side eliminate the harsh glare of the summer sun while optimising views. The building's two transparent glass ends showcase the books and the library users inside, providing views of the mountains. The building represents a source of great civic pride for the region and was an early adopter of sustainable and energy-efficiency strategies in US public architecture. At the project's start, the architects moderated a series of public engagement meetings and programming sessions with the local community, city librarian and key officials, and the team did not decide on an architectural concept until the programme and technologies were well understood. The library is organised simply as a "warehouse of knowledge" across its five levels. At the core is a 27 metre-tall (90 feet) atrium, and the fifth-level monumental reading room accommodates 320 readers below its skylight-punctured roof structure.

"Phoenix Central Library reflects the values and diligence of an engaged public, led by visionary civic leaders committed to making a mark of quality, inclusion and sustainability in the urban core of Phoenix," noted Phoenix Mayor Kate Gallego (2020).

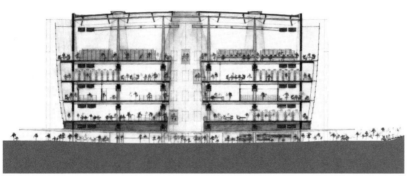

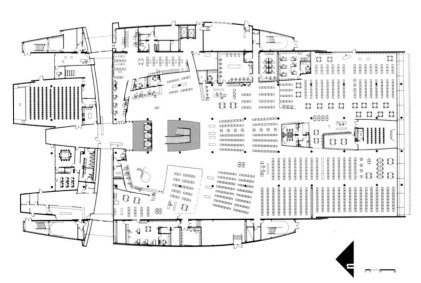

Billings Central Library, Billings, Montana, US (Will Bruder Architects), 2010–15

The form and materials of the Billings Public Library draw from local references, both natural and humanmade: the geologic uniqueness of the region's Rim Rocks, the "big sky" expansiveness of the horizon and clarity of light, the beautifully austere first settlers' homes, the modest and simple elegance of Montana pole barns, the statuesque grain elevators and the long and low storage sheds lining the region's railroads. Engaged with the urban context of downtown Billings, the two-storey public library resonates with the original and beautiful early twentieth century civic and commercial architecture that line Montana and Broadway Avenues. It makes an appropriately grand civic gesture as it rises from a foundation of golden-grey sandstone, capped with a well proportioned and finely crafted assemblage of zinc-clad wall panels, environmentally responsive glazing systems and shimmering perforated stainless steel shading panels that are calibrated to maximise views and optimise light. Day or night, the subtle transparency and glow of the grand reading room casts the library as a warm and inviting pavilion of public purpose and community pride.

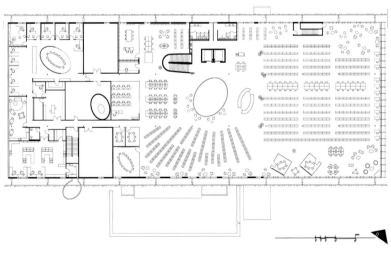

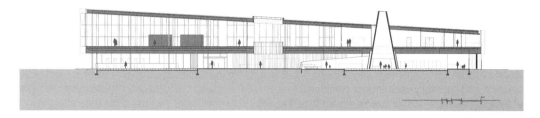

The uses of libraries, worldwide, have evolved substantially over the past 25 years. The Phoenix Central Library has proven highly adaptable to these changes and serves its purpose as well today as the day it opened. After 25 years of heavy use and necessary changes in functionality, the library still bears its architectural identity and reflects the need for libraries that can accommodate change.

— Will Bruder, 2021

Agave Branch Library, Phoenix, Arizona, US (Will Bruder Architects), 2005–09
The design of this 2,500 sqm (25,000 sqft) branch library for the City of Phoenix addresses issues of affordability in sustainable design. Impacted by a shopping centre, gas station, fast food restaurants and supermarket, the library's construction method and material pallet quietly draws from the language of its retail neighbors. Stacked bond concrete masonry units and glass enclose the simple rectangular volume of a concrete floor with sandblasted walls, exposed gang-nail trusses, glulam beams, steel pipe columns and sparingly used interior partitions. In the tradition of post offices, courthouses and city halls of fledgling western frontier towns, whose dignified, yet paper-thin street façades belie their utilitarian construction behind, the library's "false front" mediates between its two realities: one of a limited budget, the other of the civic presence expected in a public institution. The library's "cowboy front" gives scale, presence and distinction commensurate with its position in the community.

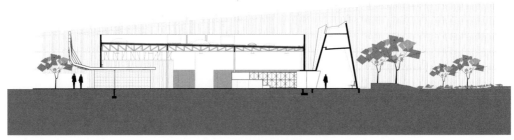

Eun Young Yi and Yi Architects

Thoughts on the Library of the Future

In the past, a church or a palace used to form the centre of a city. But in modern society, the focus is on the importance of a place for individual deepening of knowledge and enrichment of the experience. It is all the more important that a library building communicates a statement on life in the city and on the aesthetics of our age: as pure as possible, like a materialised spirit.

There have been moments in history when people initially celebrated technical innovations with great excitement. However, as soon as these innovations have spread, people rush away and quickly move on. People don't know where they want to go, but they want to achieve something as quickly as possible with this novelty. Only when the initial restless time has passed, and when one faces the story with the yardstick of the question of value, then we will recognise the real task in retrospect. Digital technologies are an exciting development, but they will not replace the classic book culture.

In the library of the future, the space requirements will become a little more individual or temporary, and certain technology-based room arrangements will still be required. However, the basic prototype of the library space will not change significantly. It first looks like poor reduction when one tries to discover the basic types and to interpret their essential conditions. But it is an asset! This reduction is one of the essential endeavors of modern architecture, in order to give it a certain perfection and generality: in terms of the purity of the spaces and in terms of the clarity of the typology.

— Eun Young Yi, 2021

Stuttgart Municipal Library, Stuttgart, Germany (Yi Architects), 1999–2011
The building takes the form of a cube with an edge length of 45 metres (150 feet). The attraction of this public library is in the inside. The cube-shaped, nine-storey "Stadtbibliothek" features an impressive atrium void in uniform pure-white, lit from the top skylight: a five-storey reading room shaped like an upside-down pyramid looks more like an M. C. Escher drawing. This gallery hall is a five-storey space, square-shaped and surrounded by a shell of books. The circulation is carefully layed out, with vistas across the central void, turning the central atrium space into a stage. There is not one grand reading room as reading is supposed to happen informally on every level. The only colour in the building comes from the books themselves. The shell of the cube is a double-layer façade with glass bricks on the outside. The symmetry of entrance of the building was inspired by the "Cenotaph for Newton" by Étienne Boullée, but the heart and core of the library follows the design of the ancient pantheon.

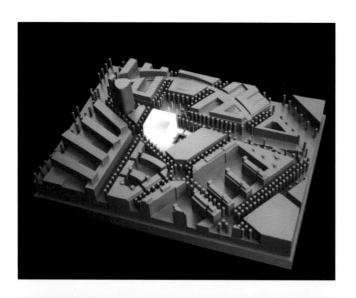

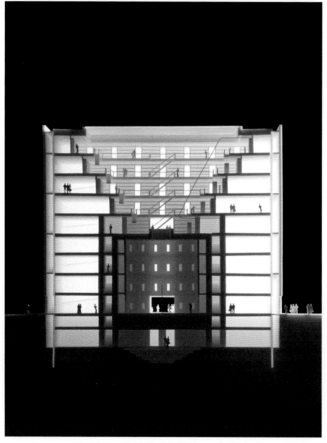

Public Library Nanjing, China (Yi Architects), unbuilt proposal, 1999
This competition scheme is for a new library in Nanjing, the third largest library in China with over 10 million items and a large collection of ancient books. The architectural idea was to create a circular "colosseum for books," with stepping terraces towards the centre, where a large glass-covered reading room is located.

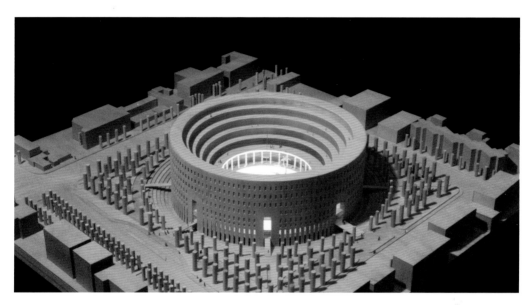

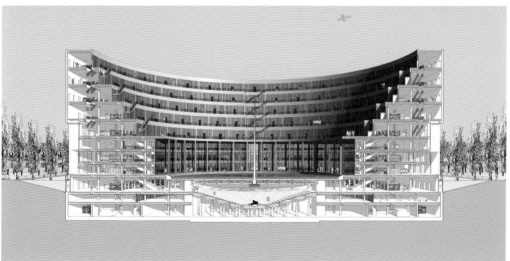

Kerry Hill Architects

City of Perth Library and History Centre, Perth, Australia (Kerry Hill Architects), 2010–16

When the library opened in 2016, it was the first major civic building to be built by Perth City Council in 35 years. Its elegant and graceful circular design with vertical louvers has seven floors and includes a 13-metre-tall (43 ft) vertical garden space with over 3,500 plants. The library also created a new public space that provides a bright, new perspective on the adjacent heritage building. Capital city libraries by their nature and location have a different user demographic from other public libraries, with a much lower residential base but high visitor base. The Library has dedicated floors targeted to different demographics. For example, a floor for very young children with appropriately designed furniture and soft surfaces, as well as a young-adult floor with study rooms and recreation areas, a History Centre for quiet study, bookable meeting rooms, hire facilities and spaces for reading, studying and relaxation.

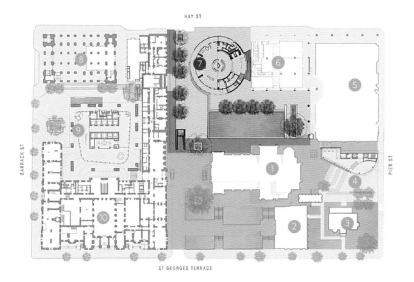

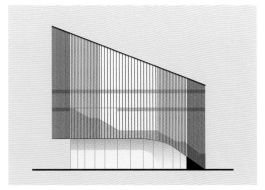

Max Dudler Architects

Thoughts on the Library of the Future

Places to Study, Flirt and Stroll
Modernity can be described as a process of creative destruction: the old loses its meaning and is replaced by the new. This also applies to the development of the city, where building types such as the ruler's palace lose their central relevance, which binds all parts of society. If you ask which buildings can represent the identity of society today and in the future through their function and their meaningful content, you will very soon come across a formerly marginal type —the library. The library as a special building of relevance within the European city also occupies a special position in the perception of the citizens as a public interior space that is equally accessible to all. Even the new media have so far hardly been able to weaken this position —perhaps on the contrary.

Precisely because reading is such a self-sufficient activity, libraries in the age of the internet have to be places of exchange and community. The library spaces not only serve the classic acts of intellectual work —reading and writing— but also conversation, encounters and strolling discovery of the flaneur. It is precisely this communicative and connecting function of libraries that will continue to gain importance in the future. In a world in which more and more areas of life are regulated via "social media", there is a need for specific places where people can actually meet face-to-face —freely, without having to consume. In the libraries designed by Max Dudler there are therefore quiet rooms for concentrated work, but also places of hospitality. There is room to dream and doze off and space for passionate sidelong gazes. The Grimm Library in Berlin, for example, created the phenomenon of the "bipster" in this way: the fashionably versed library flaneur.

The representative role that a library can play in modern society is already visible in its origins. No architectural design has captured this relationship as precisely as the design for the (first) national library by Etienne-Louis Boullée (1785), which focuses not on the book but on the person. More precisely, the architectural centre of the national library is empty. The library is actually a square cascaded around with books. This library is much more than a repository for books. This library is a forum. This is where people come together and discuss with one another. Boullée's library is therefore a public space par excellence. That is what the library has remained as an institution to this day — and will remain so in the future.

— Max Dudler, 2021

Jacob and Wilhelm Grimm Centre, Berlin (Max Dudler Architects), 2005–09

Twelve branch and departmental libraries from the liberal arts and cultural studies as well as social sciences and economics were integrated into one new central library, creating the largest contiguous open access library collection in Germany. This large library is over 37,000 sqm (370,000 sqft) in size. The debate over whether it would be better to have one central reading room or a number of smaller decentralised rooms ended with the decision to have both: all 2.5 million items in the collection are accessible from the huge, multi-leveled hall; the central reading room has stepping terraces over four levels, lit from a large skylight. This impressive main reading room reminds of the great tradition of nineteenth century libraries. The whole building is marked by a clear formal, minimal language with a reduced palette of materials and colours, all symmetrically ordered and exposing a rigid grid.

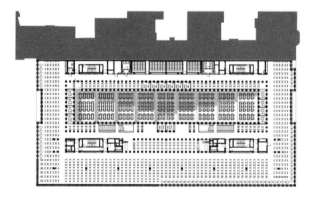

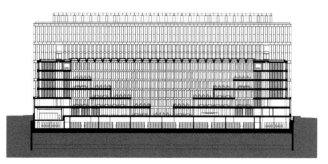

Zaha Hadid Architects

Thoughts on the Library of the Future

The library of the future has the opportunities to negotiate the contemporary heterogeneous and dynamic society of multitude. New degrees of accessibility to information and users' behaviour provide the chance to project the library beyond its physical boundaries, using the existing offering of its context and the city environment as well as remote and disconnected places with continuity. By refocusing its programme, spaces and presence, the future library will also have the opportunity to propose new interfaces between the formal and informal life of the library, amplifying the arrays of different experiences for its various users.

At the same time, the above gives the opportunity for redefining the library's typological functions and elements, and reclaiming some of the poetic symbolism that characterised the idea of library through time. The library will present itself as a statement of intellectual expression and research, such as in the in the "Future Library" project (www.futurelibrary.no) in Norway; or as a monument to the medium and the archiving of the different manifestation of knowledge, as in the Global Seed Vault project in the Arctic Circle. While both are less relevant to the immediate fruition of their content, they assume an even more relevant meaning through their presence in time.

The library of the future will act as a catalyst for programmed and spontaneous activities, becoming a public space and secret garden, borrowing museum exhibition features and archiving vault values, playing in between the hyper accessible and the private space, proposing a new scenography for knowledge sharing, archiving and universal user experience.

— Zaha Hadid Architects, 2021

Vienna University of Economics & Business Library and Learning Centre (WU-LLC), Vienna, Austria (Zaha Hadid Architects), 2008–14
At 28,000 sqm in size, the WU University Library is one of the largest economic and business libraries in the German-speaking area. It is designed to meet the specific needs of the target groups: students, faculty and academic staff. The location of the LCC is at the heart of the campus. Besides the library, the LLC comprises of a large and complex hybrid programme, including a learning centre with workplaces, lounges and cloakrooms, a language laboratory, training classrooms, administration offices, study services and central supporting services, copy shop, book shop, data center, cafeteria, event area, clubroom and auditorium. The straight lines and sharp edges of the building's exterior change as they move inward, becoming curvilinear and fluid to generate an entrance hall as free-form canyons with connecting bridges for smooth transition between the different floors. Internal circulation: from the main entrance of the LLC, visitors can walk directly to the central auditorium which also functions as a large atrium flooded by natural light. A system of ramps leads from the auditorium to the library entrance and the central services on the first floor.

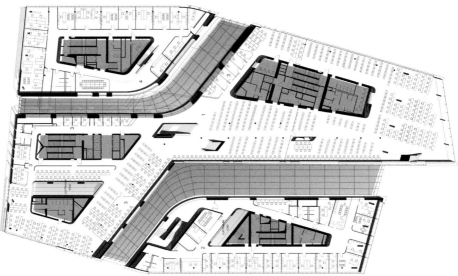

A library and learning center should be more than a mere library in the classical sense: it is a research and a service facility, a workplace and lounge, a place of communication and a traffic hub, at one and the same time. With its breathtaking architecture, the design by Zaha Hadid manages to combine all the key functions of study in a most wonderful way. It is a vision that embodies this innovative concept of a library.
— C. Badelt, **Rector of the University of Economics & Business (WU), 2008**

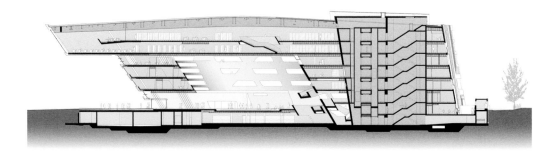

The library of the future will act as a catalyst for programmed and spontaneous activities, combining a public space with a secret garden.

— Ludovico Lombardi, Zaha Hadid Architects, 2021

Middle East Centre, University of Oxford, Oxford, UK (Zaha Hadid Architects), 2013–15
Founded in 1957, the Middle East Centre at St Antony's College serves as the University's facility for research and teaching on the Arab world, with a focus on humanities and social sciences. The research core is the specialised library, document and photographic archive covering material from the 1800s onwards. The new building provides 1,100 sqm of additional floor space and a 117-seat lecture theatre; doubling the space available and providing optimum conditions to conserve the centre's collections. The design of the expansion weaves through the restricted college site to connect to the existing protected buildings and trees; while its stainless steel façade softly reflects natural light to echo the context. The lecture theatre is located below ground and is ventilated through a thermal labyrinth. The objective for the environmental design strategy was to develop spaces that are healthy and enjoyable, where both students and staff can develop and contribute to their maximum potential.

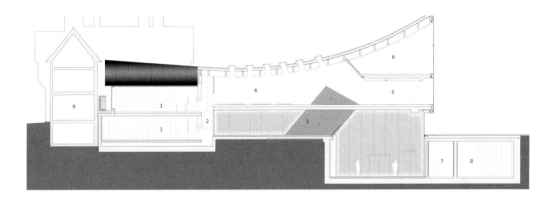

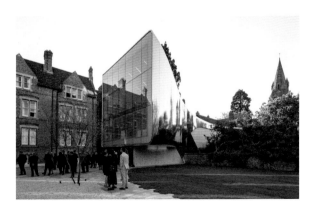

Diller Scofidio + Renfro

Thoughts on the Library of the Future: LOFt

Upon entering the Library of the Future (LOFt), you should be required to relinquish your mobile device. While such a device links to infinite amounts of information, it is also a place of derision, division and loneliness. It demands attention – attention that would otherwise be given to people, places and things. The library of the future will be a space that engineers interaction between people, and between ideas and people. The library of the future means a return to the past – it is not digital but in-real-life.

Much has been said of the library becoming the new civic center. This much seems true: libraries are archives, museums, performance spaces, conference centers, rec centers and schools all at once. Design is the silent protagonist that makes these disparate programmes work effortlessly and seamlessly together. One should not be aware of moving between activities. Rather, spaces should connect, morph, expand and contract, lighten and darken to allow a variety of activities with a variety of occupations to occur throughout LOFt. This fluidity will become both the effect and the image of the Library of the Future.

Everyone should be welcomed to LOFt. It should be accessible to all regardless of age, race, education level, gender or sexual orientation. LOFt is a safe space where the divisions found on the internet does not and cannot exist. LOFt will be a space of such diversity, dynamism and engagement that visitors will be swept up into participation. They should not be required to give their mobile devices up at the door – they will simply not feel compelled to use them.

— Charles Renfro, Diller Scofidio + Renfro, 2021

Vagelos Education Center, Columbia University, New York City, US
(Diller Scofidio + Renfro, with Gensler), 2010–16
Not strictly a library, the purpose of the Vagelos Education Center, a 14-storey tower with a total of 10,000 sqm (100,000 sqft), is a vertical campus to pursue a more holistic pedagogy in an engaging learning environment. Besides its medical and graduate student education function, the highly sustainable building offers a vertically stacked programme containing an auditorium, student commons, resources, event sky lounge, specialty labs, computer labs, classrooms office space and a simulation centre to reflect how medicine is taught, learned and practiced in the twenty-first century. The result is nothing less than a new typology for a vertical learning center with a spatially complex section including ramps, stairs and interlocking individuated spaces that favour porosity and diversified, networked pods. The building rises in rhythmic irregularity, the glazing interrupted by angled stairways, connected plateaus and open-ended boxes that pop through the glass, two of which are outdoor terraces. Could this be a vertical prototype for the next-generation library?

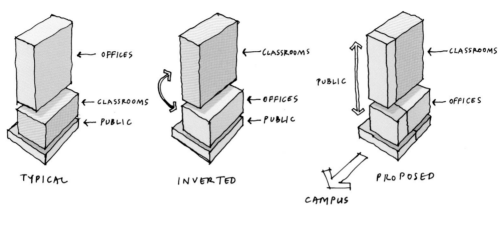

TYPICAL   INVERTED   PROPOSED

OFFICES

CLASSROOMS

PUBLIC

CLASSROOMS

OFFICES

PUBLIC

CLASSROOMS

OFFICES

PUBLIC

CAMPUS

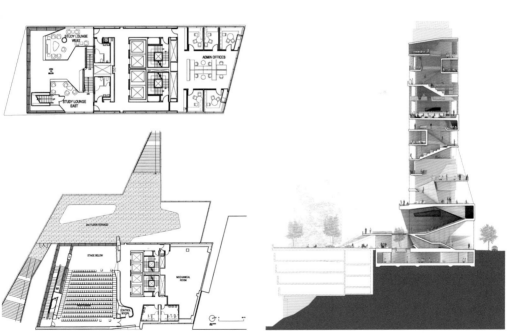

179

Steven Holl Architects

Thoughts on the Library of the Future

The library of the future should be an optimistic beacon, unlimited with an amazing balance of digital information and a love of books. It should be an environmental example of high technology, achieving ecological excellence. Today, with our supercharged clouds of information, we drink from a firehose of digital information. Our condition is comparable to Jorge Luis Borges's short story "The Library of Babel" with its books that contain every possible ordering. In Borges's library, the glut of information leaves the librarians "in a state of suicidal despair." We must balance continuous information overload with a select quality of books.

Our library of the future contains specific, quality books chosen by the staff (each library is unique). These books inspire children by their tactile and physical presence, while the whole space is digitally connected with the latest technology. In our Queens Public Library, this balance of the digital and the book is reflected in the building section.

The future library serves an important role as a community-building institution. Therefore, there should be many libraries, as there are many communities. In the community around our Queens Library, many families are immigrants and use the library for language assistance and guidance.

In our world of increasingly privatized development, the library of the future is an important social condenser —where children of the community meet other children, where seniors meet other seniors. Ongoing cultural events, such as readings, storytelling and gatherings with educational messages, provide the local community with an important place of interaction and exchange. In the recent past, churches or schoolhouses provided a public space that, like a social condenser, held the local communities together. In our digitally atomized present with multiple ethnic and religious backgrounds, the new community library provides a much-needed social institution.

The library of the future is for tomorrow, much more than its past, book-filled ancestor. It is a place where a child can find optimism for the future of our planet and the human condition.
— **Steven Holl, Steven Holl Architects, 2021**

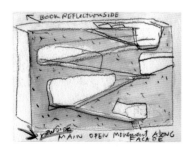  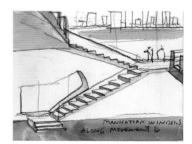

Watercolour sketches courtesy of Steven Holl, 2010

Queens Public Library, Hunters Point, Queens, New York, US (Steven Holl Architects), 2010–19

Located on a prominent site along the East River, against the backdrop of rapidly built skyscraper condominiums, the Queens Public Library at Hunters Point stands as a public building and park, bringing community-devoted space to the Long Island City waterfront. It stands independently, rising with a minimal footprint to offer maximum surrounding green space to the local community. The concrete structure comes painted in aluminum-silver, giving the small library a "subtle sparkle", says architect Steven Holl. The vertical structure reimagines the traditional library model, providing diversity of spaces from intimate reading areas to active gathering spaces. Cuts in the façade allow visitors views towards the city as they move up a series of bookshelf-flanked stairs. This compact and small branch library has a complicated section and features on 2,200 sqm (22,000 sqft) a public meeting room seating 140 people, a children's reading and activity area, an adult reading area and quiet room, a cyber centre, a teen reading area, rooftop café and roof terrace. The main Manhattan view, perpendicular to the internal movement of the library, gives the small space a dramatic experience, while the book-lined switchback stairs include small reading rooms. Natural light enters through the large windows from all sides, animating the space. The digital and the book are merged through the bookshelves and adjacent digital workstations that flow upward along a series of open stairs.

1ST LEVEL
SCALE 1/32" = 1'-0"

4TH LEVEL
SCALE 1/32" = 1'-0"

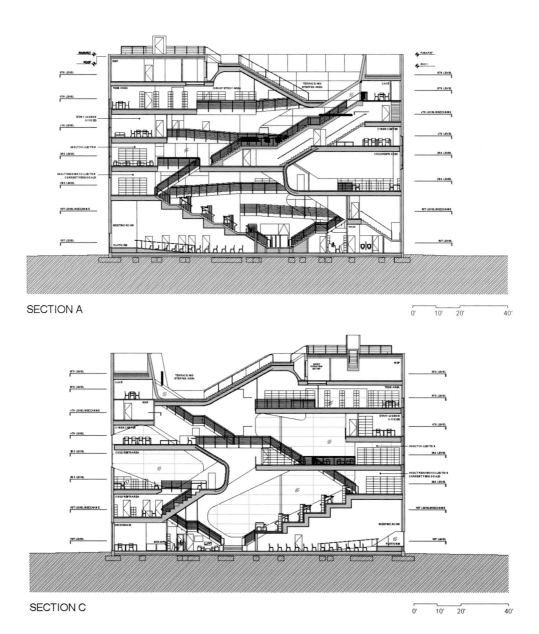

SECTION A

0'   10'   20'   40'

SECTION C

0'   10'   20'   40'

Foster + Partners

Thoughts on the Library of the Future

Long considered primarily as repositories for books and periodicals, the role of libraries in the life of contemporary communities has changed dramatically. The idea of a library of the future is inextricably linked with spaces that allow people to gather, learn and exchange ideas.

Over the past five decades, we've designed several library spaces, either as standalone buildings such as the library at the Free University of Berlin or the House of Wisdom in Sharjah; or as an integral part of the numerous educational campuses we have built. What we have found is that the most successful spaces allow for people to use the building through an extended period – a 24/7 community space that belongs to them. Alongside the libraries themselves, there should be designated spaces for talks and lectures, larger social areas, cafés for food and drink, child-friendly areas – all functions that encourage people to come together. Cultural and library aspects should be integrated to promote communication and cross-fertilisation of ideas. In our experience, overlapping uses creates a richer programme that promotes learning and fosters flexibility that will allow the building to meet future needs and changing patterns of learning. The flexible nature of a library's design is also increasingly important in terms of its potential for adaptive re-use as well as overall longevity and sustainability.

At the Free University of Berlin, we set out consciously to create a "sense of place" – a building that is both a focal point within the spreading mat-like campus and an uplifting, light-filled place in which to browse the bookshelves or to sit and read. Whereas, at the House of Wisdom, we wanted to design a flexible place of learning, encouraging people to come together and share ideas. It was important that the building and landscape were integrated. For instance, the gardens have been designed to teach people about plant species, art and sculpture, while also encouraging young children to learn through play. The building is respectful of its history, but very much looks forward to the future. Knowledge can be derived from a multitude of different avenues – online sources, lectures, exhibits, play and practical experimentation, explorations with nature, and books, and the building's design consolidates all of these opportunities into one flexible building with collaboration and openness at its heart.

— **Gerard Evenden, Head of Studio, Foster + Partners, 2021**

The House of Wisdom, Sharjah, UAE (Foster + Partners), 2018–21

Sharjah House of Wisdom conceptualises the library as a social hub for learning, supported by innovation and technology. The building creates a new publishing and research-based institution that seeks to be the catalyst for a new cultural quarter in the city.

Located adjacent to the airport, ten kilometres from the city centre, the two-storey building embodies a sense of clarity and lightness, with a large floating roof cantilevering on all sides of a transparent rectilinear volume. The 15-metre-wide overhang – resulting from the cantilever – shades the façades through most of the day, while fixed aluminium screens allow the building to filter the low sun in the evenings. Throughout House of Wisdom, there is an emphasis on establishing and retaining a connection with the outside, looking onto the gardens surrounding the building.

Dominique Coulon & Associates

Media Library, Thionville, France (Dominique Coulon & Associés), completed in 2016
This project has the ambition of becoming a new model for media libraries. The programme calls the functions of a media library into question, lending it the content of a "third place" –a place where members of the public become actors in their own condition. The 4,600 sqm building includes areas for displays, creation, music studios and a café. The various activities blend into each other, creating a dynamic arrangement. The building comes up close to the crown of plane trees –this proximity acts as a filter from the street, playing with this first colonnade of plant-life. The hollow and solid sections produce an ambiguity between inside and outside, questioning the borders of public space. Space becomes uncertain: it ceases to have clear outlines. Light spreads out along the ribbon, which distributes daylight right in the heart of the building. A garden ramp offers an escape route to the outside, leading upwards to a summer bar and the architectural promenade: the roof garden. The cocoon-like spaces contain very specific elements of the programme, such as a storytelling area and places for video games.

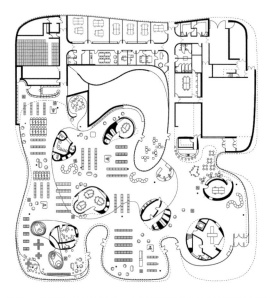

Antoine Predock

Thoughts on the Library of the Future

Bibliotheca Publica del Estado de Jalisco, Guadalajara, Mexico (Antoine Predock),
unbuilt proposal, 2015

We see our proposal for the new Bibliotheca Publica del Estado de Jalisco as an example of a library of the future. Within the shadows of La Barranca de Oblates, the new Public Library emerges from a limestone plaza, Ixtli Caliza, lined with Zapote trees. It is like a safe box "caja de tesoros" for books and media sheathed in a copper jacket of light. The library envelopes an abstract glass and media mesh Maguey (frozen fire) from the past, again awakened. This arbol de maravillas, "tree of wonders, as it is known to the Otoni people", is a source of agua miel (sweet water) and symbol of the culture, landscape and people of Mexico. For the Nahuatl people, the maguey was a divine creation representing the goddess Mayahuel. Like Juan Diego's manta enclosing divine roses, or silent walls sheltering a verdant private garden, the copper box environmentally and spiritually protects the library, selectively revealing layers of life, culture and activity within. A collector of cultures, mixing pueblo and university, casual user and academic, La Biblioteca and its plaza fill with fiesta, quinceneras and tiangis, children and jubilados, business people and tourists. Displacements of programme elements located below the theatre, auditorium and classrooms surface on the Plaza, creating a topography for shaded casual gatherings.

Viscous obsidian ramps like obsidian deposits found at Cerro Collí spiral up through the Pina, inviting visitors through the gallery and the orientation theatre up to the Biblioteca collections. From the central open core of the digital media mesh maguey, the pencas reach towards the sky, the sun, views of city and land beyond. The pencas are a deep timeline reflection of Mexican exuberance, fiesta and pachanga from Aztec cosmology to the future, from mestizaje to indigena, charting a kaleidoscope of time. Each penca, "a magical, fluid realm of memory and pueblo as in the writings of authors such as Juan Rulfo and Elena Garro", emanates from the Pina to carve through la Biblioteca. A repository of Borgesian/García Márquez/Isabel Allende - like memory and conveyor of the intellectual and spiritual flow of La Biblioteca, the pencas reach from the Cenote to the roof-top Cyber Garden, as sinuous conductors of diffuse light, illuminating and organising the collections, disseminating embedded digital technology and information, and orienting users. Pencas that escape through the roof-top garden project beams of light into the night, becoming a beacon for Jalisco. Other Pencas imprint the exterior walls of the Biblioteca, deflecting the copper skin.

Counterpoint to the exuberant glass maguey, rows of regular, precisely ordered stacks are a datum of clear organization, facilitating staff movement and overview while encouraging immersion in study or social interaction. Although the book as object is finite, a Borgesian infinity of digital/image intensity emerges through the media mesh cloaked Pencas. Through journey, procession and pilgrimage, the visitor engages the library towards individual ends, seeking that which inspires and illuminates. La Biblioteca visually culminates in the loud cry like the yellow flower of the maguey at the time of his death. A serenade to the moon. The library quintessentially celebrates place, while it simultaneously uplinks to a globalised realm.

— Antoine Predock, 2021

187

Alberto Kalach & Taller de Arquitectura X

Biblioteca Vasconcelos Public Library, Mexico City, Mexico (Alberto Kalach & TAX), completed in 2006
The library –like a giant machine– combines five different collections to one mega-library: a 250 metre-long (820 feet) super-structure with suspended, hanging bookshelves that look as if they are hovering in midair. The library sits in the middle of a lush botanical garden containing flora native to Mexico. A central linear space connects all areas of this giant 40,000 sqm (400,000 sqft) library. It is named after José Vasconcelos, who was a philosopher, politician and important cultural figure in Mexico for actively promoting literacy.

It was Jonah who, by surviving for seven days inside the whale, built in his mind a space where he could house such a creature. But the mind is always bigger inside than outside, and the space grew until it became a great vault; which Jonah was filling with his thoughts. He had thoughts of all kinds and he was organizing them according to different categories, he created a number system to catalog them and he assigned a color to each one to be able to recognize it.
— Pedro Rosenblueth, 2015

Biblioteca Publica del Estado de Jalisco, Guadalajara, Mexico (Alberto Kalach), unbuilt proposal, 2015
The visionary design of a library for the future consists of a base that supports the large unitary space, whose arrangement allows a clear and logical order of its contents. It aims to be covered in a single stroke, proposing a unique poetic spatial experience. The different levels are naturally adapted to the different sections of which it consists, offering multiple spaces, compact and easily accessible.

MVRDV

Thoughts on the Library of the Future

What happens when the internet makes the original purpose of libraries –as a central reference for information– obsolete? In 2000, MVRDV developed the Brabant Library proposal, which imagined how libraries might compete with the (then emergent) internet: a huge, comprehensive, centralised library collection serving an entire province, paired with a robust distribution system to stimulate demand with small, refined collections at places such as cafés, transit hubs and gas stations. Echoes of this proposal were heard earlier in this year: a local Brabant library, which had to close its main building, was making its collection available in partnership with a gas station.

The trends that informed the Brabant Library proposal have only intensified in the past two decades. Yet physical libraries not only still exist, they are still popular. No, they are more than popular – they are Instagrammable. In 2017, our Tianjin Binhai Library opened and was an immediate viral social media hit. The heart of the building is its expansive atrium of cascading bookcases, which form a kind of landscape of stairs and seating that curves upwards to merge with the ceiling. Passages puncture through the shelves at various levels to provide access to the rest of the library beyond, and at the centre of the atrium a large sphere houses an auditorium.

This cavernous space helps the building to go beyond the traditional role of a library –functioning as a social space, a destination in its own right, a route connecting the adjacent park and cultural district and, yes, a subject of people's social media posts. The fact that (due to a design change made despite our advice to the contrary) the upper shelves do not really hold books, but rather an image of books printed on aluminium plates is, for many visitors, unimportant. The popularity of Tianjin Library as a social media spectacle and as an entertainment destination is as much a result of symbolism and a certain aesthetic sensibility as it is a response to the library's collection of actual books.

What does it mean that physical libraries –and especially the aesthetic sensation of being surrounded by books –are romanticised in this way? What if we leverage this romantic impulse by treating the library of the future as a backdrop, or the glue that binds our everyday experiences? Shenzhen Terraces, a mixed-use project currently under construction, demonstrates a novel approach to this ideal: here, the library fills the interstitial spaces between the building's many other programmes, spread across multiple levels of two buildings. Therefore, people will interact with the library as they go about their day, and perhaps spot books they didn't know they wanted to read.

We believe that the future of libraries is an intensification of all of these designs. To adapt to our current world, libraries will need to become almost as ubiquitous as the internet itself: our libraries will become hang-out destinations, and our hang-out spots will become libraries.

— Winy Maas, MVRDV, 2021

Tianjin Binhai New Area Library, Tianjin, China (MVRDV, Winy Maas; with Tianjin Urban Planning and Design Institute), 2014–17

It is one of the most spectacular and radical library interiors of the last twenty years. The library is often a visual landmark and focal point for the surrounding area and cultural district. In this case, the external building shape is a simple box, while MVRDV was able to create an entire new library experience on the inside of Tianjin Binhai Library: a rippling wave of cascading bookcases stretches from the floor to the ceiling. These bookcases orbit the luminous "Eye", an enclosed sphere that contains an auditorium space. The library offers over 33,000 sqm (330,000 sqft) of floor area on five floors; the first two consist primarily of reading rooms, book storage and lounge areas. The upper floors offer meeting rooms, offices, computer and audio rooms and two rooftop spaces. This "instagrammable" space has been very well received and published globally.

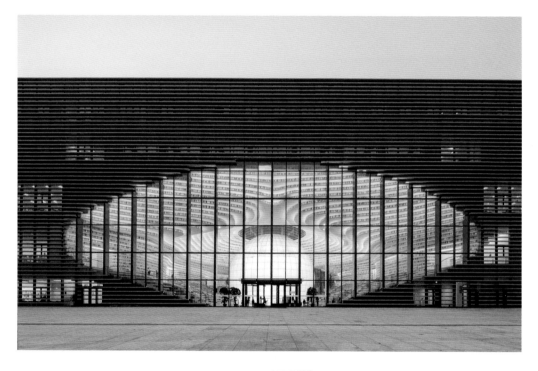

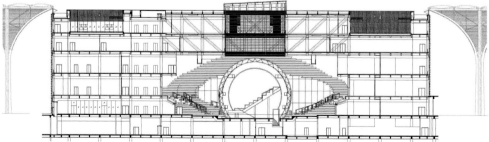

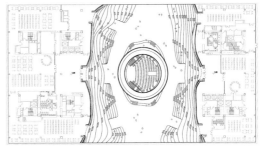

Tianjin Binhai New Area Library, Tianjin, China (MVRDV, Winy Maas), 2014–17
Terraced bookshelves that echo the form of the sphere create the interior, topographical landscape whose contours reach out and wrap around the façade. The five level building also contains extensive educational facilities accessible through the main atrium space. Public programme is supported by subterranean service spaces, book storage and a large archive. From the ground floor, visitors can access reading areas for children and the elderly, the auditorium, the main entrance, the floors above and connection to the cultural complex. It touches on the fundamental question how well-suited such a monumental space is to the function of a library, as it combines entrance hall and reading room. Architecture critic Oliver Wainwright (2021) thought that "it's a cultural building and a fairground attraction with a spectacular space for the age of Instagram; books may be present but mainly serve as background to the staircases".

195

Reimaging the Library of the Future

PART III. The Future

Reimaging the Library of the Future

PART III. The Future

Looking Ahead: Collecting and Sorting Ideas for Tomorrow's Sustainable Libraries

Not One-Size-Fits-All

The starting point of this study was to promote excellence in library design and to examine the various concepts for the next-generation library, thereby raising quality of life through better access to knowledge for everyone and the improvement of environmental, social and cultural sustainability. Of particular interest are the personal statements from leading library architects and thinkers on key issues important to the formulation of tomorrow's library, offering perspectives on how this typology might evolve.

Given the major climate, social and economic challenges, as well as the environmental degradation and social inequalities, the library of the future is also about resistance: resisting the commercialisation of public institutions and identifying new ways of doing things. At the core of it is also a resistance to the constant commodification and commercialisation of public space.

In the "Foreword" of the book, Kelvin Watson speculated that, over the next decade, the library will continue to expand its role as a free educational resource for lifelong-learning of all residents, with initiatives targeting non-traditional library users, operating as the "great equaliser of society". This means that the library of the future is not just an aesthetic statement, but also a political and planning statement on the dilemma of our public institutions and spaces.

The 40 selected cases presented on the previous pages cover a wide range in terms of size, function and location — and certainly no single example could be said to be a definitive model. However, the cases identify recent trends that manifest all that is best in contemporary library design. While each library has its own challenges and ambition, the architect's task is to prepare the facilities for unpredictable future change. Here, the presented projects give us the confidence and optimism that library design will continue to positively develop and deliver more than just a building; it gives us the hope that the library of the future will enhance the public space network (not just consume ground) and create new types of urban space.

Back to Basics, Expanding the Offerings, or Reducing the Size of the Open Collection?

When creating a new library, some basic decisions will need to be made early on. Besides the diversity of urban space, the selected cases show that the design of the next-generation library demands strong ideas for significant interior spaces. Some librarians are now asking for a return to the original purpose of the library, which is to support all the needs of the scholar and provide an inspiring place for concentration and reflection, with spaces to sit and chat, as well as an exhibition gallery space and, finally, a place where those scholars can meet, come up with ideas and make breakthroughs that would otherwise not happen. A good library provides both types of spaces: quiet spaces for concentration as well as spaces to gather, meet and discuss ideas.

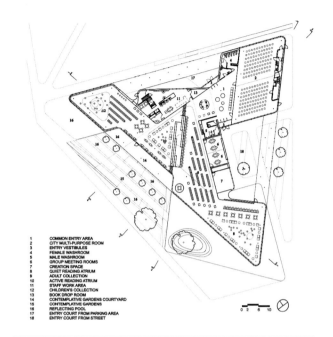

1 COMMON ENTRY AREA
2 CITY MULTI-PURPOSE ROOM
3 ENTRY VESTIBULES
4 FEMALE WASHROOM
5 MALE WASHROOM
6 GROUP MEETING ROOMS
7 CREATION SPACE
8 QUIET READING ATRIUM
9 ADULT COLLECTION
10 ACTIVE READING ATRIUM
11 STAFF WORK AREA
12 CHILDREN'S COLLECTION
13 BOOK DROP ROOM
14 CONTEMPLATIVE GARDENS COURTYARD
15 CONTEMPLATIVE GARDENS
16 REFLECTING POOL
17 ENTRY COURT FROM PARKING AREA
18 ENTRY COURT FROM STREET

Springdale Public Library in Brampton, Ontario, Canada (by RDH Architects), completed in 2019, is an interesting case for the integration into a public green space. It is located in a small public park and features an unusual triangular plan. The architects positioned the library (2,000 sqm; 20,000 sqft in size) as close to the street as possible, in order to solidify the building's presence with the street, preserve the site's natural topography and irrigation patterns, and channel interior views towards a ravine. This is also a good strategy for the library of the future, which forms a reciprocal relationship with its local context, while offering active frontages on all sides at ground-floor level. The library is a joyful place that evolves over time, purposefully designed, and it strengthens its neighbourhood. The library of the future encourages integration of nature and natural elements both inside and outside of the building. The small library at Springdale is as much about a building as it is about establishing a landscape: from the organically shaped perimeter that joins building and courtyards; and the creation of an undulating topography between the fluidly shaped ceiling and mountainous green roof; and the sloping floor slab of the interior and the at landscape of the park.

In 2011, the American Education Advisory Board released a thoughtful assessment of the future of libraries and their deep transformation, noting that "in an era when millions of books, articles, images and videos are available instantaneously via the web, libraries across all institutional types are experiencing declining demand for their traditional services, built around the storage and dissemination of physical resources". At the same time, new demand for digital information services and collaborative learning spaces promises new areas of opportunity and engagement with users, as Keith Webster argues in the Epilogue. Libraries everywhere aim to reduce the size of collections on open shelves, although many library users still value the ability to browse large-scale collections on open stacks. However, too much space is usually tied up in low-demand activities, which could better be used for collaborative learning activities.

Designing new experiences will challenge the common predictability of library use and open up new possibilities for public life. Unpredictable and unusual functions could be combined and added to the programme of the library. Introducing new amenities or cultural activities to the standard format of the programme can range from maker spaces and roof gardens, to digital training facilities and so on. The library designers reimagine the programmatic boundaries by offering new user experiences as a counterpoint to the predictability of reading books. Commonly, around 60-70% of library programmes consist of publicly accessible spaces and areas for book storage, and many libraries are now focusing on high-quality exhibition programmes for their gallery spaces. The small exhibition room at the Bodleian Library in Oxford, for example, attracts over 250,000 visitors per year, putting it ahead of many museums. Community libraries are also adding job training spaces and classrooms to their programme to remain relevant; with additional community functions, the library will continue to be an engine for research, as well as a community destination and a place for public engagement.

The Revival of the Grand Reading Room

It seems that the design of libraries can go in different directions: some libraries are moving (back) towards a model that encourages readers to stay and linger, reflecting the trend of facilitating reading as well as other functions. While an increasing number of new libraries are now using compact automated shelves that operate as a closed stack system, one can also find the revival of the traditional reading room with openly accessible stacks, frequently combined with halls and meeting rooms that promote social exchange between the users, much like a community centre or hub for social life among the local community.

One established approach that became popular in the early twentieth century was to locate the majority of the book collection on a lower level to provide an open free-flowing plan for the main floor above. This approach was frequently used for large urban libraries in the US. However, the consequence was that the reader became disconnected from most of the books. To avoid such a separation, two different approaches have emerged: either to locate the book stack in the centre of the building, surrounding it with reading rooms around the perimetre that benefit from daylight; or to disperse the collection, placing smaller parts of the collection in closer proximity to the reading areas in an open plan layout. Van Slyck (1995) noted that "as the reading space and book storage space became more integrated on each floor, the rectangular footprint of these buildings tended to grow, as did the library's dependence on air-conditioning, fluorescent lighting and flat suspended ceilings. Although the doctrine of flexible planning offered exciting possibilities in library service, the architectural spaces that it created often were monotonous".

Although space could be saved by using compact shelving in storage areas, closed stacks or automated storage systems, most of the librarians still favour open access with reading spaces located directly adjacent to, or even interspersed with, the stack areas. Many recent designs remind of the great reading rooms of the nineteenth century: a revival of the grand reading room surrounded by walls of books (e.g., Mecanoo's library in Delft). Latimer (2011) also noted this "trend back in favour of users and their spaces rather than the domination of the collection space," arguing that the library today is all about making close connections between different groups of library users and resources. Close immediate access to book stacks (to minimise "book miles") and the opportunity to freely wander around between walls of books have enjoyed a revival.

In our accelerated information-centred age, civic, cultural and educational projects are playing a new societal role, and library architecture is measuring up to this new challenge. But in the midst of all this acceleration, the slow act of reading —for the sake of knowledge, enjoyment or to explore the world of the human imagination —is still one of those experiences that gives a sense of emotional and spiritual fulfilment. Richard Francis-Jones (2021) supported this counter argument in his short essay (page 150): he contended that these times of unprecedented change in libraries urge us not to dismiss the spaces that we have valued over centuries.

Creating a space that surrounds the visitor with books on old-fashioned book shelves is undoubtedly linked to an enriched sense of public values, and this is enforced by a short distance between reading rooms and bookshelves. However, during the last six decades the ever growing extent of the collections necessitated larger interconnected storage areas in order to efficiently store the books.

A Central Reading Room or a "Free-Space" Indoor Landscape? Bringing Readers and Books Closer Together

Given the often disappointing, uninviting outcomes of new libraries in the post-war era, in the 1980s architects started to experiment with different spatial arrangements. Manuela Roth (2014) compared two recent and very different solutions that do just this: at one end is Max Dudler's monolithic Jacob and Wilhelm Grimm Zentrum in Berlin (completed in 2009), which is organised in "reader terraces"; at the heart of the library is an impressive large reading room that stretches across four floors in tiers like stepping terraces, receiving natural light from skylights above. All shelves, work places and seating areas follow the building's minimal rectangular grid layout, and this impressive space forms the "heart" of the library. At the other end is a completely different solution: SANAA's Rolex Learning Center in Lausanne (completed in the same year), a "free space" that allows visitors to wander about freely through open fluid spaces that are not separated by any partitions (similar to Toyo Ito's Sendai Mediatheque). There are no prescribed paths and along the way one can encounter a landscape of hills and valleys with integrated seating possibilities, shelves, a café and small glass cubicles to which one can withdraw for concentrated group work. There is no central single reading room because reading happens formally and informally everywhere, dispersed throughout the building. These are two contrasting types of buildings —both aiming to bring readers and books closer together again —which could not be more different!

Throughout history there have been reading rooms that offer a large, single and tranquil space with carefully placed columns, to create a feeling of openness reminiscent of the outdoors, like being in a grove or forest. One of the most well-known example of such a space is the main reading room at the Bibliotheque Nationale in Paris, designed by Henri Labrouste in 1850. For its columns and arches, the architect used the most advanced iron construction technology of the nineteenth century.

True to their slogan, "we create happy and adventurous places", one of the most eye-catching contemporary examples is the spectacular Tianjin Binhai Library (2014–17) designed by Rotterdam-based architects MVRDV. Questioning its entertaining design, Elizabeth Farrelly (2021) wrote in the Sydney Morning Herald: "This library entertains the masses with scores of undulating bookshelves that snake in around its amorphous interior, which centres on a giant white golf-ball of an auditorium. But many of the shelves are inaccessible and fake; the 'fun' amorphous interior resonates with the sound of crowds at a funfair and anyone wishing actually to read or study is consigned to the dully utilitarian spaces around the edge. No sense of sacred learning here; in fact, almost the opposite. This is a building that elevates easy popularity over scholarship." And she goes on, "we need to lose the threadbare assumption that everything must be popular, dumbed down and profitable. Some things are beyond price."

I think the main dilemma at Tianjin Binhai Library is the lack of a quiet grand reading room; everything happens in the central entrance hall. As we have seen, numerous recent cases presented in this study strengthen again the key role of the grand reading room. It is a renewed focus on the reading room as the central main space that provides visitors with soft, diffuse lighting (often daylight from the top) and a pleasant, comfortable experience to sit and read. Visitors may stroll through the stacks and browse the titles on display, and the access from shelves to the reading room is never far. To avoid long circulation paths, a close relationship between the open-shelf area and the reading room is still importtnat. In Alvaro Siza's libraries, for example, the readers and the books always share the same spaces; according to the man himself, this is a lesson he learned from visiting the libraries of Alvar Aalto. Such a central reading room allows people to experience the joy of reading while surrounded by a treasure trove of books, which can have a powerful physical presence —something that the convenience of electronic and digital books cannot offer. The reading room represents a continuous relationship that brings humans and books together even as it changes and evolves, transcending time and history.

Developing a Detailed Programme Through User Engagement
Broad engagement with the librarians and trustees is essential before any basic design concept can be decided. Paul Goldberger (2004) noted, in regard to Seattle Central Library, that the architects, before commencing with any design, started out by first investigating how libraries actually work and how they are likely to change. "They went with Seattle's chief librarian and several trustees and staff members to look at libraries around the country, and then they held a series of seminars about the future of the book with scholars and representatives

of Microsoft, Amazon, Media Lab and other organisations. They concluded that people are not ready to give up on books and that they are not ready to give up on libraries, but that they find most libraries stuffy, confusing and uninviting. Patrons wanted a more user-friendly institution, and librarians wanted one that was more flexible, and would not require constant rearrangement as collections expanded" (Goldberger, 2004). It became quickly clear to the team that older libraries, where books are stored on endless rows of shelves on separate floors and collections are arbitrarily broken apart, were not particularly attractive or user-friendly. It was at this point that OMA came up with the solution of the "Book Spiral", where the shelves continuously wound up and up in a spiral, allowing for an uninterrupted presentation. The stacks were designed in the manner of a parking garage, with slanted floors joined in a series of zigzagging ramps —a new library typology was created.

New Community-based Programmes, the Case of Finland

Concerning libraries, Finland is a particularly interesting case: it has the highest number of registered book borrowers per capita in the world, and the Finnish people are probably the world's most enthusiastic users of libraries: the population of 5.5 million people borrow close to 68 million books a year –just over 12 items per person. Finland was ranked the world's most literate nation in a 2016 study. Public libraries play a central role in Finland's civic life, and access to public library services is a statutory right for all citizens. The Finnish enthusiasm for libraries goes back a long time: Finland's first Library Act was passed in 1928. In the early twentieth century, the leaders of the newly independent country embraced the public library as an investment in human capital and as a means to promote education and economic development in a region without a wealth of natural resources or an established industrial base. Today, Finland is an advanced economy, and access to public library services remains a statutory right, protected by law. Early on, public libraries in Finland began to explore new community-based programmes and a broad range of services in addition to the core activity of lending books. It is not uncommon for libraries to provide amenities ranging from music rehearsal and recording facilities, to community space and child care facilities.

Oodi Central Library, Helsinki's newest public library (completed in 2019), is part of a new era of libraries in Finland that respond to the country's 2017 update of its Library Act, which established a mandate for libraries to promote lifelong learning, access to culture, active citizenship, democracy and freedom of expression. Oodi's Maker Space, equipped with technologies such as 3D-printers and laser cutters, extends the tradition of lifelong learning by giving citizens the opportunity to access and experiment with new technologies that are likely to shape design and manufacturing in the digital economy of the twenty-first century. Oodi is not exactly a normal library. Given its breadth of services, different civic purposes and expansive technological offerings, one might be forgiven for wondering whether it should be considered a library at all. Thomas Rogers (2018) commented with some amusement in the *New York Times* that "Helsinki's new library has 3-D printers and power tools (and some books, too)". Obviously, new libraries are an ambitious attempt by one of the most literate and digitally savvy nations in the world to build social infrastructure. Nordic and Scandinavian countries place a high premium on social integration and education, emerging as leaders in library design. With their generous funded programmes, the Finnish government spends more than one and a half times as much per capita on libraries as the United States.

The main entrance to Helsinki Central Library Oodi, completed in 2018 (designed by ALA Architects) faces the steps of the Finnish parliament building on the other side of the road.

The Joe and Rika Mansueto Library at the University of Chicago, designed by Helmut Jahn and completed in 2011, reflects the institutions guiding ideals —the designer argues. It features a day-lit 180-seating grand reading room underneath a glass dome and an underground high-density automated storage and retrieval system (ASRS) for 3.5 million books. However, part of the joy of a library is wandering the stacks and occasionally finding books accidentally (which is impossible in this automated system).

With Oodi Central Library in Helsinki, we took into account the fact that libraries will always be changing. Already, their use is different now from what it was 10 years ago.

— Samuli Woolston, ALA Architects, 2019

Community Library, SESC Pompéia Cultural Centre, São Paulo, Brazil (Lina Bo Bardi), 1977–86
When Lina Bo Bardi visited the derelict metal barrel factory in São Paulo's working class district of Pompéia with plans to build a new sports and cultural center, the space had already been occupied spontaneously by neighbours who spent the weekends amidst the empty warehouses of the industrial complex. For Bo Bardi, this meant that the priority was to maintain and support this vital informal activity, without demolishing the existing factory concrete structures. Still today, the SESC Pompéia represents social openness and stands for bottom-up artistic independence and a lively neighbourhood, offering free use of the community library, exhibitions, a space for the community, theatre and sports activities. The main space has the flexibility to completely change in atmosphere and quality depending on the time of day, usage or occupation.

University Library Biblioteca Disposit de les Aigues for UPF, Barcelona, Spain
(Clotet, Paricio & Associates), 1992–99
Having first suffered as the digital trends took over in the early 1990s, academic libraries have now returned as a trendy and popular destinations for study and reading spaces. Unsurprisingly, many of the most creative libraries can be found on university campuses, as they continue to form new spaces for study, shaped by multiple-discipline users, and plenty of options for self-study or group work. This academic library reuses a nineteenth century water reservoir. The main reading room of the 65-metre-long vaulted brick structure built in 1874 is 12 metres (40 feet) high. The new library offers quiet isolated spaces to study. In order to bring natural light into the central part of the dramatic space, the architects introduced a linear skylight.

**Municipal Library and Historical Archive – Biblioteca del Mediterraneo, Alghero, Sardinia, Italy
(Giovanni Maciocco and Department of Architecture of the University of Sassari), 2010–15**
The Biblioteca del Mediterraneo is located in the adaptive reuse of the former church of Santa Chiara
that, since 1647, has housed the cloistered convent of the Isabelline nuns. In 1868, the whole estate
became property of the municipality of Alghero who turned it into a civic hospital, serving this function
up until 1970. After more than thirty years of abandonment, the entire complex was restored and the
run down area transformed into an exceptional centre of culture, including the Department of Architecture,
Design and Urban Planning of the University of Sassari. The small library hosts 50,000 volumes; staircases
are running on both sides of the three-storey vaulted main hall, and the walls are covered with books.

The ecologically sustainable library integrates greenery in all its forms.
The library of the future will be greener than ever. The next generation library will be a super-green building with green entry courtyards, roof gardens and green walls to reduce the urban heat island effect and to create a calming ambience. It integrates vegetation and greenery to form new relationships between the urban and natural worlds.

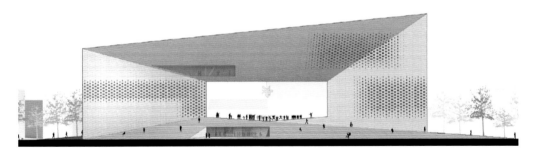

Mediatheque MECA, Bordeaux, France (BIG Architects), 2013–19
The main feature of the 18,000 sqm Maison de l'Économie Créative et de la Culture en Aquitaine (MECA) is its new public space, an urban terrace overlooking Bordeaux's river and revitalised waterfront. MECA creates a frame for the celebration of contemporary art, film and performances. The building was conceived as a single loop of three cultural institutions and a new public space by extruding the pavement of the promenade to become the ramp that leads into the 1,100 sqm "outdoor living room"; this space forms a large gate (window) between the city and the river that can be transformed into a stage for concerts and theatrical performances. Bjarke Ingels said: "At MECA, it's hard to say where the public space stops and the cultural institution begins, because both are intrinsically linked together." (2014) MECA is blurring typological boundaries and an example for an always evolving typology: while it is not really a "library" per se, it is a genre-bending hybrid that combines a Cinematheque with the performing and visual arts. However, it also creates an impressive indoor/outdoor public space and a community destination (features that will also shape the library of the future).

The Three Main Trends We can Identify in Recent Library Design
More recently, three main trends in library design (and combinations of these trends) can be identified:

- The adaptive reuse of an existing structure as a library;
- The library as a highly sustainable building that integrates nature and greenery;
- The library as a programmatic hybrid and community destination.

Let us examine these three main trends further.

Libraries as Adaptive Reuse Projects: Refurbishment and Building Adaptation
The examples on the previous pages (pages 205–207) show three libraries that are adaptive reuse projects in existing structures. Buildings often last longer than the purpose they were designed for, and adaptive reuse offers interesting opportunities in which the new can relate to the old, can pay respect, but can also speak of its own age with integrity and without pastiche. In times of ecological necessity and holistic approaches, it has become increasingly questionable to justify completely new-built library structures, when an adaptive reuse solution would, most of the time, be so much more sustainable. Reusing and adapting existing structures has emerged as a significant way to accommodate new libraries in a sustainable way: reducing the embodied energy, maintaining a sense of memory and place, and making the reused structure part of the wider urban renewal while requalifying the existing city through its reuse. We need adaptable buildings that can accommodate multiple uses within their lifecycle through retrofitting, adaptability and as a catalyst for the reuse of brownfield sites. Some good examples of the trend to repurpose existing structires include:

- The Community Library at the SESC Pompéia Cultural Centre, São Paulo, Brazil, designed by Lina Bo Bardi, reuses a former metal barrel factory space (1977–86);
- The Library in Eichstaett, Germany, designed by Karljosef Schattner, reuses a former palace as the new Eichstätter Universitätsbibliothek —Ulmer Hof (1976–80);
- Municipal Library and Historical Archive, used by the public and by the Department of Architecture, Design and Urban Planning, University of Sassari in Alghero, Italy: the reuse of a former seventeenth-century church as a small public and specialised college library (2015);
- University Library for UPF Biblioteca Disposit de les Aigues in Barcelona, Spain, which reuses a nineteenth-century water reservoir (architects: Clotet, Paricio & Associates, 1992–2009);

Do libraries have a future? There is no doubt they do, as the current wave of library building across the world confirms. However, new designs for libraries will be much more site-specific in their future configurations, and their programme will be adapted to meet local social and demographic circumstances, along with the likelihood of more shared or co-located facilities and funding partners. In the USA the grand city library has become a focal point of urban renewal, and the same is true in Europe. These new libraries are no longer service-stations but destination buildings in their own right, and require architectural imagination to succeed. In an otherwise highly commercialised urban centre, the public library acts as a beacon of civility and will be increasingly valued as such.
— Ken Worpole, Library Historian, London, 2015

- LocHal Public Library in Tilburg, the Netherlands, which reuses a converted locomotive shed (architects: Mecanoo and others, 2017–19).
- Marrickville Public Library and town square in Sydney, Australia, which reuses a former hospital building (2018–20), designed by BVN.
- Stanbridge Mill Library in Wimborne, Dorset, UK, which reuses a former farmhouse and water mill (2020–21), by Crawshaw Architects.
- Public Library in Mechelen, Belgium, which reuses a former baroque monastery (2021), designed by Korteknie Stuhlmacher.
- Central Library Permeke in Antwerp, Belgium, which repurposes a former garage (2005), designed by Aequo Architects.

The Library as a Hybrid Urban Place, Community Destination and a Leader in Sustainability

Designing for the cultural sector is always a creative endeavour in terms of how to create a building that truly expresses and shows respect for what will be represented and displayed inside. As discussed, libraries of the twenty-first century are about more than just books: they are about place-making —creating urban places that have a positive, long-lasting impact on users and the community. A place for tourists to visit on a rainy day. Simply put, these new libraries are places that people enjoy spending time in, and that are buzzing with activity.

Elizabeth Farrelly (2021) asks, "Does a library of the future even need books? No one seems certain. Indeed, for a while, the book-free library seemed a real possibility and librarians were encouraged to think of this as 'reinvention.' But we all knew it for what it was; the triumph of the Neoliberal bums-on-seats barbarians over any kind of respect for scholarship." There it is: the counterargument, suggesting that not every library should be turned into a community centre or childcare facility, because it could diminish its value. So, what is appropriate and makes sense? When is too much additional function too much?

Redefining the boundaries of library design begins with questioning what is possible and practical. Introducing soft amenities, additional functions and cultural activities to the traditional library programme can be the right solution. It could range from gallery spaces and roof gardens, to digital training facilities. And some of these additions might make the library part even stronger. The most promising of current metaphorical trends in library design that are likely to influence the library of the future, can be identified as:

- The library as a public space and catalyst for urban regeneration;
- The library as a large neutral flexible shed to deal with any future change;
- The library as a public pavilion in a densely vegetated garden;
- The library as a terraced vineyard;
- The library as a civic theatre and stage for urban life;
- The library as an inserted urban monolith that forms the context of, and background to, public life;
- The library as a continuous spiral, helix or ramp space for entirely new spatial experiences.

Deep Green and Highly Sustainable Libraries: Renaturing the City and the Library

Sustainable design principles are now a key component and major driver of any contemporary building, introducing new ways of designing with the aim to minimise the environmental impact (a good example of how sustainable design strategies can directly shape the library of the future is the "The Brain" in Berlin by Foster + Partners, completed in 2005, see pages 88–89). The need to preserve resources, minimise waste and ensure low-cost operation is a powerful driver of the design of any new project.

In terms of user comfort, the most common complaints in libraries are about temperature (overheating), glare and acoustic problems, with users commenting that the buildings are either too hot or too cold, too day-lit (which can lead to glare on computer screens), or too noisy (for more details on this, see the IFLA building guidelines). Latimer (2011) noted that "In the past, libraries often had uniform lighting throughout, but it is now recognised that areas of activity can be defined by varying the level of lighting. As readers, and indeed library staff, like to work in natural light, seating areas are often now placed around the edges of a building with maximum daylight penetration throughout deep-plan buildings being provided by an atrium".

Over the next decade, we will most likely see continuous improvement in the fields of energy-efficiency and sustainability. There will be an increase in adaptive reuse projects, where libraries are not entirely new-built but instead adapt an already-existing structure, as well as an increase in refurbishment and remodelling of existing libraries (Mecanoo's recent remodelling of libraries in Washington, D.C. and New York City are good examples of this). The potential of a new library for the urban regeneration of an entire neighbourhood is significant. Designers must ask how to repair and restore damaged ecosystems, by activating nature-based solutions and reconnecting the human-made with the natural. There are numerous new ways to integrate greenery into libraries and reframe the conversation with clients and policy-makers on the possibilities of regenerative design.

Ecological Turn: Regenerative Library Design

The next-generation library will be designed for an ecological future, with a concern for the flows of energy, water and materials (waste). It will be a key part of the economic redevelopment of urban centres, and based on circular-loop thinking and principles of sustainable design. It will not only be a library building that encourages encounters between readers and books, but an institution that goes far beyond this by reconnecting the user with nature. It will be an immersive experience: the experience of nature will be a key element of the future library, which could be a building that allows visitors to experience being in a garden or next to a tree. Moreover, it will be made of natural ecological materials: the library as a timber building, using the latest technology in innovative mass timber engineered construction systems.

Designing buildings in partnership with nature, the new urban library will not only be biophilic, but it will be bio-centric: a shift from human-centric to bio-centric starts with the replication of processes and patterns commonly found in nature (without imitating them literally). In "Low Carbon Cities" (2015), I argued that bio-centricity often starts with the recovery and repair of damaged brownfield sites where soil and water systems are degraded. Here are a couple of thoughts on the regenerative design for libraries:

- Urban form becomes polycentric, rather than the monocentric as seen today. Instead of centralised energy power plants, the city will operate many small decentralised systems and nodes, operating at the scale of the building. At least 50% of its energy needs will be generated on-site by the library itself, using renewable energy sources. Roofs, canopies and façades will become gardens and solar-powered collectors. The library will capture rain and recycle grey water; excess water from roofs will be diverted to landscape features that hold and clean the water. Close-by natural areas, such as parks, gardens or wetlands, will be integrated to manage hydrological flows.

- The library of the future is likely to programmatically stack its different functional sections and be connected with the surrounding urban fabric at different points. Buildings will be elevated on pilotis to keep the ground plane open so as to prioritise public space and blue-green networks. Elevated community decks will be connected to public space below and, by extension, with, the surrounding neighbourhood. This includes a rethink of hard urbanism to include soft socio-ecological landscapes and systems.

- Cities need new infrastructural systems and buildings that can generate, capture, process, recycle, upcycle, distribute and store resources. Construction materials and components will need particular attention to avoid material waste and high embodied energy, using modular off-site manufacturing where possible. As outlined in *Cradle to Cradle – Remaking the Way We Make Things* (2002), as well as in *The Principles of Green Urbanism* (2010), and the work published by the Ellen MacArthur Foundation (UK), circularity is the reorganisation of resource flows into closed-loop systems so that the waste from one becomes a resource for another.

Self-sufficient cities have closed-loop systems that eliminate the constant demand for virgin materials, decoupling consumption from material needs, and the metabolism of cities from planetary systems. Some of this depends on the infrastructure, and some on new roles for existing adaptively reused structures, while much depends on new business models for manufacturing and the behaviour change of urban populations.

The Library as a Public Garden and Social Space — Embedding Culture within Landscape
Over 80% of the US population currently live in urban areas, with a large portion of the population "estranged from nature" (Office for National Statistics, 2016, 2). Today, we spend over 90% of our lives in controlled interior environments (ASHRAE, 2010) with increasing amounts of our time constituting "screen-time" online and for most of this time being isolated. With an increasing number of people living in urban areas (often suffering from loneliness and depression), the need to create and enhance public spaces and civic facilities within cities has never been greater. At the same time, city life is becoming increasingly synonymous with technology and disconnectedness from nature, neighbours and the public sphere. Cities have formed the backdrop of these trends and have been substantially influenced and shaped by them. Hence, the wider theme of the next-generation of public buildings should include a discussion on renaturing and regreening our cities.

Michelle Jeffrey Delk noted in the *Prologue* of this book that "it is not about any specific technology, but about how people interact with technology or access resources" (Delk, 2021), arguing that a library could also be read as a "landscape of knowledge", similar to a public garden or ecosystem. There are numerous ways for a library to integrate natural elements and be like a garden. This garden could be a rooftop garden, urban farm, or a community garden in a courtyard, as a productive landscape element that brings together people from different backgrounds.

Greened building envelopes and vegetated roofs are ways of repairing and renaturing the city fabric. Greened building envelopes can reduce a library's operating and cooling costs. Public green spaces and roof gardens have a series of positive impacts besides the recreational and ambience effect: integrating greenery into library design will help to reduce air pollution, decrease the build-up of the urban heat island effect, lower noise levels and enhance the wellbeing of library users. This could include ground-based green areas such as in a courtyard, or green walls inside, terraced contemplative gardens, or a public roof garden as a consumption-free roof space with a panoramic view. There are a number of good examples of this trend:

- Warsaw University Library (Poland) features a large public roof park measuring 10,000 sqm (100,000 sqft);
- TU-Delft University Library (Netherlands) has an accessible sloping green roof (5,000 sqm);
- Ballard Library in Seattle (US) offers a gently curving green roof of 2,000 sqm (20,000 sqft);
- Vancouver Public Library in Vancouver (Canada) has a 2,600 sqm (26,000 sqft) green roof.

So, the possibilities for greening a library can range from courtyard gardens and communal urban farming, to low-tech potted plant terraces, green walls in entrance halls, or plant shelves, or extensive roof gardens —all contributing atmospheric and climatic benefits. Today, green roofs are essential, as they reduce the urban heat island effect; importantly, the vegetated library roofs should be made accessible to library users, so that people can enjoy the view and read outside, or have meetings on the roof.

Thus, the library of the future is a project that is as much about a public building as it is about regreening and establishing an urban landscape. The goal is to create a library that is an inclusive gathering place, a counterpoint to the otherwise suburban areas, and as a point of pride for the city. The library's role as a symbol of shared cultural and community values will remain and become stronger. Given the physical disintegration of the city centre, one could say that the library of the future is likely to become a microcosm of the city —a social network— in and of itself.

A book is like a garden, carried in the pocket.
— Chinese Proverb

What could be Add-on Design Components of the Next-generation Library?
New libraries will increasingly follow a pattern of strategic calculation similar to investment-driven economic operations: indoor and outdoor design elements (selected from an inventory of scalable and exchangeable components) can be selected and bundled together in section and plan, to create an attractive offering of spatial sequences.

Philosophy exercises a strong influence on contemporary architectural thought and the understanding of the built environment. Discussions of architects and academics are heavily loaded with theoretical ideas, concepts and views imported from the works of philosophers and from other disciplines. Influenced by the ironic work of the Austrian team Mörtenböck & Mooshammer (2021), who developed an inventory of future urban elements (the "must-haves" of every design project today), these components are emblematic of the current innovation economy and design trends. Under the banner of "place-making", said components could become today's ubiquitous ingredients for any competition-winning future library design. Adapted as "components of the future library" and illustrated by 15 current trends in library design globally, these include:

- The public space in front of or inside the library: this "Instagrammable" forecourt, square or entrance hall offers free Wi-Fi connection for everyone and is an area of high visibility
  that blurs the boundaries between private and public; the building typology is reframed in service of urban morphology and a revival of the courtyard type;
- The inclusion of a domesticated public space and courtyard: this can further blur the boundaries between public and private, indoor and outdoor, by creating outdoor spaces that feature interior design elements that create intimacy with objects for individual library users;
- The concept of the library as a shared warehouse: the high flexibility and staged urban atmosphere of the warehouse appeals to startups and younger library users, who want to be part and move in; additional services are offered outside the usual library functions;
- Meeting pods: these create unusual spaces for meetings or concentrated work that can be inserted everywhere, as sound proof spaces with glass walls that can vary in size;
- Free public Wi-Fi connection: offering connectivity to everyone and everything is likely to be part of the future, but could create a conflict with privacy policies and data management;
- Open ceilings: these create a technical look and enable rapid installation, adding a casual "high-tech" vibe to any library space;
- Stadium seating and landscape furniture: this consists of large-scale steps for sitting that suggest openness and allow for social moments such as sudden meetings and encounters; this could also take the form of an interior built landscape that seamlessly merges floors and walls, signalling collaboration and non-hierarchical space;
- Themed spaces: different from the traditional library space, these lessen the feeling of "work" by creating a different experience; the more eccentrically they are designed, the more interest they will create, communicating an image of "enjoyable productivity";
- A viewing platform on the green roof: a special roof location that provides an elevated panoramic view and a place where people can socialise, chat and enjoy the sights as a shared immersive experience;
- Whiteboard walls or graffiti walls: these allow for rapid markings that can be quickly erased or left for days to foster the dynamic exchange of ideas;
- A circulation loop: connecting various activities along a ramping pathway in a non-hierarchical way can foster social encounters and a sense of continuity;
- Green walls, screens or a vertical garden: trendy in cities globally, they bring relaxing feelings of nature and can transform the experience from a collective to an individual one;

they can also improve internal acoustics. However, if not done well, the integration and irrigation of a green wall can require constant and costly maintenance duties;

- DIY furniture: the unique and casual appearance of DIY furniture is always very popular and looks cool on social media; it could include upcycling of materials as an ecological statement and will create a sense of identification with the library environment;
- A climbing wall: these unique exercise spaces can be integrated into the entrance hall or atrium and are usually located next to the café;
- A must-have component for all libraries today is a maker space, a 3-D printing and laser-cutting workshop facility to introduce library users to digital manufacturing.

The Role of the Library in Improving People's Lives and in Shaping Meaningful Civic Space
There have been plenty of spectacle-driven libraries. But what might the next-generation library really look like? Bringing various functions and elements together in one compact complex, the Sendai Mediatheque by Toyo Ito, designed between 1994 and 2000, combined an art gallery, a library, and a centre for the visually and auditory-impaired, with a media centre of visual images; twenty years ago, this building embodied a fresh way to look at the library. Similarly, at SANAA's Rolex Learning Center in Lausanne, the library is just one of a number of different learning spaces (including even some retail spaces) combined in one building. Most likely, the trend of including unusual programmatic elements will just become stronger.

Huis van Eemnes in Donderen, the Netherlands (completed in 2020), is marketing itself as a new type of "hospitable library and culture house for a small town": an inspiring third place to meet, create and participate, where organised and spontaneous activities can take place. This library combines two opposing functions: the peaceful surroundings of the library with the dynamics of a culture centre, and the noisy brasserie and bar. The entities are openly connected to each other and surrounded by multifunctional rooms, including a theatre, a sports hall and event rooms.

Here, the risk is, of course, that the functionality of a serious library is compromised. However, it seems that, with financially constrained times ahead and a growing need to market libraries in the face of competition from other information providers, such hybrids will probably become a more common model. Moreover, it is also likely that architects will become even more concerned with new design concepts and library planning on very limited budgets.

The built structures reflect and shape the aspirations and expectations of changing societies and the aim to improve people's lives; libraries do this probably more than any other building. Architecture, urbanism and the creation of public space can be exemplary vehicles to enhance the health, sustainability and vibrancy of communities. In reflecting on the appropriateness of a commercial programme for the next-generation library, it is helpful to consider the following concerns:

- How are new environmental, social and technical challenges addressed through innovative approaches in the design?
- How will principles of inclusion and diversity (pluralism) be articulated through the architectural design and everyday usage of the library?
- How does the library and its public space react to the current condition of our public space networks, shaped by excessive globalisation, commercialisation and the uncontrolled surveillance of the public realm and identify another pathway?

Conclusion: a Super-Flexible Hybrid Building Type Serving Multiple Uses

What are the new trend-setting ideas, or at least refinement of already known ideas in library design? Architecture must always look to the future, anticipate the changing contexts and imagine the libraries that are ahead of their time. The next-generation libraries will be socially inclusive of the needs of the wider community and perform well environmentally; they will be designed for their entire life-cycle to ensure that tomorrow's libraries can stand up to the rigours of the next generation's demands.

One of the key take-away messages of this study is that we will still need libraries in the future, but these must now be super-green buildings. It is a positive trend that green roofs, living walls and gardens have become a popular feature to be integrated in in all architecture worldwide. Besides its positive impact on the urban microclimate and water management, contact with nature is essential for human existence, urban wellbeing and good quality of life. The importance of applying the concept of regreening to the library of the future is only now better understood and recognized as essential.

The public and academic library remains an uplifting and important feature in the community and on campus. Libraries are not dying, but evolving. Libraries are important cornerstones of any healthy community; they give people the opportunity to find jobs, explore scientific research, experience new ideas and get lost in wonderful stories, while at the same time providing a sense of place for gathering. Appearing effortless, the extraordinary libraries of Snøhetta, Mecanoo, FJMT and others (presented in this publication) demonstrate an extra-ordinary ability to uncover the real and often contradictory issues and potentials of each project by a very careful analysis of purpose and place, often resolving these in a building of ease and elegance. These libraries represent themselves and their users —carefully balancing the need to express a sense of *civitas.*

Seattle Central Library, which opened in 2004, was designed before e-books and the iPad even existed. The post-digital age requires our civic spaces and public buildings to become more agile, malleable and adaptive to change, able to respond to the complexity and unpredictability of our urban situations. It is most likely that the library of the future will be an indoor extension of a public space or green space —a civic "living room" that offers a variety of facilities such as recording studios and maker spaces, with access to public services, exhibitions and community events —in addition to providing books. The future concept that emerges is a library as a public resource, civic space and a place for ideas and contemplation. Instead of suffering "death", the library is very much alive, and the speculative idea of what a library *is*, is in accelerating re-definition.

The library is experiencing a strong comeback and is now firmly established as a "third place" —a place away from both the workplace and the home —to study, collaborate or socialise. Contrary to predictions, the digitisation has had largely a positive impact on library design. However, serious challenges remain: the ever-changing user needs, reduced funding and declining user numbers will pose ongoing challenges that future library design has to recognise.

The user-focused (rather than collection-based) library of the future must also strike a thoughtful balance between quiet, contemplative spaces for concentration and conversational spaces for lively communication and collaboration. It will be more fluid between formal and informal spaces, between the individual and the collective. The library of the future must serve those who want to work alone or collaboratively in groups, in silence or in a lively café atmosphere.

Furthermore, a climate-neutral building as the library of the future will be a must, as greenhouse gas (GhG) concentrations are already too high. Bold, fast and comprehensive action is needed to rapidly end anthropogenic GhG-emissions, and at the same time to improve and regenerate landscapes in and around the cities, such as forests, agricultural soils and wetlands to the extent that they retain or regain their ecosystem services and carbon management function.

Pages 230 and 231 present a final thought of what might be possible: a temporary structure in a park in India or a tiny micro-library along the river in Indonesia. Could these small interventions actually be the most innovative concepts for a library of the future? In the end, a temporary structure or a micro-library, both located in the Global South, could emerge as the most flexible and innovative ideas for the next-generation library to instill reading in young people.

In conclusion, it has become evident that, as a vital and continuously evolving building type, the library remains alive and with a bright future. There is obviously no formula for a library of the future. First and foremost, a library for tomorrow must enable and inspire the imagination of its users. It might well be that the ideal type of library has not yet been realised. Jorge Luis Borges wrote in 1975: "*I have always imagined that Paradise will be a kind of library*".
—I am inclined to agree.

Notes:
More background on sustainable design principles and the impact of climate change on cities and buildings, including libraries, can be found in the writings of Banham, Reyner (1969); Buckminster Fuller, Richard (1969); McHarg, Ian (1969); Meaddows, Donna et al. (1972); Hall, Peter and Pfeiffer, Ulrich (2000); McDonough, William and Braungart, Michael (2002); Lehmann, Steffen (2010, 2015 and 2019); Haas, Tigran (2012); Crawford, Jane and Davoudi, Simin (2012); Hawken, Paul (2017);
and in publications by the UN-Habitat (2020).

More background on urban design and the evolution of cities and their public space can be found in the writings of Jacobs, Jane (1961); Mumford, Lewis (1961); Banham, Reyner (1969); Rowe, Colin and Koetter, Fred (1974); Pevsner, Nikolaus (1979); Whyte, William (1980); Lynch, Kevin (1981); Alexander, Christopher (1987); Kostof, Spiro (1991); Ockman, Joan (1993); Koolhaas, Rem and Mau, Bruce (1995); Lehmann, Steffen (2010); Glaeser, Edward L. (2011); Unwin, Simon (2014); and Burdett, Ricky and Rhode, Philipp (2018).

Further background on the practicalities of library design and the history of libraries can be found in the writings, articles and handbooks of: Wheeler, Joseph Lewis, and Alfred Morton Githens (1941); Thompson, A. (1963); Metcalf, Keyes DeWitt (1965); Brawne, Michael (1970 and 1997); Ellsworth, Ralph (1973); Thompson, Godfrey (1973); Oehlerts, Donald (1991); Worpole, Ken, Greenhalgh, Liz and Landry, Charles (1992); Kito, Azusa (1995); Browning, John (1995); Van Slyck, Abigail (1995); Kaser, David (1997); Bieri, Susanne and Fuchs, Walther (2001); Arets, Will (2005); Futagawa, Yukio (2006); and Latimer, Karen (2007 and 2011).

Reimaging the Library of the Future

PART IV. The Design Studio

In other words, if the library is, as Borges put it, a model of the universe, we must try to transform it into a universe on a human scale, and, I would remind you, a human scale also means a light-hearted scale, with the chance of a coffee, even with the chance for two students to sit down on a couch on an afternoon and, if not to indulge in indecent behavior, at least enjoy the continuation of their flirtation in the library as they take down or replace some books of scientific interest from their shelves.
— Umberto Eco, 2019

A Design Studio on the Library of the Future

In 2021, the author led a design studio at the University of Nevada, Las Vegas that explored the dilemma of public buildings and public space in the age of post-pandemic social isolation and climate change. The studio used the public library as a catalyst for upgrading urban space and enhancing climate resilience and social inclusion. This studio has a long-term research interest in urbanism and is engaged in the architectural explorations of typologies and the future of public buildings, such as the library, as an anchor for entire neighbourhoods.

A group of twelve enthusiastic students in the 4th Year Bachelor of Science in Architecture programme developed design proposals for a local public library at a prominent downtown corner site on Charleston Boulevard in Las Vegas, over a period of four months. I am grateful for the support by library experts, including Michele Brigida (East Las Vegas Library), Antoine Predock (Las Vegas Central Library and Children's Museum), Maggie Farrell, dean of Libraries (UNLV Lied Library), Richard Saladino (UNLV) and Windom Kimsey of TSK (Sahara West Library, Summerlin). Visiting critics at reviews of the student projects included eminent academics: Mark Mueckenheim (San Francisco), Iman Ansari (Los Angeles), Annette Condello (Perth), Eric Farr (San Diego), David Erdman (New York), Samia Kirchner (Baltimore), Sergio Lopez-Pineiro (Cambridge), Ed Vance (Las Vegas), Igor Peraza (Barcelona), Niccolo Casas (Bologna), David Turnbull (London), Will Bruder (Portland), and Richard Marshall of Perkins+Will (Los Angeles).

With a series of lectures, precedent analysis and field trips, the students were introduced to the complexity of the design project and asked to develop their final programme for their library of the future. The size of the library was 7,000 sqm (70,000 sqft); it had to facilitate the creation of new forms of knowledge production and knowledge sharing that build capacity and resilience in communities. Following here are a couple of selected projects from this intensive studio.

The three selected projects from the studio, presented on the following pages, were designed by my talented undergraduate students: Jose Rodriguez, Rebeca Rivera and Martin J. Ebro.

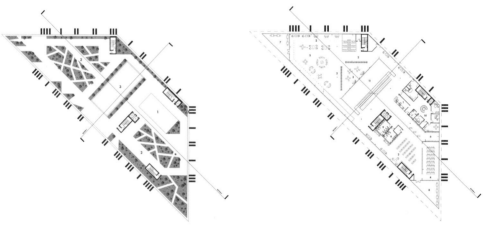

Jose Rodriguez

SOUTHWEST ELEVATION

0' 25'   75'   175'

SECTION 1

0' 25'   75'   175'

Jose Rodriguez

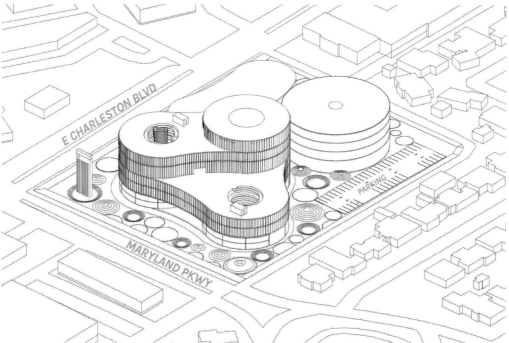

Rebeca Rivera

FIRST FLOOR

KEY
1. MAIN ENTRANCE
2. FOYER
3. LOBBY & RECEPTION DESK
4. ACTIVE READING
5. ROCK CLIMBING COURTYARD
6. COFFE SHOP
7. RESTROOMS
8. STAFF MEETING ROOM
9. STAFF OFFICES
10. STAFF RESTROOMS
11. QUIET READING
12. CHILDRENS COLLECTION
13. CHILDRENS PLAYGROUND COURTYARD
14. CHILD CARE
15. SEMINAR ROOMS / MAKER SPACES
16. ATRIUM
17. STORAGE CLOSET
18. FIRE ESCAPE STAIRS
19. SPIRAL RAMP
20. STUDY ROOM
21. DESERT GARDEN

BAR SCALE

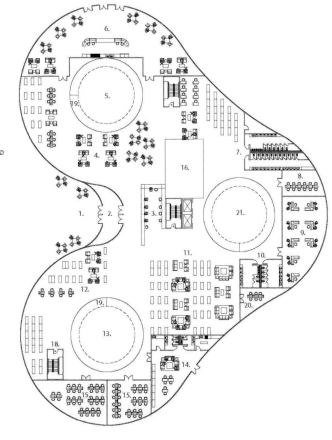

FOURTH - FIFTH FLOORS

KEY
1. QUIET READING
2. BOOK STACKS
3. COFFEE SHOP
4. SPIRAL RAMP
5. FIRE ESCAPE STAIRS
6. ELEVATORS
7. STORAGE CLOSET
8. REFERENCE DESK
9. OUTDOOR READING/ GARDEN -
RECREATION SPACE
10. VOID

BAR SCALE

SIXTH FLOOR

KEY
1. QUIET READING ROOM
2. BOOK STACKS
3. ROCK CLIMBING
4. VOID
5. SPIRAL RAMP
6. FIRE ESCAPE STAIRS
7. ELEVATORS
8. REFERENCE DESK
9. OUTDOOR READING / GARDEN

BAR SCALE

a

223

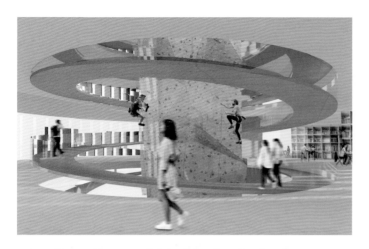

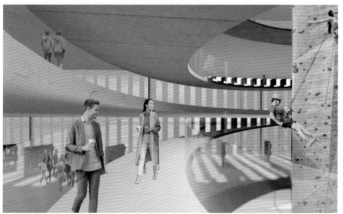

Rebeca Rivera

The last 15 years has bared resonance—an evolution of libraries' value and role to the community. Libraries no longer just hold value in being repositories of information resources, but with an intended focus on space as a place for equitable access, management and utilisation of information in the knowledge economy. I foresee the library as a typology in 20 years, continuing this trajectory. The digital age has led to a surge in information creation. This manifests itself in re-designing spaces in meeting the ever-evolving diverse and equitable needs of its users. In terms of information resources, libraries have a responsibility in procuring and stewarding information resources based on the strategic goals of the institution and community they serve. Libraries of the future will continue to advocate for the relevance of these resources to research, as well as, continue to set standards on the processing and stewardship of these types of information resources, providing equitable access to all users for both print and electronic resources.

— **Richard Saladino, Art, Architecture and Design Librarian, UNLV, 2021**

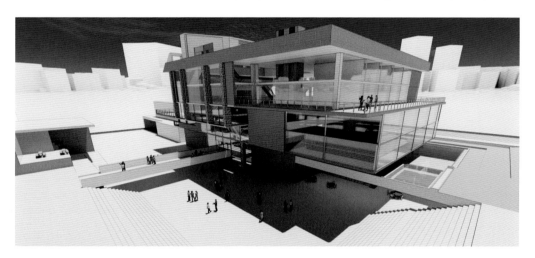

Martin J. Ebro

Epilogue

The Future of the Library and the Library of the Future

Keith Webster

Almost 30 years ago, the Follett Report on the future of British university libraries was released (Joint Funding Council's Libraries Review Group, 1993). Within the report was a scenario set in the year 2001, describing the lives of a number of personas on a university campus. Many of the technological projections in the scenarios are commonplace today, including digital delivery of texts and streaming of multimedia resources. However, the report's predictions of the demise of the library building, "some of the old University Library had been given over for parking since the building was extraordinarily strong, and had successfully resisted the installation of so much cable", have not stood the test of time. The account continued, "One architect had been bitter: '...libraries were the last great symbols of society for my profession to design. Now even you offer no certainty!'"

From the perspective of the early 2020s, what seemed plausible, if not desirable, three decades ago has not been realised. Libraries are busier than ever, and universities are expanding and remodelling existing libraries, and constructing new facilities at great pace.

The Follett Report was right to anticipate the shift to digital content. In most disciplines today, all new content arrives electronically, in the form of online journals and e-books, and large parts of the historic scholarly record have been digitised. While it remains too early to predict with certainty the demise of the printed book, the need for large print collections housed in libraries at the heart of campus steadily declines. The response to this is seen in the approach of many universities: as libraries are remodelled, collections are transferred to offsite stores. Some new libraries are equipped with an Automated Storage and Retrieval System, a robotic facility that allows large collections to be held in densely packed bins, with titles retrieved rapidly on demand. Such a facility greatly reduces the footprint of the collection, maximising the space available to support students and researchers.

The rapid reduction of openly accessible print collections is commonly understood among (most) librarians, but is often viewed as surprising to the general public. Surely, they opine, a library is a building for books. For them, if the digital shift forecast by the Follett Report was to prove true, then the need for libraries indeed goes away. The opportunity to solve the biggest shortage on most campuses, accessible car parking, could indeed be realised!

Before the digital age, the purpose of most academic libraries was straightforward: to assemble collections, and provide expertise, tools and space to support their use. In a typical research university, the bulk of library space was allocated to housing collections, and reader spaces were primarily set aside for quiet and individual study. This supported the prevailing model of scholarship, and created the environment required to support close reading of academic texts.

However, the digital delivery of texts has prompted a shift in information consumption, and this has been accelerated by the lockdown phase of the COVID-19 pandemic. Trends that were already underway have been advanced by the opening up of publishers' platforms, free access to online textbooks, and emergency access to digitised texts from the Hathi Trust and others. As universities reopen, it is clear that the convenience of immediate access to library materials, wherever, and whenever they may be required, is something that students and faculty value.

The same technologies that have allowed greater delivery of content in digital form also have supported a shift in research and in teaching and learning. Pedagogical approaches such as the flipped classroom have seen direct instruction move from the classroom to an individual's learning space, and class time used to form a dynamic and interactive environment where students and professors debate, discuss, create and present. This places a number of learning space demands on the campus environment: adequate space is required both for individual and group engagement with instructional materials, space for pre- and post-class group work and discussion, and flexible classroom environments. Further, affordable access to basic digital fabrication technologies, such as 3D-printers and laser cutters, provide a means to achieve another aspect of contemporary education. Students, professors, and employers all recognise the importance of interdisciplinary approaches, helping students understand the problem-solving approaches and habits of mind of their peers from other fields. Programmes such as Carnegie Mellon's IDeATe (www.ideate.cmu.edu) use maker education as the backdrop to interdisciplinary education.

It is against this backdrop that one changing role of the library can best be seen. It is viewed as an open, accessible and neutral space on campus. The library and those who work within its walls support all disciplines, but are part of none. Students collaborating across academic fields report that the library is the only place where they can all feel at home; working in any one departmental space would leave some students feeling that they are in a space they regard as "other". The library also is viewed as a non-judgmental space, where scholars can seek help from experts without feeling embarrassed by any perceived lack of expertise. For most students, though, the library is viewed as an inspirational destination. Surrounded by books, even if they are never consulted, students feel a sense of academic place. They are building on the shoulders of those who preceded them. The library is the primary non-classroom academic space on campus, and it is here that students come, seeking serious space for serious work.

One of the major challenges for library leaders is anticipating the types of learning spaces that will be needed today and in the future. We have all been confronted by a sense that students want more: more quiet, individual space, more group study space, more maker spaces and more collaboration and discussion space. Few universities will be able to meet all of these demands at all times, but perhaps there will be opportunities to ride the tidal wave of the semester, designing spaces that can support peak demand for collaborative space in the first part of term, and being converted to quiet space as finals draw near.

The sense of the library as an open and neutral space aligns with the model of the public library as civic space. The university campus should be a place of debate, and a place that advances diversity, equity, inclusion and social justice. As we think about the future of the academic library, we must plan for spaces that allow the campus community to come together, both in a planned and programmed way, and informally, to debate the issues of the day, exchange ideas and offer a safe space for critical conversations.

All of these demands are clear on most campuses, but a provocative question emerges: "Why the library?" In an environment where general collections attract increasingly diminished use, will the library truly be able to save itself? Undoubtedly, the students and researchers of the digital age have answered that challenge: they report an inner essence of libraryness that must be preserved. Librarians and architects working together can respond to shifts in the academic environment in the years ahead, securing a continued role for one of the oldest and most cherished of campus institutions.

The emergence of digital collections of books and journals has made it possible for every library, subject to funding, to provide access broadly to the same collections. There is a greater degree of homogeneity of collections across libraries, and this has prompted many to focus on their distinctive collections of rare books, manuscripts and archives. It is these unique materials that distinguish one library from another, and high quality facilities to support their storage and use, and to host exhibitions, are increasingly in demand.

As a professional futurist, I often look at a domain through the alternative future scenarios of growth, constraint, collapse and transformation. Building scenarios, somewhat like those in the Follett Report, give us a sense of possible futures, helping us prepare today for the long-term. This work often begins by gathering drivers and signals, pointers that show what might eventuate. As I look at the particular landscape of the university library, I see many reasons to be optimistic: inspiring libraries are being designed and constructed, and opened to vast acclaim. The scholarly information landscape has evolved from the locally owned collection that is stored on library book stacks to a vast collection of digital materials offered by publishers, policy institutes, libraries and museums, and the resources of digital archives such as the Hathi Trust. This allows librarians to take a bold approach —to reimagine the library as a space truly at the heart of the academic community. One clear lesson from the pandemic has been the importance of preparedness. We need bold visions of the libraries we need in the future, spaces to excite and inspire, and to allow us to reimagine our human experience for the century to come.

Today, the library has a bright future at the heart of the community it serves!

Reference
Joint Funding Council's Libraries Review Group: Report (The Follett Report) (1993). Published December 1993, Bristol, UK. Available online at: https://www.ukoln.ac.uk/services/papers/follett/report/intro.html

Keith Webster is an experienced higher education leader and librarian. His particular interests are in the future of universities, higher education systems and in libraries, the transformation of scholarly communication, research data management and the design of learning spaces. He was appointed Dean of University Libraries at Carnegie Mellon University in July 2013, and is also Director of Emerging and Integrative Media Initiatives since 2015. Previously, Keith was Vice President and Director of Academic Relations and Strategy for the publishing company John Wiley and Sons. He was formerly Dean of Libraries and University Librarian at the University of Queensland in Australia, leading one of the largest university library services in the southern hemisphere. Earlier positions include University Librarian at Victoria University in New Zealand, Head of Information Policy at HM Treasury, London, and Director of Information Services at the School of Oriental & African Studies, University of London. Keith has held professorships in information science at Victoria University of Wellington and City University, London. He is a fellow of the Chartered Institute of Library and Information Professionals (UK). He became chair of the National Information Standards Organization in July 2018.

For more information, please visit Keith's blog: www.libraryofthefuture.org

Architectural quality less and less depends on the skill of the craftsman, or on a common architectural language that is based on a shared understanding of established typologies. We are living in a time when form is less and less connected to anything, such as logic, programme, historical precedence, or site specificity. But this new "design freedom of anything goes" exposes also new responsibilities.
— David Chipperfield, 2020

Final Thought: two Small-scale Libraries as *the Library of the Future?*

Nudes Architects, Mumbai, India

Temporary Library "BookWorm", Mumbai, India (Nudes Architects), 2019
Indian architecture studio Nudes has designed the meandering BookWorm pavilion in the park to encourage reading among children and adults. Located in the gardens of a Museum in Mumbai, the temporary pavilion has been built as a response to the United Nations' Sustainable Development Goal that all youths and a substantial proportion of adults achieve literacy by 2030. The 35-metre-long pavilion winds its way through the museum gardens, providing space for 12,000 books. It is made of two simple, modular structures based on wooden ladders that stretch outward to create undulating forms at either side of a central pathway. A temporary structure that allows for an entirely new daring concept of the "Next- Generation Library".

Shau Architects, Jakarta, Indonesia

Micro-Library, Bandung and Semarang, Indonesia (Shau Architects), 2016 and 2020
A series of low-cost micro-libraries have been initiated by the architects and built in Indonesian towns in an effort to boost literacy and combat the country's high school-dropout rates. This was the first prototype, and so far, five micro-libraries have been built. The entire project was completed on a budget of USD 40,000. The reading facility is supported by stilts with a sheltered space for gatherings at ground floor; the stairs double up as seating. The façade is composed of 1,800 repurposed ice-cream containers allowing for diffused light to enter. Sliding polycarbonate doors on the inside protect against tropical storms. Supported by the local municipality and charitable organisations, the project has been enthusiastically received by the community and several more micro-libraries are planned for other Indonesian towns.

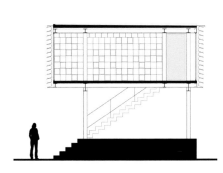

References

Alexander, C., Neis, H., Anninou, A. and King, I. (1987). *A New Theory of Urban Design,* Oxford University Press, Oxford.

Arets, Will (2005). *Living Library*, Prestel Publishing, London.

Banham, Reyner (1969). *The Architecture of the Well-tempered Environment.* University of Chicago Press, Chicago.

Beck, Ulrich (2000). *Risk Society. Towards a new Modernity*. Sage, London.

Becker, Lynn (2005). *Sleekness in Seattle – the New Seattle Public Library*, Chicago; article available online.

Black, Alistair and Dahlkild, Nan (eds) (2011). "Library Designs: from Past to Present", *Library Trends,* Vol. 6(1), Summer, Illinois.

Browning, John (1995). "Libraries without Walls - For Books without Pages", *Wired*, Vol. 1.1, New York.

Brudvik-Lindner, Richard (2021). "Reimagining a new Nelson library", opinion piece in the *Nelson Mail,* May 1, 2021, New Zealand, available online.

Buckminster Fuller, Richard (1969). *Operating Manual for Spaceship Earth* (reprint 2008), Lars Mueller Verlag, Baden.

Burdett, Ricky and Rhode, Philipp (eds) (2018). *Shaping Cities in an Urban Age*. Phaidon Press Ltd., London.

Caygill, M. (2000). *The British Museum Reading Room*, The British Museum Press, London.

Club of Rome/Meaddows D. et al (1972). *Limits to Growth*, report to the United Nations.

Crawford, J. and S. Davoudi (2012). *Planning for Climate Change: Strategies for Mitigation and Adaptation for Spatial Planners*. Routledge, London.

Education Advisory Board, EAB (2011). "Redefining the Academic Library", US report available online: www.eab.com/research/academic-affairs/study/

Edwards, B. (2009). *Libraries and Learning Resource Centres*, Oxford Architectural Press, Oxford.

Fainstein, Susan, Gordon, Ian and Harloe, Michael (2011). "Ups and downs in the global city: London and New York In the twenty-first century". In: Bridge, Gary and Watson, Sophie, (eds) *New Blackwell Companion to the City.* Wiley-Blackwell, Chichester, 38–47.

Farrelly, Elizabeth (2021). "How can Libraries Improve our Lives? Do They even Need Books?", *Sydney Morning Herald* (10 Sep. 2021), Sydney, Australia.

Florida, Richard (2002). *The Rise of the Creative Class*, Basic Books, New York.

Giddens, Anthony (1999). *Runaway World*; Profile Books, London.

Glaeser, EL. (2011). *The Triumph of the City: How our Greatest Invention Makes Us Richer, Smarter, Greener, Healthier, and Happier,* Penguin Press, New York and London.

Goldberger, Paul (2004). "High-Tech Bibliophilia", *The New Yorker*, May 16, 2004, New York.

Haas, T. (Ed.) (2012). *Sustainable Urbanism and Beyond*, Rizzoli, New York.

Hall, Peter and Pfeiffer, Ulrich (2000): *Urban Future 21. A Global Agenda for Twenty-First Century Cities*. London.

Hawken, Paul (Ed.) (2017). *Drawdown. The Most Comprehensive Plan Ever*, Penguin Books, New York.

Herzog, Jacques (2020). "Jacques Herzog: letter to David Chipperfield", *Domus*, Oct. 2020, Milan, Italy.

Hessel, A. (1925). *Geschichte der Bibliotheken*, Goettingen.

Isozaki, Arata (2006). "About my Method", in: Yuki Futagawa (Ed.). 2006, *GA Contemporary Architecture*, Vol. 03: Library, ADA Edita, Tokyo, Japan, 206-207.

Jacobs, J. (1961). *The Death and Life of Great American Cities*, Cape/Random House, London/New York.

Kito, Azusa (Ed.) (1995). *Libraries. New Concepts in Architecture and Design*. Meisei, Tokyo.

Koolhaas, R. and Mau, B. (1995). *S,M,L,XL*, Monacelli Press, New York.

Kostof, Spiro (1991). *The City Shaped. Urban Patterns and Meaning through History*. London.

Lamba, Manika (2019). "Marketing of academic health libraries 2.0", *Library Management,* Vol. 40 (3/4), 155-177.

Latimer, Karen (2011). "Collections to Connections: Changing Spaces and New Challenges in Academic Library Buildings", in: *Library Design*: From Past to Present, edited by Alistair Black and Nan Dahlkild, 2011, 112-133, University of Illinois, Chicago.

Latimer, K. and Niegaard, H. (eds) (2007). *IFLA Library Building Guidelines: Developments and Reflections*, Saur Verlag, Munich.

Lehmann, Steffen (2010). *The Principles of Green Urbanism. Transforming the City for Sustainability*. Earthscan Publisher/Routledge, London.

Lehmann, Steffen (2019). *Urban Regeneration. A Manifesto for Transforming UK Cities in the Age of Climate Change*, Palgrave MacMillan, London.

Lynch, K. (1981). *A Theory of Good City Form*, MIT Press, Cambridge, MA.

Mazzucato, Mariana (2018). *The Value of Everything. Making and Taking in the Global Economy*, Hachette Book Group, New York.

McDonough W, Braungart M. (2002). *Cradle to Cradle: Remaking the Way We Make Things,* North Point Press, New York.

McHarg, Ian (1969). *Design with Nature*, Double Day, New York/Falcon Press, Philadelphia.

McParland, E. (2001). *Public Architecture in Ireland, 1680–1760*, Yale University Press, New Haven.

Mumford, Lewis (1961). *The City in History. Its Origins, its Transformations, its Prospects*, Penguin Books, London

Muschamp, Herbert (2004). "Architecture; the Library that puts on Fishnets and Hits the Disco", *New York Times*, May 16, 2004, New York.

Nevarez, Julia (2021). *The Urban Library. Creative City Branding in Spaces for All,* Springer, Amsterdam.

Ockman, Joan (Ed.) (1993). *Architecture Culture 1943–1968*. A Documentary Anthology, New York.

Pevsner, Nikolaus (1979). *A History of Building Types,* Princeton University Press. Page 91 gives an overview of the history of the library.

Pickles, Matt (2015). *How Do You Design the Library of the Future?*, University of Oxford, UK.

Ramus, Joshua (2004). "Seattle Central Library", in: Yuki Futagawa (Ed.). 2006, *GA Contemporary Architecture*, Vol. 03: Library, ADA Edita, Tokyo, Japan, 310–314.

Rowe, Colin; Koetter, Fred (1974/1978). *Collage City,* MIT Press, Boston.

Schmitz, Karl-Heinz (2016). "Form and Function in Library Design", in: *Libraries: A Design Manual*, Birkhäuser, Berlin/Boston, 30-37.

Sennett, Richard (1977). *The Fall of Public Man,* Penguin Books, London

Stevens, Philip (2021). "Interview with Mecanoo's Francine Houben", online, *designboom* (June 13, 2021).

Thompson, A. (1963). *Library Buildings of Britain and Europe –An International Study*, Butterworths, London.

UN-Habitat (2018). "Brief on Migration and Cities", *The United Nations Human Settlements Programme* (UN-Habitat), Nairobi.

UN-Habitat (2020). *The Value of Sustainable Urbanization. World Cities Report,* published by the United Nations Human Settlements Programme (UN-Habitat). Nairobi.

Unwin, Simon (2014). *Analysing Architecture,* Routledge (4th Edition), New York/London.

Urry, John (2011). *Climate Change and Society*, John Wiley & Sons, London.

Van Slyck, Abigail A. (1995). *Free to all: Carnegie Libraries and American Culture, 1890–1920,* University of Chicago Press, Chicago.

Whyte, W. (1980). *The Social Life of Small Spaces*, Conservation Foundation, Washington, DC.

Wingert-Playdon, Kate (2019). *Library as Stoa*, ORO Editions, San Francisco.

Wong, Liliane (2016). "The Library in its Social Context", in: *Libraries: A Design Manual,* Birkhaeuser, Boston and Berlin, 10-15.

Zaera Polo, Alejandro (1992). *El Croquis:* "OMA / Rem Koolhaas 1987–1993", *El Croquis*, 53, 1992, Madrid.

Bibliography: Further Reading and Resources on Library Design

Here a selection of relevant books and key texts on libraries and their design methods.

Bieri, Susanne and Fuchs, Walther (2001). *Bibliotheken bauen*, Birkhäuser, Basel.

Black, Alistair, Pepper, Simon and Bagshaw, Kaye (2009). *Books, Buildings and Social Engineering: Early Public Libraries in Britain from Past to Present*, Ashgate, Farnham, Surrey.

Bosser, Jacques (2003). *The Most Beautiful Libraries in the World,* Harry N. Abrams Publishing, New York, and Thames and Hudson, London.

Brawne, Michael (1970). *Libraries: Architecture and Equipment*, Praeger Publishers London.

Brawne, Michael (Ed.) (1997). *Library Builders*, Academy Editions, London; and Lanham, Maryland.

CABE (2003). *Better Public Libraries,* Commission for Architecture and the Built Environment (CABE), London.

Campbell, James W. (2013). *The Library: A World History,* University of Chicago Press, Chicago.

Eco, Umberto (2019). *Libraries: Candida Hoefer*, Schimer Verlag/Mosel, Prestel Gmbh, Munich.

Ellsworth, Ralph E. (1973). *Academic Library Buildings: a guide to architectural issues and solutions*, Associated University Press, Boulder.

Futagawa, Yukio (Ed.) (2006). *GA Contemporary Architecture,* Vol. 03: *Library*, A.D.A. Edita, Tokyo, Japan.

Hille, R. Thomas (2018). *The New Public Library: Design Innovation for the Twenty-First Century*, Routledge, New York/London.

Johnson, Alex (2015). *Improbable Libraries: A Visual Journey to the World's most unusual Libraries,* The University of Chicago Press, Chicago.

Kaser, David (1997). *The Evolution of the American Academic Library Building*, Scarecrow Press, Lanham, Maryland.

Lushington, Nolan, Rudolf, Wolfgang and Wong, Liliane (2019). *Libraries - A Design Manual*, Birkhäuser, Berlin/Boston.

Metcalf, Keyes DeWitt (1965). *Planning Academic and Research Library Buildings*, McGraw-Hill, New York; 2nd edition, by Philip D, Leighton and David C. Weber (1986). Republished by the American Library Association, Chicago.

Murray, Stuart A. (2009). *The Library: An Illustrated History,* Skyhorse Publishing , New York; ALA Editions, Chicago.

Oehlerts, Donald E. (1991). *Books and Blueprints: Building America's Public Libraries*, Greenwood Press, New York.

Roth, Manuela (2014). *Masterpieces: Library Architecture + Design,* Braun Publishing, Berlin.

Ruppelt, G., and Sladek, E. (2018). *Massimo Listri: The World's Most Beautiful Libraries*, Taschen, Cologne.

Schlipf, Fred and Moorman, John (2018). *The Practical Handbook of Library Architecture: Creating Building Spaces that Work,* ALA Editions, Chicago.

Thompson, Godfrey (1973). *Planning and Design of Library Buildings,* Architectural Press, London.

Wheeler, Joseph Lewis, and Alfred Morton Githens (1941). *The American Public Library Building*, Scribner, New York; and American Library Association, Chicago.

Worpole, Ken, Greenhalgh, Liz and Landry, Charles (1992). *Libraries in a World of Cultural Change*, UCL Press, London.

Worpole, Ken (2013). *Contemporary Library Architecture: A Planning and Design Guide*, Routledge, London.

Websites on library design

Designing Libraries (UK) website and blog: www.designinglibraries.org.uk

Library of the Future blog by the American Library Association: www.ala.org/tools/future/blog

Documentation of examples of library buildings by e-architect: www.e-architect.com/library-buildings

Top 100 Largest Libraries in the World: a project by the World Creativity Science Academy (WCSA World): www.wcsa.world/news/world-copyright-academy/top-100-largest-libraries-in-the-world-p99-princeton-university-library-usa

100 Famous Universities in the World: www.worldkings.org/news/world-top/top-100-famous-universities-in-the-world-university-of-basel-88

Photographer documenting library architecture: www.thomasguignard.photo/libraries

Other Sources and Library Websites

The International Federation of Library Associations and Institutions (IFLA) is the leading international association of library organisations. It is the global voice of the library and information profession, and its annual conference provides a venue for librarians to learn from one another. IFLA is based in The Hague, Netherlands. www.ifla.org

The American Library Association (ALA) is a nonprofit organization based in the United States that promotes libraries and library education internationally. It is the oldest and largest library association in the world, with more than 57,000 members, and it is based in Chicago. www.ala.org

Library Journal (published in New York) has since 1945 devoted its December issues to articles on library architecture

A recent design showcase on libraries:
https://americanlibrariesmagazine.org/2020/09/01/2020-library-design-showcase/

Previous years and a few podcasts are available here:
https://americanlibrariesmagazine.org/tag/design-showcase/

Library journal provides some trends:
https://www.libraryjournal.com/?page=year-in-architecture-2020

Article by the AIA on five American Libraries:
https://mail.google.com/mail/u/0/?pli=1#inbox/FMfcgxwLttDKrXvQkTQcdSjTcZNTXksz

List of Featured Architects (Selection)

The book introduces libraries designed by over 20 international firms. The author would like to express his gratitude to the following design studios for rethinking the library typology:

- Arata Isozaki & Associates, Tokyo, Japan
  www.isozaki.co.jp

- Toyo Ito & Associates, Tokyo, Japan
  www.toyo-ito.co.jp

- Snøhetta, Oslo, Norway, and New York City, US
  www.snohetta.com

- Mecanoo, Delft, Netherlands
  www.mecanoo.nl

- FJMT Studio, Sydney, Australia
  www.fjmtstudio.com

- Will Bruder Architects, Portland, Oregon, US
  www.willbruderarchitects.com

- Antoine Predock Architects, Albuquerque, New Mexico, US
  www.predock.com

- Herzog & de Meuron, Basel, Switzerland
  www.herzogdemeuron.com

- Kerry Hill Architects, Singapore and Perth, Australia
  www.kerryhillarchitects.com

- Eun Young Yi Architects, Cologne, Germany, and Seoul, Korea
  www.yiarchitects.com

- Zaha Hadid Architects, London, United Kingdom
  www.zaha-hadid.com

- Foster + Partners, London, United Kingdom
  www.fosterandpartners.com

- Diller Scofidio + Renfro, New York City, US
  www.dsrny.com

- Steven Holl Architects New York City, US
  www.stevenholl.com

- BIG, Copenhagen, Denmark, and New York City, US
  www.big.dk

- David Chipperfield Architects, London, United Kingdom, and Berlin, Germany
  www.davidchipperfield.com

- Alberto Kalach & Taller de Arquitectura X, Mexico City, Mexico
  www.kalach.com

- MVRDV, Rotterdam, Netherlands
  www.mvrdv.com

- OMA, Rotterdam, Netherlands
  www.oma.com

- Bolles+Wilson Architects, Muenster, Germany
  www.bolles-wilson.com

- si_architecture + urban design, Barcelona, Spain, and Dubai, UAE
  www.si-architecture.com

About the Author

Dr. Steffen Lehmann (born in Stuttgart, Germany) is based in London and Las Vegas. He is the full professor of Architecture & Urbanism and former director of the School of Architecture at the University of Nevada, Las Vegas. He is founding director of the interdisciplinary Urban Futures Lab and CEO of the Future Cities Leadership Institute. Previously, Steffen has led three architecture schools, as head of school and executive director in Las Vegas (US), Perth and Brisbane (Australia). He has been a full professor since 2002, has taught, researched and practiced architecture for over thirty years, and defines all three as one activity.

Education and background: Steffen graduated from the Architectural Association School of Architecture in London in 1991, after securing a two-year DAAD scholarship. In 2003, he completed a Ph.D. in Architecture and Urbanism at the Technical University of Berlin, Germany. An ambassador of sustainable design principles and holder of the inaugural UNESCO Chair, Steffen's thinking is deeply influenced by three experiences: first, studying at the Architectural Association School in London in the 1980s; second, by British and Japanese modernism and the years he spent working as a young architect with James Stirling in London and Arata Isozaki in Tokyo; and third, the privilege to have been able to design and build significant urban and architectural contributions to the "New Berlin", after the fall of the Wall, in the 1990s and 2000s.

Leadership in practice: Before establishing his own multi-awarded practice, *Steffen Lehmann Architekten + Stadtplaner GmbH*, in 1993 in Berlin, he worked with Pritzker Prize-winners James Stirling in London and Arata Isozaki in Tokyo, both recognised as leading library architects. Steffen became a licensed architect in 1993 in Berlin with the aim to pursue a more ethical practice.

In 2021, Steffen co-founded the global firm *si_architecture + urban design LCC* with studios in Dubai and Barcelona. He has a deep understanding of architectural practice, having been lead architect of large public and private buildings. Between 1993 and 2003, he delivered as lead architect a construction budget of over $1 billion. Most of his built work is the result of winning design competitions for historically significant places, including large mixed-use complexes at Potsdamer Platz and the Quarter at the Museumsinsel in Berlin, both acknowledged as examples of excellence in sustainable design. His buildings and project designs have been published extensively, and the subject of two monographic books including "Steffen Lehmann: Breite x Hoehe x Tiefe" (Junius Verlag) and "Steffen Lehmann: Works" (AEDES). His work was shown in numerous exhibitions throughout the world, including solo exhibitions at the Bauhaus in Dessau, AEDES Gallery in Berlin, Plan '99 in Cologne, and at QUT in Brisbane.

He has advised more than a dozen cities on sustainable urban development, including the cities of Berlin, Stuttgart, Hamburg, Dresden, Shanghai, Singapore, Sydney, Melbourne, Adelaide, Brisbane, Abu Dhabi, Ho-Chi-Minh City, Oslo, Helsinki, Brighton, Southend-On-Sea, Las Vegas, Reno and Honolulu.

Professional memberships: In 2019, he became a member of the American Institute of Architects and joined the AIA Board of Directors of the Las Vegas Chapter. In 2016, he was elected to the UK's Academy of Urbanism and became a member of the Royal Institute of British Architects (RIBA). In 2003 he joined the Australian Institute of Architects (RAIA). In 1995, he was appointed "Freier Architekt BDA" in Berlin. In 1993, he became a licensed architect, first in Germany, then EU-wide.

Strategic leadership in research and teaching: Over the last twenty years, Steffen has been a tenured chair professor at four research-intensive universities on three continents (in the US, the UK and Australia), leading and transforming schools of architecture. He led three schools of architecture and established four highly successful research institutes, managing over $15 million in external research grant funding. This experience has provided him with a unique insight into different cultural and organisational contexts and models of architectural education. Since 1991, he has continuously taught urban and architectural design studios and research methods, and developed effective design teaching methods, for which he received the Award for Teaching Excellence, the *Top 100 Global Leader Award* (2021) and the *Athena City Award* from KTH Stockholm (2021), for two decades of integrating principles of sustainability in the teaching-research nexus. In recognition of the international significance of his work, Steffen was appointed in 2008 as the inaugural chair holder of the UNESCO Chair for Sustainable Urban Development in the Asia-Pacific.

Since 1990, he regularly travelled to China and witnessed the enormous urban transformation of Asian cities. He was invited as visiting professor to prominent universities worldwide to lead Global Studios, including at the University of California, Berkeley; TU Munich (as DAAD Professor); TU Berlin; NUS Singapore; Tongji University, Shanghai; Tianjin University; Iberoamericana University, Mexico City; University of Portsmouth (UK); Xi'an Jiaotong University as a Distinguished Visiting Professor; and in 2022-23 at Keio University in Tokyo.

His main research focus is in the field of twentieth-century architecture, urbanism and resilience, sustainable architectural and high-performance urban design. His work has received funding from the NSF, ESRC, Innovate UK, AHRC, Belmont Forum, British Council and other prestigious funding bodies. In the field of scholarly research, Steffen is best known for his pioneering work in and holistic view of green urbanisation, and for actively promoting environmental sustainability. He always maintained an active role in publishing as an architectural researcher, author and critic. The significance of his contribution to research is supported by over 4,000 citations in academic journals, a high h-Index in Google Scholar, and by over 500 conference presentations in 40 countries (including over 100 invited keynote presentations), at important institutions such as the Harvard University, University of Oxford, University of Sydney, MoMA New York, the Chinese Academy of Sciences, UNESCO Paris and TEDx.

He was the principal investigator of several large multidisciplinary research grants, leading international teams of researchers, including "CRUNCH: Climate Resilient Urban Nexus Choices". Over the last 30 years, he has published 23 books with prestigious publishers, and more than 400+ articles and papers on architecture and sustainable urban development. His research includes seminal works on sustainable architecture and the concept of the *Zero Waste City*. He is acknowledged for introducing the concept of *Green Urbanism* in the late 1990s. Since then, he developed large-scale urban design projects, exploring the concepts of *Density without High-rise* and *The City of Short Distances*.

For more information, please visit: www.city-leadership.com and www.si-architecture.com

Introducing a selection of former Ph.D. Students

To illustrate the diversity of reserach themes explored by the author, we introduce a selection of former Ph.D. students who worked and reserached in his research centres and successfully completed their thesis:

Dr. Wenli Dong
Lecturer in Architecture at Zhejiang University, Hangzhou, China

Ph.D. completed in 2013
Dissertation topic: "An Integrated Decision Framework for Density and Sustainability in Regenerating Chinese Cities", supervised by Prof Steffen Lehmann.
This thesis at the University of Newcastle (NSW) explored the density and urban form of regeneration projects in China and established a methodology for holistic evaluation for decision-makers.

Dr. Atiq U. Zaman
Senior Lecturer in Environment & Climate Emergency at Curtin University, Perth, Australia

Ph.D. completed in 2015
Dissertation topic: "A Strategic Waste Management Framework and Tool for the Development of Zero-Waste Cities", supervised by Prof Steffen Lehmann.
This thesis at the University of South Australia investigated waste management and avoidance strategies, establishing a new analytical framework for Zero Waste Cities, the "Zero Waste Index".

Dr. Ehsan Sharifi
Lecturer in Architecture and the Built Environment at the University of Adelaide, Australia

Ph.D. completed in 2016
Dissertation topic: "Public Spaces for Liveable and Sustainable Cities: the UHI Effect and the Urban Microclimate of Australian cities", supervised by Prof Steffen Lehmann.
This thesis at the University of South Australia explored the effectiveness of urban cooling strategies and urban greening in public space and place-making practice.

Since 2003, Professor Steffen Lehmann has been supervising and mentoring the research of numerous Ph.D. candidates and post-doctoral fellows through his interdisciplinary research centres. He has been a primary Ph.D. advisor in the US, UK and in Australia; a member of twelve Ph.D. committees and appointed as external reviewer for eight research-intensive universities in five countries.

Dr. John Shiel
Managing Principal and Lead Consultant at EnviroSustain, New South Wales, Australia

Ph.D. completed in 2018
Dissertation topic: "Low-carbon Affordable Retrofits of Australia's Existing Building Stock for Climate Change and Scarce Resource Scenarios", supervised by Prof Steffen Lehmann.
This thesis at the University of Newcastle (NSW) explored the parameters and analysed the experiences from case studies for the most cost-effective for low-carbon retrofitting.

Dr. Monika Szopinska-Mularz
Lecturer in Architecture at Rzeszów University of Technology, Rzeszów, Poland

Ph.D. completed in 2020
Dissertation topic: "The Adaptive Reuse of Inner-city Car Parking Structures for Urban Farming", supervised by Prof Steffen Lehmann.
This thesis at the University of Portsmouth (UK) investigated the potential of urban parking garage structures for the adaptive reuse as food growing and urban farming hub.

Mr. Fortino Acosta, MLA
Landscape Architect in Mexico City; Instructor at the University of Nevada, Las Vegas, US

Ph.D. to be completed in 2022
Dissertation topic: "The Food-Water-Energy Nexus in a City-Region Framework: the Role of Landscape Design Narratives", supervised by Prof Steffen Lehmann.
This thesis at the University of Nevada, Las Vegas explores how landscape characterisation and regenerative circular economy goals contribute to Food-Water-Energy Nexus' strategic solutions.

Index

List of names mentioned in the study, in alphabetical order, with the page number when the name is mentioned the first time.

Books to the ceiling, Books to the sky, my pile of books is a mile high. How I love them! How I need them! I'll have a long beard by the time I read them.

— Arnold Lobel, 1969

When knowledge is no longer present, physically, tactilely "comprehensible"...what should the libraries look like then? Should they resemble huge data servers? The question also arises, how digital systems at some point will be such that knowledge does not simply disappear in the event of a power failure or data storage problems. Most likely, there won't be a Mac or Windows in 100 years. On the other hand, there is an insurmountable advantage of the traditional book...I can leaf through it in seconds, get a quick overview. Digital does not offer this quality; maybe not yet. Isn't every smartphone and tablet actually a library, available anytime, anywhere, filled with an enormous quantity of information and knowledge?

— Gabor Kovacs, 2021

With digitisation, the library was declared dead, a wildly premature prediction as we know today. The opposite is the case. The library of the future is setting new standards in sustainability: it's a building that produces more energy than it consumes over its lifespan, including construction (embodied energy), operation and demolition.

— Steffen Lehmann, 2021